CITIZEN
MURDOCH

CITIZEN MURDOCH

by

THOMAS KIERNAN

Dodd, Mead & Company

New York

Copyright © 1986 by Thomas Kiernan

Published by Dodd, Mead & Company, Inc.
79 Madison Avenue, New York, N.Y. 10016
Distributed in Canada by
McClelland and Stewart Limited, Toronto
Manufactured in the United States of America
Designed by Kay Lee
First Edition

1 2 3 4 5 6 7 8 9 10

Library of Congress Cataloging-in-Publication Data

Kiernan, Thomas.
  Citizen Murdoch.

  Includes index.
  1. Murdoch, Rupert, 1931–   . 2. Publishers
and publishing—Australia—Biography. 3. Publishers
and publishing—Biography. 4. Newspaper publishing.
5. Broadcasting. I. Title.
Z533.3.M87K53 1986   070.5′092′4 [B]   86-16503
ISBN 0-396-08523-7

Contents

Foreword

Not since the days of the robber barons and William Randolph Hearst, Jr., has a big-business media tycoon captured the attention of the public the way Rupert Murdoch has. Nor has such an individual generated so much feverish dispute. Notorious around the world for his controversial newspaper and broadcasting practices, his aggressive accumulation of wealth and political power, and his increasingly strident right-wing social and economic principles, Murdoch in recent years has become a singular influence on the American cultural scene. The *Columbia Journalism Review* has cited him as "a sinister force" in our lives, and the chief editor of *The New York Times* has called him "an evil element." Yet throughout the rising public debate about him, Murdoch has remained for the most part a mystery man, his real goals, motives, and methods hidden behind a phalanx of public relations mouthpieces, legal apologists, and propagandists.

Rupert Murdoch and I have known each other, at times well, for the past ten years. This book springs from that relationship, and in the early stages of its preparation it had Murdoch's full cooperation. Much of the factual material contained in the pages that follow is based on intimate information, recollection, anecdote, and impression I received directly from Murdoch himself between 1976 and 1985. Our relationship also brought me into varying degrees of close personal contact with members of his family, and some of the material derives from those sources.

Further sources were the numerous individuals I also got to know who have worked, or still work, in Murdoch's vast international organization, most in close proximity to Murdoch himself. Many of them depend on him for their livelihood, or anticipate doing so in the future, and have requested anonymity in the event

I used material they provided, whether by quotation or other reference. I have honored similar requests from certain social friends of Murdoch and his family who gave me other valuable information and insights.

In addition to gathering material from such "inside" sources, I have done an exhaustive amount of separately sourced research on Murdoch's life, and it is upon this that the book is also based. In summary, the book is not an authorized biography but represents, for the most part, my own independent work and effort as supplemented by the information I have received over the years from Rupert Murdoch personally and from those intimately connected with him.

—T.K.

Rupert Murdoch is very good at what he does. The question is: is what he does any good?

—*Theodore Kheel, a New York attorney who has worked for and against Murdoch*

CITIZEN
MURDOCH

MURDOCH

AUSTRALIA

"Lord Southcliffe"

The first widely recorded instance of Rupert Murdoch's propensity to play fast and loose with established rules of conduct occurred when he was a student at England's Oxford University in the early 1950s. He had arrived at Oxford from Australia in 1949 as a brash, chubby eighteen-year-old. Depending on which on-the-scene witness one is willing to credit the most, he was at worst "a raving flat-out Communist," at best "a teenaged male version of the Jane Fonda of the seventies, all radical rant and no substance." What is clear is that Murdoch was of a decidedly youthful—"immature and juvenile," he admits today—left-wing bent. "Red Rupert" and "Rupert the Red" were, alternately, his principal nicknames.

Oxford was second only to Cambridge as a hotbed of upper-class university leftism in postwar England. While Cambridge was the longtime breeding ground of Britain's Communist underground, Oxford tended to produce more mainstream left-wing political talent, along with the usual harvest of conservative establishmentarians. The country's Labour Party was the national political organization to which most of Oxford's left-leaning students subscribed. Within the university, the Labour Club was the principal student offshoot of the party. Membership in the club was tantamount to formal party apprenticeship, and the elected leaders of the club often went on to distinguished political and government careers.

By his third year, Rupert Murdoch was sufficiently mature to aspire realistically to a leadership post in the Labour Club. Accordingly, he managed to get himself nominated, along with several others, as a candidate for the club's secretaryship.

Once nominated, candidates for any office were forbidden by club charter from actively campaigning for votes. Annual elections were conducted solely on the basis of the vying candidates' past performances and their reputations for seriousness and political acuity. The rules were strictly enforced.

Murdoch ignored the rules. Secretly, he and a few supporters had electioneering leaflets printed up and distributed among the student body. They also traveled about the university soliciting votes, often through not-too-gentle methods of persuasion and, according to some members, bribery or intimidation. Murdoch and his cohorts were eventually exposed. As a consequence, he was disqualified from the election by the Labour Club's board, censured, and formally barred from future office.

One Oxford contemporary of Murdoch's remembers that the thing that struck him most about the incident was how blatant the offense was. And how readily Murdoch shrugged off the accusations of untoward conduct brought against him, even while acknowledging them by calmly accepting the punishment.

According to Murdoch today, he did nothing that his competitors for the position weren't doing. Everybody broke the rules against campaigning, he claims. It was simply a matter of being the one who was caught.

Why was he caught?

"I had plenty of enemies even then," he told me when we were talking about this book.

Was he comfortable being a man with so many enemies?

"Of course not. It's not pleasant at all when I find myself under attack all the time from so many quarters. On the other hand, it's very valuable. It invigorates me."

Did he understand why he had so many enemies?

"A few particular enemies, yes. But I don't care about them. What I don't understand is why I incite so much hostility from those who don't know me, who I've done nothing to hurt. I'll never understand that."

The conventional wisdom among most analysts of Rupert Murdoch's career is that he was compulsively—pathologically—driven to outdo the considerable journalistic and financial achievements of his late father, all for the purpose of proving to the rest of his family, and by extension to the world at large, that he was undeserving of the lack of confidence his father often voiced, not always privately, in and about his character.

If there is ever any hard truth in psychobiography, such analysis is way off the mark. As a youth, Rupert cared little about his father, except insofar as the older man was a constant thorn in his side. Although his father provided the professional grubstake, it was Rupert's mother who seems to have supplied most of the genetic fuel and psychological impetus of his success.

It is accurate to say that Murdoch has succeeded far beyond his mother's dreams for him. Like any mother, she is publicly proud of her only son's achievements. Privately, though, she is often unsure of their value. "It can be very tiresome indeed being known as the mother of Rupert Murdoch," she told me.

Murdoch, today accustomed to her frequent admonishments about his aggressive business style and tainted reputation, has a couple of standard, good-natured ripostes when he overhears such utterances. One of them is, "Just taking after your own dad."

Rupert Greene, Murdoch's maternal grandfather, was an engineer by training and one of the leading figures in Australia's wool trade during the early decades of this century. A garrulous man of Anglo-Scottish blood, he was known as an inveterate gambler, drinker, womanizer, and sportsman.

Greene's favorite sporting activities were cricket and horse racing, the trademark leisure-time interests of colonial Australia's small upper class, which self-consciously emulated and mirrored its English forebears. He became most prominent socially as a steward of the Australian racing establishment which was centered in Melbourne, the south coast city that, of all of Australia's growing metropolises, hewed most closely to the "home" traditions of Britain. It was in and around Melbourne that the Greene family settled after it emigrated from the British Isles in the mid–nineteenth century.

But Rupert Greene was no playboy. Operating in an environment that was still part-frontier and saturated with a survival-of-the-fittest reality, he was a tough, shrewd, thrusting businessman who was eventually knighted by England's King George V.

An impulsive wheeler-dealer, says one modern-day member of the family. "He fought and scratched for every penny he made, and he made quite a lot. He was not the most ethical of men, but he was colorful."

Sir Rupert Greene was in sharp contrast to his wife Marie, Rupert Murdoch's maternal grandmother. "She was—well, rather strange," recalls the same family member. "Colorful, too, in a fashion, but only because of her natural eccentricity. She was rock-ribbed, stern, a bit dotty, a woman of very strict principles. In another incarnation she might have been a nun. She was totally subservient to her husband and yet thoroughly independent of him. She tolerated his excesses—no, actually she remained airily above them. She was like a feather made of steel, if you can imagine it. Her one great achievement in life was her daughter. She doted on Elisabeth."

Elisabeth is Rupert Murdoch's mother—today, Dame Elisabeth Murdoch, having been "knighted" in 1963 by the Queen of England for her aggressive charitable work. Elisabeth Joy Greene was born in Melbourne in 1909. Raised in comfortable surroundings but in strict fashion by her stern Victorian mother, she was schooled in the traditional niceties of Scottish womanhood and was trained to settle for nothing less than a canny Scotsman for a husband when she grew up.

A canny Scotsman she got—well, almost. His name was Keith Arthur Murdoch. Physically imposing and mentally astute when he met and began to court Elisabeth Greene in 1927, and already somewhat of a celebrity in Australian society, the stocky, ski-nosed Keith Murdoch was the first-generation son of Scottish parents who had emigrated to Camberwell, near Melbourne, in 1885.

A grim Calvinist-Presbyterian clergyman from near Aberdeen—that part of chilly northern Scotland known for producing the most dour and fatalistic of the Scottish clans—Keith Murdoch's father, as well as his mother, had led a near-penurious church existence in the old country. Their settlement in southern Australia's Victoria Province had improved their financial lot only marginally. That their son Keith would become both well-to-do and celebrated throughout the new land was something they could never have anticipated, or even contemplated, when he was born the year after their arrival.

Keith Murdoch came into the world on August 12, 1886. By all accounts he had a most uneventful childhood in the sunny Melbourne area, a region in stark contrast to Scotland's often gloomy, misty Aberdeenshire. He was just another mouth to be fed in a refined but churchmouse-poor family of eight. Once he was old enough for serious education, he was, like his siblings, forced to work his way through school.

Few who knew Keith Murdoch at the turn of the century would have predicted a career of much distinction for him. Terribly timid as a young boy and afflicted with an almost paralyzing stutter, he remained diffident well into his teens and seemed destined for a conventionally humdrum life in colonial Australia. Only a sharp natural analytical intellect, along with a talent for writing that he had developed to compensate for his deficiencies in oral expression, belied such a bleak future.

His interest in writing propelled Keith Murdoch into the newspaper business after he graduated from high school in 1903. For six years he toiled as an apprentice reporter for the Melbourne *Age,* working his way up to a suburban correspondent's position by 1908. During that period, he managed for the most part to conquer his stutter. He also became known as a "comer" in Melbourne's highly competitive newspaper community.

The Melbourne *Age* regularly offered a promising young member of its apprentice staff the opportunity to travel to England for a year for further seasoning on a paper there while attending a course at the influential London School of Economics. In 1909, when he was twenty-three, the offer was made to Keith Murdoch and he accepted it without hesitation. (In that same year, as Murdoch sailed from Melbourne, Elisabeth Joy Greene was born there.)

His stay in London expanded the young Murdoch's horizons immensely. Not only was the city the core of the vast and powerful British Empire, but England represented the world's richest expression of early twentieth-century industrial enterprise and technological achievement. Murdoch received a solid grounding in contemporary economic and political theory. At the same time, he learned at first hand some of the more rambunctious and sophisticated methods of the fiercely competitive Fleet Street newspaper trade. Upon his return to Melbourne a year later, his apprenticeship at the *Age* was declared at an end. He was installed as a regular staff reporter and assigned to cover the workings of the Australian government, Melbourne still being the capital of the Commonwealth.

Forging a reputation as a forceful and increasingly well-connected journalist, Keith Murdoch remained with the Melbourne *Age* for four years after his return from London. Then, with the outbreak of World War I in Europe—an event of profound interest to Australians, since so many Australian youths were

conscripted to fight for Britain—he became the Melbourne correspondent for the Sydney *Sun.*

Much like New York and Chicago in the United States,
Melbourne and Sydney were engaged in a lively rivalry over the
issue of which was Australia's most important city. Although
Melbourne was the nation's capital and cultural seat, as well as
the more populous of the two, Sydney, with its great natural harbor, had become the principal gateway to the world beyond and
was fast overtaking Melbourne in population and cosmopolitan
character. Keith Murdoch's switch to the *Sun,* aside from adding
a few shillings each week to his meager newspaperman's salary,
symbolized his recognition of that fact.

Soon after the start of the war, large numbers of Australian
and New Zealand ANZAC troops were transported to the Middle East to shore up the British in the fight there against the Ger-
mans and their Turkish allies. In the early summer of 1915, the
twenty-eight-year-old Murdoch followed as a special government
correspondent and captain in the Australian army. His first stop
was in Egypt, a major staging area for Britain's Middle East operations. From there he sailed to the Dardenelles. A few months
before, the British, using mostly ANZAC troops, had launched
an invasion of southwest Turkey's Gallipoli peninsula. Murdoch
had picked up rumors in Egypt that the campaign was going
badly, so he decided to see for himself. When he arrived at Gallipoli, he found a major debacle in progress, with thousands of
ANZAC soldiers being sacrificed by their English commanders in
pointless fixed battles with the Turks.

Outraged, Murdoch repeatedly tried to send a dispatch back
to the Australian prime minister describing the months of needless slaughter. Because of the censorship imposed by the British
military authorities, however, his attempts were blocked. Equally
appalled and frustrated was a British war correspondent named
Ellis Ashmead-Bartlett. He, too, had been stymied from sending
reports to his newspaper in London, which would have exposed
the deadly folly of the British commanders on the scene.

Murdoch resolved to leave Gallipoli so that he could freely
communicate the horrors he had witnessed. When Ashmead-
Bartlett learned of his intention, he hurriedly wrote a long report
addressed to a member of the British war cabinet with whom he
was friendly. He then begged Murdoch to smuggle the report out
of Gallipoli and carry it to London as quickly as possible. After

reading the document, Murdoch agreed. He was persuaded by Ashmead-Bartlett that its delivery to London would produce a much more rapid remedial response than his own plan to alert the government in Australia.

Once off Gallipoli in September 1915, Murdoch managed to catch a ship bound for Britain. However, another British correspondent on the peninsula, having learned of the plot between Murdoch and Ashmead-Bartlett, had alerted the British military authorities. Murdoch was intercepted when his ship put in at Marseilles, and he was forced to hand over his secret cargo.

Undeterred, he continued the voyage to England. Using the time aboard ship, he composed his own version of the confiscated Ashmead-Bartlett report, which he had practically memorized before reaching Marseilles. In the process he added his own flourishes, putting it all in the form of a top-secret letter to the prime minister of Australia. He resolved to mail it immediately he arrived in London and to deliver a copy to the British government. His only problem was how to ensure that the letter fell into the right hands in London.

After reaching the English capital, Murdoch, through his Australian press contacts, engineered an audience with Alfred Harmsworth, who by then was known as Lord Northcliffe.

The British equivalent of America's Joseph Pulitzer and William Randolph Hearst, Northcliffe was an all-powerful newspaper publisher who had revolutionized British journalism during the previous twenty-five years. The owner of the stately *Times* of London, of the more lively *Daily Mail,* and of a spicy pop-tabloid called the *Daily Mirror*—all of them national papers that together came close to dominating Fleet Street's circulation charts—Northcliffe was almost a separate branch of government unto himself.

What's more, he was a harsh critic of Prime Minister Herbert Asquith and his Minister for War, Lord Kitchener. Kitchener, at the behest primarily of the young Winston Churchill, had approved the invasion of Gallipoli and appointed the aged General Sir Ian Hamilton to command it.

It was Hamilton's incompetence that Ashmead-Bartlett and Keith Murdoch had made the centerpiece of their respective reports. Murdoch's letter called for Hamilton's dismissal and an immediate evacuation of all British forces from Gallipoli before any more ANZAC lives were wasted.

Anything that was damaging to the Asquith government and damned its conduct of the war was grist for Lord Northcliffe's mill. He received the agitated Keith Murdoch and looked over his report. Six years later, Northcliffe recalled the encounter in this fashion:

> He [Murdoch] brought a dispatch, a very terrible dispatch, which I believe was intended to be sent to Australia. He showed that dispatch to me, and I suggested that the time which would be spent in carrying that ghastly record to the Antipodes could be better used for the purpose of immediate action. He will correct me if I am wrong, but I think I asked him to take it to Mr. Lloyd George.*

David Lloyd George, a member of the Asquith war cabinet, was one of Northcliffe's pet politicians and his first choice to succeed Asquith. Northcliffe arranged for Keith Murdoch to meet with Lloyd George and show him his Gallipoli report. No doubt the fine manipulative hand of the notorious Northcliffe was behind what happened next.

Lloyd George promptly had Murdoch's report printed and distributed to every member of the cabinet, including Asquith and Kitchener, as a state paper. Asquith, who had entrusted most of the conduct of the war to Kitchener, was stunned by the detailed on-site descriptions of British military bumbling at Gallipoli and the resulting carnage among the ANZAC corps. Kitchener denounced Murdoch's account as being ridden with falsehoods and distortions. Lloyd George defended it as true in every respect, pointing to the fact that it was the product of two separate witnesses.

Debate raged for several days. Then Asquith appointed a special committee to study the charges further. It did not take long for the committee to affirm their general thrust. General Hamilton was immediately dismissed and another top commander sent to Gallipoli to organize and supervise its evacuation.

As a result, Keith Murdoch won instant fame as an Australian patriot and intrepid Commonwealth journalist. That some later branded him a disloyal gadfly and pesky, self-aggrandizing exaggerator mattered not at all. Under Northcliffe's grateful embrace, he became the toast of Fleet Street.

* From *The Times,* London, July 2, 1921.

Murdoch finished out the war as a reporter in England and France for several Australian papers. After the Armistice in 1918, he remained in London as the British correspondent for the Sydney *Sun* and Melbourne *Herald.* A year later, he also became the chief London manager of the United Cable Service, which supplied Australia, New Zealand, and other domains of the Southwest Pacific with most of their news from Europe. During that stint, he learned the crafts of brevity and conciseness in composing his cable dispatches. The cable service, which charged by the word, was extremely expensive.

Such skills were highly valued by Lord Northcliffe. With linguistic color, raciness, and innuendo, he had built his newspaper empire on tabloid brevity and conciseness. He was unable to do much to change the sedate, long-winded *Times,* which he had purchased ten years earlier principally as a monument to his self-esteem. But with the *Daily Mail* and the *Mirror,* both of which he had started from scratch, and with his stable of rancidly spicy regional papers throughout Britain, he had created what became known in Fleet Street as the "New Journalism."

The fact that Northcliffe had borrowed most of his ideas from the Pulitzer-Hearst "yellow journalism" of America was of no concern to Britishers. What interested them was the fact that a new mode of news dissemination had entered their lives—saucy, sensationalist, easy-to-read coverage of local crime and scandal. In other words, peep-show journalism, reportage that stimulated "the vicarious thrill," as one commentator of the time put it.

When Herbert Asquith was forced to resign as prime minister in 1916, to be succeeded by Lloyd George, Northcliffe took much of the credit. Although it would be inaccurate to attribute Asquith's downfall to Keith Murdoch's Gallipoli report alone, that document, along with the anti-Asquith and anti-Kitchener passions it aroused, clearly were contributing factors.

Northcliffe had used Murdoch to his own political ends. Perhaps out of gratitude for the opportune fodder the Australian newsman had provided him, when the war was over and Murdoch settled in London as an Australian correspondent, Northcliffe "adopted" him. He took him under his professional wing and drilled into him the techniques and tricks of his new pop-journalism.

Murdoch's attitude toward Northcliffe was nothing short of hero worship. The British press baron, more than twenty years

older than the thirty-two-year-old Australian, regularly surrounded himself with sycophantic employees from his various
papers. Murdoch became a charter member of Northcliffe's postwar entourage, a devoted disciple who soaked up his elder's professional tips and consciously modeled himself on him. Their
relationship very quickly became one of mentor and protégé—on
the personal level, one almost of father and son.

Thus, when Keith Murdoch returned to Australia in mid-
1921 to become editor-in-chief of the sagging Melbourne *Herald,*
he very soon was nicknamed "Lord Southcliffe" for his rampant
praise and espousal of Northcliffe's editorial formulas. The ambition he brought back with him was to become no less than the
Northcliffe of Australia—the country's premier press baron and,
as it were, a branch of government unto himself. He was only
thirty-five. Melbourne's population had grown to about 800,000.

Notwithstanding the good-natured ribbing he took, Murdoch, faithfully following Northcliffe's journalistic prescriptions,
transformed the *Herald* into Australia's most influential and prosperous paper over the next few years. He did so by "populariz-
ing" the once dull paper's tone and layout, while at the same time
expanding its serious news coverage—especially news from overseas, which he used his experience in cable writing to sharpen and
improve. Already somewhat of a national hero for his Gallipoli
exploits, he quickly became a leading and respected voice in the
country's development during the 1920s. And, as his influence
and authority spread within the *Herald*'s parent company, he
found himself well on his way to becoming a wealthy man.

By 1927, Keith Murdoch was a pillar of Melbourne's business elite. The bitterly and often violently combative atmosphere
of Australia's newspaper industry had left him little time for, or
interest in, a social life. A toughened, opinionated, highly principled "workaholic," to use the modern expression, he had given
little thought to marriage and family in his climb toward the top
of the Melbourne establishment. A man's man in what was altogether a man's world, he had had no close experience of women
and usually remained exceedingly shy in their presence; his residual childhood stutter often reappeared at the first hint of inti-
macy. His friends thought him likable but increasingly eccentric
in his stiff-necked obsession with work, and all were sure he
would never marry. "A more unsuitable prospect for matrimony
cannot be imagined," said one to an inquiring Australian reporter
in 1927.

Another unsuitable prospect for matrimony in Melbourne that year was the eighteen-year-old Elisabeth Greene, recently graduated from a prim, starchy girls' school. Such, at least, was her recollection as conveyed to me some fifty-five years later. "No one lived up to her name more aptly than I," she confided to me in 1982. "Oh, I was such a 'green' young girl!" Be that as it may, she and Keith Murdoch, having met at a Greene family social gathering in Melbourne late in 1927, were married the following June.

"Oh, That Little Nuisance"

When Keith Rupert Murdoch was born on March 11, 1931, his father had already fallen into the habit of remaining for long periods away from the home in which he'd settled his young wife and first child, a girl named Helen. The home was a colonial farm-estate at Langwarrin in the countryside thirty miles south of Melbourne. Keith Murdoch had called the place Cruden Farm, after the village in Scotland, near Aberdeen, from which his parents had emigrated. Although Murdoch gave his infant son his own first name, the boy quickly became known by his middle name—Rupert. This naturally delighted Elisabeth Murdoch's father, who proceeded to dote on his namesake grandson and ply him with expensive toys and other gifts.

The busy Keith Murdoch, only a few years younger than Rupert Greene, by 1933 thoroughly disapproved of his father-in-law's profligate ways. He was sure the wealthy, free-spending sportsman, if allowed to, would set a miserable example for Rupert's juvenile sense of values. Thus, he was forced repeatedly to admonish Rupert Greene. No matter what he said, though, the older man found increasingly devious ways to bestow his largesse on his grandson, often with the connivance of Elisabeth Murdoch.

Growing in-law tension thereby became a regular feature of life in the Murdoch household. Soon Keith Murdoch buried his frustration and resentment in his work, leaving most of the rearing of his two children to his wife. He became a proxy father, distant and somewhat morose when he was in the presence of his offspring, yet insufferably boastful of them to his newspaper and business friends in Melbourne.

Keith Murdoch had been made managing director of the Melbourne *Herald* just after his marriage, a major step up from the mere editorship. Under his wing, as well, came the *Weekly Times,* a paper that served the outlying areas of the city.

Thereafter, throughout the 1930s, he thrust himself full tilt into the task of expanding the *Herald* company's leadership and influence in Australian journalism. He started or acquired papers in other cities and fought circulation battles with Northcliffian gusto. He inserted himself in both national and state politics with the bulldog ferocity of a Churchill. He orchestrated the *Herald* company's investments with the zeal of a Rockefeller. Almost single-handedly, he created a domestic wire service—the Australian Associated Press—and a newsprint industry. He started several magazines. He pioneered in the use of cable and radio photography and was always the first to take advantage of new printing technologies. By the end of the thirties, the senior Murdoch was so thoroughly identified with the *Herald* chain that many believed he was its principal owner.

That was not the case. Although Murdoch *was* the *Herald,* the *Herald* would never be his. Indeed, the family that owned the majority of shares in the company frequently became annoyed at Murdoch's increasingly proprietary attitude toward what was theirs. On at least two occasions during that time, they made halfhearted attempts to oust him, only to abandon their efforts when they realized they'd be losing their most valuable asset— him.

Instead, although they paid him well, they made sure they kept his shareholdings to a minimum. Nor would they entertain the periodic offers he made to buy the company, even though they would have profited handsomely.

During that period, Keith Murdoch suffered two major surprises, one pleasant, the other bitterly demoralizing. The first, in 1933, was a knighthood; he was now Sir Keith Murdoch.

The second was a savage heart attack that laid him low for nearly half a year and left him a more remote father than ever. It seemed a bitter reward for his lifelong adherence to the precepts of hard, honest work in which he'd been raised by his own stern father. It did not shake his faith in the value of such toil, however. After he recovered, he plunged back into the newspaper business with even greater obsessiveness than before. Having had a premature confrontation with his own mortality, it was as if he were now compelled to pack as much achievement into the remainder of his life as he possibly could before the real end, which he sensed was close at hand, arrived.

Rupert Murdoch's first remembered awareness of his family surroundings was during the time subsequent to his father's first coronary problems. His memories are of a frequently absent Keith Murdoch who, when he was on the scene, was a brusque and intimidating figure—frightening, even, though without necessarily meaning to be. Then there was Rupert's mother, almost always present in his life, a bundle of contradictions, at once flighty and severe, alternately demanding and succoring, the real authority figure as opposed to the phantom one his father represented. Finally there was his sister Helen, two years older, whom he simultaneously despised and adored in the way five-year-olds always seem to do. Well, not finally, for there had been a recent addition to the family—another daughter born to Elisabeth and Keith Murdoch the year before. Her name was Anne, but she really didn't count yet in Rupert's juvenile consciousness. A last child, Janet, would make her appearance three years later, in 1939.

And then there was the farm, with its semirural ambience, its animals, toys, nannies, and an assortment of male cousins as occasional playmates. One of those cousins was Ranald MacDonald, himself destined to become an eminent newspaper publisher in Australia, though on a much smaller commercial scale than Murdoch. "I played with him as a boy," MacDonald was quoted as saying when the grown-up Murdoch was angling to take over the *Times* newspapers of London in 1981. "I know him. He cannot be trusted. It's always the same. Everybody thinks that this time he'll behave. But it will never work."

The words could have been those of a single disaffected—perhaps steeply envious—cousin and thus might properly be dismissed as unfairly selective. Yet every one of Murdoch's male childhood contemporaries with whom I spoke had similar recollections of him. As a boy he was clearly not well liked, and such perceptions carried over even more vividly to his school environment. Before he was ten, the young Murdoch was sent off to Australia's prestigious but harshly rigorous Geelong boarding school, much against his wishes. There he spent nine years and is recalled by most in negative terms.

"Oh, that little nuisance," the headmaster, Sir James Darling, was reported to have said when queried about Murdoch years after his graduation.

Other recollections combine to paint a portrait of an unhappy, timid boy who verged on academic failure throughout his school career and turned to various forms of social rebellion and reckless attention-getting to make his mark. In his later years at the school, just after the end of World War II, he also suffered from his father's prominence throughout Australia as an outspoken anti-Communist and wartime press censor.

Remembers one classmate, "Rupert took quite a lot of needling from the older boys because of his father. Sir Keith was using his newspapers to carry on his own personal cold war against communism. He was sort of the William F. Buckley of his time in Australia. The mood in the school, of course, was just the opposite—all postwar liberal idealism and such. So Rupert, who wasn't very popular anyway because of his emotional immaturity and rather obnoxious personality, got a lot of additional teasing on account of his father.

"So far as I could see, he didn't get along very well with his dad. The old man was tough on him all through his boyhood, and the more he pressured Rupert to excel, the more Rupert did the opposite. So, that anticommunism business of his own father was a perfect reason for Rupert to take the opposite tack, especially when he was so mercilessly goaded about it by his schoolmates. In his last year or two, Rupert became the school's leading radical, with the possible exception of a couple of chaps on the faculty. It was not something he thought out rationally, though. It was simply a matter of going overboard in wanting to be accepted by his mates, plus rebelling against his father."

It might have been more than just reaction against his father, however. Rupert's mother had always had a strong streak of rebelliousness in her character and was becoming notorious in the Melbourne area—some bluenoses would have said odiously so—for her charity work among the poor. By all independent accounts, her charitable concerns were genuine and her work was not just the leisure-time social hobby it was of other wealthy women.

A genuine interest in improving the lot of the poor and disenfranchised suggests a humanism that is often susceptible to political manipulation of the Socialist, even Communist kind. Thus Rupert Murdoch's teenage adoption of left-wing ideals may well have been as much a function of his mother's humanist idealism as it was a rebellion against his father's increasingly right-wing posturing, and a need for acceptance by his schoolmates.

Rupert, however, was strictly a privileged left-wing ideologue in his last years at Geelong. He was not an "activist" who went into the streets to spread the Socialist message. Nor would he attempt to argue politics with his steeltrap-brained father, for he knew he could never best the impatient, quick-tongued, dismissive Sir Keith.

Another teenage acquaintance recalls that "Rupert was afraid of his father. He was totally overwhelmed by him. He was always trying to please Sir Keith, but to no avail. Sir Keith had little patience with Rupert and perpetually gave the impression of being disappointed in him. Sir Keith was this great respected figure, and Rupert ached to have his approval, some expression of pleasure or pride. So Rupert turned to trickery and deceit to try to get his father's attention.

"I don't think Rupert was born with the traits that have sullied his reputation as a grown-up. He developed them out of his desperation to encourage his father's approval when he was growing up. Or, on the other hand, to discourage his father's disapproval.

"You know what I mean. Today Rupert is reviled for being a newspaper publisher who has made his fortune by pulling the wool over other people's eyes—mainly readers'. It was those traits he picked up back in the forties, when he was trying to influence the way his father thought about him. He felt terribly compartmentalized by his father. So he began to make up things about himself to make himself look better in Sir Keith's eyes, or at least to gain his sympathy. He would do it in such a way that he thought he could not get caught out, believing that his father would never inquire further. Telling his father, for instance, that he'd won a medal for something in school when in fact he hadn't. That sort of thing. Little lies, innocuous lies, all for the purpose of getting Sir Keith to give him a pat on the back.

"But of course Sir Keith was not the type to show his pleasure, even over Rupert's real achievements. If Rupert said he'd won a race by five yards, his father would bark: 'Why not by ten?' There was no way Rupert could please him. So he went the route of trickery and deceit, either creating favorable facts about himself or concealing unfavorable ones.

"If you ask me, the Rupert Murdoch of today is very much a

creation of his father in that negative way. It's not that Sir Keith taught Rupert that dishonesty is the best policy. It's that Sir Keith's cold judgmentalism unconsciously instilled in Rupert the idea that deception, trickery, and dishonesty are the only ways to survive and flourish in this world. Rupert has merely taken what he learned out of the pressure of being a self-perceived second-rate kid and applied it to his circumstances as an adult."

When asked to respond to such analyses, the Rupert Murdoch of today first of all denies imputations of personal dishonesty and deceit, whether then or now. As for such frequent descriptions of his boyhood and school career at Geelong, he says, "I simply can't understand why all these people remember it so differently than I do."

He maligns the Geelong headmaster as an incompetent who had the contempt of just about everyone connected with the school.

As for those who describe him as unruly, poor at sports—so important at such a boarding school—and friendless, he has a mixed response. He admits to deficiencies at sports: "I hated organized sports and was no good at them. That was mainly because I hated being organized. It was also due to the fact that I was lazy, I suppose.

"But to say I had no friends, that's pure rubbish. It's true that I was on the rebellious side. There was a group of us at the school who were kid rebels, who didn't like the regimentation. They were my friends. Talk to them—I think you'll get a different opinion."

I tried, but couldn't find any.

Geelong was in part a military school. Murdoch insists that his youthful left-wing proclivities derived solely from that fact. "All the military training they imposed on us, that's where it came from," he told me. "Couldn't stand the warmongering, so we rebelled by becoming pacifists."

Pacifism is hardly a mark of the adult Murdoch's personality. Bellicosity and retribution are, though. Which is more consistent with this Murdoch recollection of his school days: "At Geelong they had the old English-school tradition of prefects who would take a cane to you for the slightest breach of discipline. I took issue with this, particularly as I was so often the object of the caning. I can remember one particular Fascist type who let me have it with special brutal delight on a couple of occasions. Later, when I was out of school, I drove by him waiting in a downpour at a bus stop. I got a great deal of pleasure in passing him by, not stopping to give him a lift."

Murdoch's only soulmate as a youngster was his sister Helen. Although they saw little of one another after he was sent off to boarding school, "We were one of a kind in many ways. Both rebels, she more against our mother, me more against my father. Both outcasts in a certain sense. Both bristling with undirected energy."

If anything, Helen Murdoch was more clever and innately intelligent than her brother, as well as more defiant and independent of spirit.

"Helen was the real Socialist in the family," says a Murdoch family friend. "Unlike Rupert, she was one who really thought out her position and could defend it with telling logic. What's more, she practiced it, going out and doing things. I think their father took pride in her sincerity and resoluteness, whereas he viewed Rupert's proclaimed socialism as insincere. Especially when Rupert took up gambling."

According to other reports, the young Murdoch had become an inveterate schoolboy gambler by the time he was sixteen.

"It was another way for him to be accepted at Geelong," says a student from the period. "Gambling was sport, and he was no good at any other sport. He would gamble at anything, from horse racing to finger-tossing. He always seemed to have money, and the gambling allowed him to assume a certain arrogant, cocksure attitude.

"Of course gambling assumes a profit motive, which put Rupert at odds with his pseudo-Communist stance. But the funny thing is that he was no good at it. He was regularly fleeced by those with whom he made bets and became even more of a laughingstock than ever. No one would laugh at him directly, though. Since he always seemed to have money to lose, they didn't want to discourage him."

Richard Searby, today among Murdoch's closest friends and business allies, and a top lawyer in Melbourne, was at Geelong with him. Although they were not particularly close at the time, Searby remembers Rupert as being a young man without distinction except for his politics. Even at that, "No one took him seriously," Searby has been quoted as saying. "It seemed incongruous that Sir Keith Murdoch's son could be a rampant Socialist. It was, everyone agreed, just a boyhood aberration that would pass."

Rupert the Red

Although an undistinguished student at Geelong, Murdoch managed to graduate in 1949 and, through the help of influential friends of his father's in England, gained admission to Oxford University.

As with Geelong, Murdoch's matriculation at Oxford was against his wishes. He had no desire to leave Australia; indeed he had no interest in further education. He was hoping that his father would start him off straightaway with a job on one of his newspapers. It was not that he had any fierce ambition at that time to follow in his father's footsteps. He simply believed, he told me, that such was in the natural order of things.

Thus his dismay—his bitter agony, even, since some recall that he fell into a profound depression—when his father pulled the rug on his fantasy and ordered him off to Oxford. By most accounts, Sir Keith, although he had not foreclosed entirely on the notion of Rupert one day taking a place in the *Herald* organization, profoundly doubted the prospect. During Rupert's last years at Geelong, he had tried on occasion to tutor the boy in the nuts and bolts of newspaper work. He had seen little interest on Rupert's part, however, and less in the way of aptitude.

By then, because he had been unable to obtain a controlling share of the *Herald* company despite his nearly three decades at the helm, Keith Murdoch had acquired for his own account two small newspapers in the provincial cities of Brisbane and Adelaide and was running them, through surrogate editors, from his base in Melbourne. He had bought the papers primarily to provide himself with something to do once he was forced to retire from the *Herald* organization, but also as a potential legacy for his still-young wife and children.

Logically, this modest family newspaper venture would have been the place for Rupert to start, Sir Keith believed, had Rupert shown any inclination for newspaper work. But because he hadn't, and because the eighteen-year-old appeared to his aging father still to be drenched in immaturity, Sir Keith grew resolute in his insistence that Rupert go to college.

Elisabeth Murdoch, agreeing that the "confused" young man had to "find himself," supported her husband's demand, although for the usual maternal reasons she argued against sending her only son as far away as England.

"Rupert was brimming with energy," she told me. "He simply did not know how to channel it. Not an uncommon trait in young men of that age, is it?"

Energy, yes—but according to Murdoch, there was still some question about his ambition.

"Oh, I had plenty of ambition," he says. "Only it was into areas far different from those my father thought I should have. It's fair to say that my ambition was locked up, so to speak. I guess my only palpable goal at that time was to change the world. And avoid going to Oxford."

But go he did, being admitted into Worcester College, academically one of the university's less exalted schools. He arrived with a chip on his shoulder and a bust of Lenin in his luggage. He installed the likeness on the windowsill of his room—a talisman of his left-wing fervency.

Murdoch quickly discovered that he was out of his depth at Oxford. "He was a pudgy, awkward, attention-seeking bloke," says one of his classmates today. "Very Aussie, very provincial, a horrible accent. Smart, no doubt, but thoroughly rough around the edges as compared to most of the young English nobs in his class—snooty lads from the best schools, Eton, Harrow, Charterhouse, that sort. Early on, everyone I knew gave him a wide berth. We learned that he was the son of this important Aussie newspaper chap, but that was of no moment. Important Aussie newspaper chaps were about on a par in significance to Oxford Street clothing merchants.

"But Rupert had a quality. I don't know how to describe it, exactly, but he had a knack for getting the attention he sought. One's first impression was of a total nerd. But then, when one got to know him a bit, he turned out to be fairly likable. He had a tremendous desire to be liked, to be respected, to be accepted.

And he went about it in such a pitiably obvious way that one couldn't help but like him in the end."

A once-leftist Australian who was at the university at the time commented on Rupert's politics. "Frankly I found Rupert an embarrassment. He was this wild-eyed pretend radical who nattered on endlessly about the virtues of the working class and the treachery of the capitalists and the need for revolution. Now all those things might have been true. But he recited them as if he'd been the first to discover them. And he had this way of rattling off his arguments like he'd memorized them from some textbook on Marxism.

"But the real embarrassment was that after all that, he'd spin down to London to spend a weekend with some rich relatives he had there. He'd come back on Mondays filled with chat about how much he'd enjoyed the tea service and all those other little rituals of the English upper classes. One could tell then that his radicalism was more a pose than anything else. Rupert had grown up on a certain tough regimen imposed by his mother and father, and he liked to impart an air of toughness. But behind the toughness he was subjected to at home, there were plenty of creature comforts he could fall back on, take refuge in, when he grew tired of the regimen.

"He used to tell us of how his father forced him to sleep in a shack on the family estate when he was home for weekends from Geelong. And how at two in the morning, when his father was sleeping, he would sneak into the house and make straight for the downy warmth of his bed. And how his father never caught on. So it was all an artificial toughness and sense of deprivation. Behind it was the downy warmth whenever he needed it."

Murdoch admits today that he might have been somewhat of a papier-mâché radical when he arrived at Oxford, but insists that he matured very rapidly into a sincere and deep-thinking one. If so, it was under the tutelage of two figures who had the greatest personal impact on him while he was in England. The first was Rohan Rivett, an Australian who had been sent to London by Murdoch's father as the Melbourne *Herald*'s British correspondent. Still in his twenties, Rivett was, like Murdoch, the son of a distinguished Australian family; his grandfather was among Australia's most celebrated scientists.

But unlike Rupert, Rohan Rivett had already packed what seemed like a lifetime of experience into his relatively short life.

During the recent war he had been captured by the Japanese while broadcasting from Singapore and spent three years as a prisoner in Burma. He had later served as a correspondent for the *Herald* in China and Malaya. He was an Oxford graduate. He had become a much-valued protégé of Sir Keith Murdoch, and his assignment to London was in part a reward for his journalistic promise and in part a commission from Sir Keith to look after his son.

Rupert simultaneously hero-worshiped Rivett and resented him for the high esteem in which he was held by Keith Murdoch. It was as though the tough-minded Rivett were the son Sir Keith wished he'd really had.

Rupert was smart enough, though, to sense that if he modeled himself on Rivett, his father might eventually feel the same way about him. And so he did.

During his first two years at Oxford, Murdoch was a regular weekend visitor at the home the lanky, red-haired Rivett shared with his wife Nancy in the London suburb of Sunbury-on-Thames. Rivett was himself a man of a decidedly radical and crusading bent—apparently no impediment to Sir Keith Murdoch's admiration of him—and a booster of British Labour Party politics. It was Rivett who first encouraged Rupert's tainted, unsuccessful run for office in Oxford's Labour Club, and through out his three years in England, he did much to inculcate in his young charge a more mature, refined, and intellectually tempered left-wing outlook. Many of the positions Murdoch took in upperclassman debates at Oxford were as much Rivett's as his own.

Despite Rivett's influence, though, Murdoch still seemed unable to make any headway with his father. Keith and Elisabeth Murdoch traveled to Oxford to visit him toward the end of his second year. So discouraging were the reports Sir Keith received about his son's academic performance that he proposed to pull him out of the university and drag him back to Australia with them. Only Elisabeth Murdoch's intervention saved Rupert—not that he would have minded being yanked from the school. She was convinced that such a measure would be a shattering blow to her son's shaky pride and confidence, and she persuaded her husband to give him another chance.

She made it clear to Rupert, though, that she expected him to do his part to justify her faith in him. She subjected him to the sternest lecture she had ever delivered, assuring him that if he failed her this time she would "lose the last shred of respect" she still had for him.

The warning shook Murdoch to his bones, he says today. There was something about his mother that always fired him with a desire to please. It was a desire much easier to fulfill than his need to please his father. This was no doubt due to the fact that, in reality, there was no pleasing his father, whereas his mother was always ready to praise him, however stiffly, for his slightest accomplishment.

The heart condition that had felled Sir Keith Murdoch in the 1930s was now back and haunting him. At sixty-four, he seemed even older and more pessimistically out of touch with Rupert's crass youthfulness than ever. Elisabeth Murdoch, on the other hand, was still only forty-one and brimming with vitality and optimism. She believed she possessed a special insight into Rupert, one beyond that created by the ordinary mother-son bond. She saw much of her own father in him and was convinced that the superior "Greene genes" would prevail to lift him out of his college-boy behavioral difficulties. Soon she would find herself in a position to bet her entire future on it.

Chastened by his parents' visit, Murdoch resolved to turn a new leaf. One of his father's conditions for allowing him to stay at Oxford was that he work at a summer job with an English newspaper to get his feet wet in the business. Rupert was agreeable, but wondered why he couldn't go back to Melbourne for the summer and work on the *Herald* or some other paper.

"Absolutely not," said Keith Murdoch. "Back home they'll pamper you, knowing who you are." He added that he wanted no personal at-home embarrassment at the failure he half-expected Rupert to be at this test of his mettle.

"You'll go up to Birmingham," the elder Murdoch said. He told Rupert that he'd already talked to a friend, the publisher of the Birmingham *Gazette,* and that a summer spot had been set aside for him there. Rupert didn't have to guess that his father had also already demanded that the *Gazette* people be as tough as possible on him.

Keith Murdoch bought his son a small car and saw him off to Birmingham, in the heart of Britain's grimy industrial Midlands. There, Murdoch reported to Patrick Gibson, the *Gazette*'s chairman and the man Keith Murdoch had prevailed upon to provide the job. Gibson turned Rupert over to Charles Fenby, the paper's editor.

Fenby was a "cool, remote operator who ran his paper with a perpetually arched eyebrow and a quizzical smile," as one former *Gazette* staff member remembers him. "He was a tough customer to deal with because one never knew what he was thinking. He wasn't a bad editor, but with his superior, condescending manner he could be hard to like as a person."

Rupert—or Rupe, as he was commonly called during his Oxford years—took an instant dislike to Fenby. The editor relegated him to the most menial, meaningless jobs around the newsroom and then, when he took notice of him at all, criticized Murdoch's performance with icy glares and acidic mutterings of disgust.

Fenby's attitude was partly due to his commission from Keith Murdoch, via Patrick Gibson, to put Rupert ruthlessly through his paces. It derived also from the fact that Fenby resented being forced to serve as a functionary in what was nothing more than an experiment to see how the privileged son of Sir Keith Murdoch took to everyday newspapering. Fenby had struggled his way up the hotly competitive ladder of British journalism and had a high opinion of his own worth. It nettled him to have the young Murdoch around. Rupert was a reminder that there were those in the newspaper game who would never have to struggle to achieve success.

The situation was not helped by Murdoch's attitude. Immediately upon his arrival at the *Gazette*, rather than play the eager-to-learn apprentice, he adopted a superior pose of his own and made it quickly apparent that he was there only under duress. He constantly let it be known that he thought the work he was given to do—basically "gofer" chores—was far beneath him. And he took to criticizing the *Gazette*, comparing it unfavorably to newspapers in Australia.

In the words of another who was on the scene that summer, "He was an all-round obnoxious mutt and general pain in the ass."

Nevertheless, it was a watershed experience in Murdoch's life. On his own for the first time in the bowels of a big-city newspaper, he discovered that he enjoyed the business and camaraderie of newspapering.

Back at Oxford at the end of the summer, he communicated

his discovery in a long, enthusiastic letter to his father in Melbourne. Keith Murdoch was encouraged, but in his reply he took a "we'll see" approach to Rupert's epiphanic missive. He also ordered him to write a letter to Patrick Gibson, thanking him for his summer at the *Gazette.*

Murdoch sent such a letter to Gibson, but he was not content just to thank his father's friend. He then analyzed the weaknesses he perceived in the *Gazette,* pinned most of them on Charles Fenby, and urged Gibson to replace Fenby as the paper's editor.

Gibson did little more than chuckle at what he later called "young Murdoch's collegiate cheekiness." But Rupert had been quite serious, albeit motivated by revenge for Fenby's cavalier treatment of him. When asked today to confirm that he lobbied for Fenby's ouster, Murdoch says, "Sure I did."

Murdoch resumed his studies with a new seriousness and sense of direction. The Birmingham *Gazette* had been a hothouse of street-level left-wing dogma. He'd had his first immersion in the politics of trade unionism during the summer and his first experience of the burgeoning grassroots socialism that was preoccupying most of postwar England. All this was far different from the mélange of theoretical material he had half-learned during his previous two years in the insulated atmosphere of Worcester College.

"There was no doubt that Rupert was a confirmed, hard-core Socialist," recalls another Oxford classmate. "And he had a lot of good things to say—trenchant, relevant points. But he had an insufferable manner about him that always worked against whatever it was he had to say. 'Red Rupe' was his nickname. This was given more to characterize his political style than his political substance.

"He was grossly impatient and brooked no disagreement. He tended to lord his so-called experience over everyone. He knew more about the real world because of his newspaper background—that was his line. He blithely ignored the fact that many other leftists in the school were the offspring of working-class families—miners, railroadmen, and such. He took a dictatorial approach to his politics, and if you dared to disagree with him on some minor point he would banish you from his small circle.

"He was a debating bully and would often resort to *ad hominem* attacks when his logic and clarity of language faltered. Most of us viewed him as a caricature of some young Russian commissar who, like Stalin, would simply have you shot if you deviated from his party line.

"Actually, with Rupert there was really no need, no room, for debate. He had all the answers, and if you didn't go along with him you were nothing. You were a 'putrid little shit,' or some such expletive. That was his style. He could be very charming and 'nice-chappy' to those who sucked up to him for whatever reason they did. But woe if he turned on you.

"At school, politics was practically his whole life. He was good at little else, interested in little else except wagering. So he tried to make his mark with his politics. But his manner was so blindly and bloody offensive that although his politics were acceptable, he could never get much respect. He could never become the leader he so desperately wanted to be."

Interested in little else? Not according to Murdoch. He says that he was a normal, red-blooded college student who had many friends, chased girls, went on the usual drinking binges, engaged in slapdash horseplay, tried at sports, and never had enough money, no doubt due to his gambling. He received a monthly allowance from his father, which "was adequate but certainly not lavish."

He is proud of the material modesty of his university years. Part of it had to do with his proletarian outlook; it would have been unseemly for him to have lived and spent up to his family's economic station. The other part stemmed from his father's tight-fistedness.

"No one could say I was spoiled," Murdoch asserts. "I never had a bit of the good life. I was surrounded by students who had much more to live on than I. They spent every penny on social diversions. I led a rather Spartan existence."

Murdoch's seriousness upon his return to Oxford from the Birmingham *Gazette* did not extend to his formal studies. Enrolled in a program of politics and economics, his attitude toward classroom work remained indifferent, although he began to do extracurricular research and writing on his own. As a consequence, toward the end of his third year he was once again in danger of washing out.

"There was always something more interesting to do than attend to the course work. I worked hard in the courses I was interested in. Unfortunately, there weren't many of those. Actually, I was impatient by then to get back home and start doing newspaper work."

Much of his impatience stemmed from the fact that his combined mentor-rival, Rohan Rivett, had returned home. He had been called back to take over the editorship of Sir Keith's own paper in Adelaide, the *News.*

Many in Australia were perplexed by the elder Murdoch's choice of Rivett to run the Adelaide *News.* Although the younger man was widely perceived as a future star of that country's newspaper scene, he was known to be poles apart from Sir Keith politically. What they didn't know was that the appointment was Rivett's reward for his two-year stewardship of Rupert in London. Sir Keith credited Rivett, much more so than he did the Birmingham *Gazette,* for stirring Rupert's nascent journalistic ambitions.

Furthermore, the Adelaide *News,* a small-circulation afternoon daily that Sir Keith had taken over soon after the war, was struggling under its stale, prewar-style editorship. Adelaide was 350 miles from Melbourne. Murdoch, still in charge of the Melbourne *Herald,* had been unable to revitalize the *News* from such a distance. Nor had he been able to mount the traditional circulation battle with the *News*'s main competition, the Adelaide *Advertiser.* The *Advertiser,* as it happened, was owned by the Melbourne *Herald,* and Murdoch would have been caught in a conflict of interest had he sought to push his own paper over that of the company that paid his considerable salary.

But in 1951, at the age of sixty-five, Murdoch was preparing to retire from the *Herald* organization. He intended to devote his time thereafter to building up the *News* and its weekend version, the Adelaide *Sunday Mail,* and his other paper in Brisbane, the *Courier-Mail,* in which he had also acquired a controlling interest just after the war. His goal was no less than to create a smaller model of the profitable *Herald* newspaper chain. In this regard, he was also involved in an attempt to purchase a major interest in the Melbourne *Argus,* which was owned by a British press conglomerate headed by Cecil King, the eccentric nephew of Murdoch's onetime mentor, Lord Northcliffe.

It was in this context that Murdoch offered the Adelaide job to Rohan Rivett. Rivett was too outspokenly left-wing to be brought back to the conservative Melbourne *Herald.* Besides, perceived throughout the *Herald* organization as a personal protégé of Sir Keith's, he would be treated as a pariah by those who succeeded Murdoch at the *Herald.*

Murdoch had in fact been grooming Rivett for a future not

at the *Herald,* but in the separate and private newspaper organization he had been putting together since the war. Sir Keith had satisfied himself that Rivett was a newspaperman first and a political animal second. A further heart-to-heart talk with Rivett, when Keith Murdoch went to England to visit Rupert, brought Rivett's reaffirmation of this.

It was then that Sir Keith offered Rivett the editorship of the Adelaide *News* and an important executive future with News Limited, the holding company under which Murdoch operated the Adelaide papers and planned to expand his mini-empire.

The void created in Rupert Murdoch's student life by Rohan Rivett's return to Australia in 1951 was gradually filled by the emergence of a new mentor. His name was Asa Briggs, and he would have a crucial impact on the further formation of Murdoch's personality and ideas, if not his character.

Briggs was a brainy, dynamic honors graduate of Cambridge University. Ten years older than Murdoch, he was the son of Yorkshire parents and had served with distinction in British Intelligence throughout much of the war. At war's end, when he was still only twenty-four, he had settled at Oxford to teach and write. By the time Murdoch enrolled at the end of the 1940s, the pudgy, bespectacled Briggs was a popular young professor of history and economics with fashionable but moderate, craftily thought-out, left-wing views. Though tough-minded and blunt, he was loaded with charm and sophistication and was famous around Oxford for his colorful style of teaching.

When Keith Murdoch and his wife visited Oxford near the end of Rupert's second year, Sir Keith had solicited Briggs's advice about his struggling son's prospects. Up to then, Briggs had scarcely noticed Rupert. But he was impressed by the senior Murdoch, having already known him by reputation, and he promised to take a special interest in Rupert if Sir Keith allowed the young man to continue at Oxford.

As it happened, Briggs was writing a book about the social and industrial development of the city of Birmingham. He mentioned that he'd be spending much of the coming summer there working on his research. It was then that Murdoch hit upon the idea of Rupert's also spending the summer in Birmingham.

Briggs agreed to take the younger Murdoch under his wing and give him individual tutoring in Birmingham. Still living on an assistant professor's modest salary, the thirty-year-old Yorkshireman was happy to have the extra money the elder Murdoch offered him.

During that summer in Birmingham, a close relationship developed between the charismatic Briggs and the cocky Rupert Murdoch. Many who knew them say that as a result, Murdoch's personality began to evolve along twin, often contradictory, tracks. On the one hand, he retained much of his innately raspish, petulant, attention-seeking manner. On the other, he gradually assumed a more suave, droll, and loftily superior style that seemed consciously modeled on Briggs's.

Although Briggs originally looked upon Murdoch as little more than a between-terms tutorial client, he gradually came to enjoy the young Australian. In the beginning, he was flattered, no doubt, that the son of the celebrated Keith Murdoch should try so hard to emulate him. But over the next two years, Murdoch began to evince signs of independent intellectual maturity and emotional stability. He became in Briggs's eyes "genuinely endearing in many respects."

"Between Murdoch's second and third years at Oxford," recalls another who knew him well, "he went through a sea change in personality. He became much cooler, much calmer. He affected a more sober, thoughtful demeanor. His latent aggressiveness, theretofore so bloody-minded unpleasant, turned into stubborn but relatively subdued arrogance. He never had the stuff of a born leader, but he developed the attributes of a boss.

"Socially, he remained fairly much his old self. He was never at ease, never spontaneously forthcoming, and that did not change. He was still a bit oafish. He seemed to have little interest in the opposite sex—indeed, so far as any of us could tell, he was frightened of women, had no use for them.

"But on another social level—by which I mean the politics of university life—he changed enormously. He asserted himself, fought for his beliefs, stood up to others, made himself abundantly visible, all of these in a much more clever way than he had before. Not always nicely. But certainly in a more grown-up fashion.

"Perhaps it was simply the process of natural maturation taking hold—after all, we were all going through sharp changes as we approached adulthood. But a great deal of it had to do with Asa Briggs's influence. They were as close as a hand in a glove at the end there."

Today, Murdoch readily acknowledges Briggs's influence on him. "He certainly had no Svengali effect on me, as I've often heard it bruited about," he told me. "Nor was he really a mentor. But doesn't everyone who goes to university encounter a great teacher or two who influences his way of thinking? Briggs was that to me, certainly. And it happened that we became good friends."

The Beaverbrook Factor

Murdoch's life was about to undergo its most radical change as he began his final year at Oxford in the fall of 1952. Early in October, his father suddenly died.

Sir Keith had all but retired from the Melbourne *Herald.* He had spent much of 1952 involved in the long and often heated process of selecting his successor, while at the same time unsuccessfully attempting to add the morning Melbourne *Argus* to his small stable of personally owned papers.

The man he had trained to succeed him as the *Herald* company's managing director, his longtime assistant and close friend, John Williams, had incurred Murdoch's disfavor at the last moment by some act of real or imagined disloyalty. At the start of October, Sir Keith had sought to persuade the company's board of directors to pass Williams over and find someone else. This brought an acrimonious confrontation between Williams and Murdoch in Sir Keith's office on Melbourne's Flinders Street, the *Herald*'s headquarters.

The next morning, Sir Keith was dead of a heart attack. He was just sixty-six. Williams, in the end, succeeded him. The Murdoch family never forgave him.

Sir Keith's death came at Cruden Farm in the early hours of a Saturday. Rupert made the long flight home to Melbourne for the funeral. Once home, he was loath to return to England. But after a brief interval, his mother insisted on it. It would take time for Sir Keith's convoluted financial affairs to be sorted out and for his will to be probated. Rupert must complete Oxford, Elisabeth Murdoch insisted. He must, she implored, finish for her.

Murdoch obeyed. And finish he did, but only by the skin of his teeth. By the time he returned, he'd missed a massive amount of important course work. Coupled with his previous academic deficiencies, that fact lessened the likelihood of his being able to pass his final examinations for a degree.

It was Asa Briggs who saved him. Murdoch arrived back at Oxford with a large cash bankroll. Whether this represented an interim bequest from his father's estate or his winnings at the Melbourne race course while he was there for his father's funeral, or a combination of both, I have not been able to determine.

Whatever the case, Rupert, for the first time in his life, had plenty of money on his hands. As the end of the school year approached, he and Asa Briggs left Oxford for several weeks of travel together. During their trip through France, Briggs crammed Murdoch with the volumes of catch-up material the Australian needed to know to pass his examinations. After they returned, Murdoch managed to graduate with a third-class degree, the lowest awarded by Oxford.

During that time in England, Murdoch's fate was being shaped in far-off Melbourne. The probating and settlement of Sir Keith's estate had become a much more nettlesome—and in many ways more dismaying—problem than anyone anticipated. Sir Keith had died a well-to-do but not wealthy man. In fact, he was far less wealthy than anyone supposed, including his wife and children. Most of his personal holdings were tied up in his ownership of the still-struggling papers in Adelaide and Brisbane. He had left those holdings in a trust to his family, with his forty-three-year-old widow as chief beneficiary and administrator of the children's eventual shares.

But as crafty a financial manipulator as Keith Murdoch had been in life, particularly on behalf of the *Herald* organization, he had been inept in arranging for the survival of his personal estate. He had placed his family's future in the hands of uncreative, unimaginative lawyers and bank fiduciaries who became the administrators of his will on behalf of Elisabeth Murdoch. As a result, there were considerable death taxes to pay before Sir Keith's estate could be settled. And those taxes threatened, if not to wipe out the modest fortune he had left, certainly to decimate it.

Murdoch, in England, did not become fully aware of the problem for several months. His father's death had galvanized his theretofore lukewarm ambition to follow in his footsteps. With the senior Murdoch's regular litany of misgiving and doubt over his son's aptitude a thing of the past—it was a litany that Sir Keith had often recited publicly, much to Rupert's increasingly bitter resentment—Murdoch felt there was nothing to stop him from stepping directly into his father's shoes. He had extracted a promise from his mother at the time of the funeral that if he went back and finished Oxford, she would use her authority to install him as Keith Murdoch's successor as operating head of what was now the family newspaper company.

Based on that expectation, Murdoch, just after his graduation from Oxford, went to see Cecil King in London. King was the nephew of Keith Murdoch's long-dead mentor and idol, Lord Northcliffe. In the 1930s, he had inherited much of the Northcliffe empire, whose principal papers remained London's tabloid *Daily Mirror* and *Sunday Pictorial,* by then the most widely read and profitable publications in the world. King was building from that rich domestic base the International Publishing Company (IPC), which would develop into the biggest conglomerate of its kind on the globe, with controlling interests in more than a hundred newspapers and other media properties around the world.

Among those newspapers was the Melbourne *Argus,* which Sir Keith Murdoch had tried to buy to provide his small News Limited chain with a Melbourne flagship. Seeing himself about to assume his late father's command of News Limited, Murdoch set out to succeed where his father had failed.

King's personal eccentricities and near-maniacal psychic phobias would later bring him profound discredit in England. For example, in 1968, when the country was beset by a monetary crisis under the Labour Party government of Prime Minister Harold Wilson, he attempted to organize what would virtually have been a coup d'état had it succeeded. His idea was to oust the Wilson government forcibly and replace it by a permanent government of high-level businessmen, which, presumably, would save England from the dire fate envisioned for it by King. When the plan was exposed, largely as a result of Lord Louis Mountbatten's refusal to join the cabal, King was roundly excoriated throughout the nation. Soon thereafter, he himself was the victim of a coup d'état of sorts when he was unceremoniously ousted from his position as the head of IPC.

But in 1953, the powerful King was a model for the young Rupert Murdoch. The trouble was that King made no secret of his contempt for Murdoch's father. It was a contempt born of jealousy over the fact that Keith Murdoch had been an apple of King's famous uncle's eye, whereas King himself had enjoyed no such favor as a young man. When the fifty-two-year-old King deigned to give Rupert an audience to discuss the Melbourne *Argus,* his contempt spilled over in barely concealed fashion on Sir Keith Murdoch's son. Murdoch was unfazed, though. He pressed his case with some financial sophistication and even, for a moment, got the scornful, autocratic King interested.

Between the periodic lectures of his father and the lessons he learned at Birmingham, Murdoch had absorbed well the first financial principle of newspaper proprietorship: cash flow. Popular newspapers were fountains of weekly cash flow, which, when the papers' production and circulation costs were kept to a minimum, made it possible for their owners to live exceedingly well and at the same time plow their surpluses into new publishing enterprises. Murdoch, nervous and earnest in this first major venture into the world of the newspaper business, tried to persuade King that he could turn the ailing *Argus* around and would be able to pay the considerable purchase price out of future cash flow and profits. He went so far as to appeal to his presumed sense of King's spiritual kinship with his father—after all, he offered, both had built their illustrious careers in journalism under Northcliffe's guiding light.

It was all King could do to keep a straight face at Murdoch's "brass," as he later described it. Yet perhaps out of amusement at the young Australian's naïveté, he deferred decision on his proposal and promised to think it over. Murdoch left King's office "walking on air," sure that the imperious press magnate would consent to sell the *Argus* on his simplistic terms. He began to consider whom he'd install as the paper's new editor, and he couldn't wait to cable his mother in Melbourne to announce that he'd accomplished what his father had tried and failed to do for so many years.

But trouble loomed. Murdoch's decision to visit King had been a unilateral one. He'd neglected to inform the men handling his father's estate of his intention and doesn't recall if he'd so much as forewarned his mother. As a consequence, when Keith Murdoch's executors heard of Rupert's offer, after King sent an inquiring cable to Melbourne about the financial condition of the Murdoch estate, they angrily confronted Elisabeth Murdoch and demanded that she put a stop to her son's blithe entrepreneurship. Sorting out the estate was a complex enough task without adding further complications and financial obligations. Indeed, it appeared that the Murdoch holdings in the Adelaide and Brisbane papers might have to be sold to meet the estate's tax and other financial liabilities. Talk of buying a third paper was absurd.

Murdoch was called off by his mother, but his meeting with Cecil King prefigured the business style that would later become his hallmark: opportunism combined with off-the-top-of-the-head strategy. Although today he likes to hire business school graduates to manage his vast complex of subsidiaries, the methodical MBA approach to doing business is personal anathema to him.

Elisabeth Murdoch had made a promise to her son, but that was before she was fully aware of the financial difficulties attendant upon her husband's estate. Now, in 1953, she was being entreated by his executors to sell off Sir Keith's holdings in the Adelaide and Brisbane newspapers to pay estate taxes and other debts and to invest the surplus in annuities that would provide modest financial security for her and her daughters in the years to come.

There was little point in keeping the papers, they argued. Mrs. Murdoch had no personal interest in them, and Sir Keith had repeatedly made it plain before his death that he judged young Rupert to be unsuitable for a career in newspaper management. As fiduciaries, their primary duty was to ensure that whatever remained of Sir Keith's assets were preserved and allocated most favorably for his heirs' benefit. Selling his interests in the Adelaide and Brisbane companies, in their view, constituted the most prudent preservation of his assets.

In any event, it was now clear that at least one of those properties would have to be sold simply to pay the immediate estate taxes and other debts. Until those obligations were discharged, the estate could not be settled. And since one of the papers had to go, why not both? In fact, the Melbourne *Herald,* Sir Keith's former company, was prepared to take them together at an attractive price.

Elisabeth Murdoch was torn between her promise to her son and her confidence in the wisdom of her husband's executors. It was true that she had little or no desire to keep the newspapers for herself. Nor was Helen, her oldest daughter, captivated by the idea. Her two younger daughters, then only fourteen and eighteen, were still too young to take into consideration, but even so, they had shown no personal interest in their father's profession.

Only Rupert, still in England, was urging her to keep the papers—no, demanding that she do so and reminding her of her promise. She, too, was mindful of her husband's pessimism about Rupert's aptitude. Yet she also recalled why she had made her promise to him, for despite Sir Keith's attitude, she still had faith in Rupert. And, as promised, he had finished Oxford.

Elisabeth Murdoch finally resolved her dilemma. With Helen's consent, she told the executors that she would agree to the sale of the Brisbane paper, but that she intended to retain the Adelaide publications for Rupert, at least until he proved himself incapable of running them.

Not only did the executors disagree, so, more vehemently, did Murdoch. "We could have borrowed on both papers' assets to pay off my father's death duties," he says, "then repaid the loans from the papers' excess cash flow. Easiest thing in the world, even then. I was furious that my mother gave in on Brisbane."

But his mother was able to keep her side of their bargain. She told Murdoch that she would install him as her operating surrogate on the Adelaide *News* and *Sunday Mail* as soon as the estate was settled. In the meantime, she wanted him to remain in London for a while to get a deeper grounding in the operation of a popular newspaper, somewhat in the fashion his father had done thirty-five years earlier under the tutelage of Northcliffe.

Grudgingly, Murdoch agreed. There was no longer a Northcliffe around to seek out, however. And he was embarrassed to go back and ask Cecil King for training.

"Beaverbrook, then," his mother suggested. "He liked your father. I'll write him, then you go see him."

Lord Beaverbrook, born William Maxwell Aitken in Canada in 1879, was—even more so than Northcliffe—a legend in his own time in England. He had reverse-immigrated to Britain in 1910 after amassing a fortune as a young man in Canada's burgeoning industrial revolution. Like Keith Murdoch, the son of a Scottish clergyman, he was totally dissimilar to Murdoch in his penchant for dishonesty and trickery. Many of his contemporaries were certain that his fortune had been built on a vast Canadian business swindle and that his arrival in England was more of an enforced bid for sanctuary from those he had fleeced than a voluntary return to the land of his forebears.

Whatever the case, once settled with his riches in London, Beaverbrook took the country by storm. Almost immediately, he managed to power his way into a seat in Parliament. When that proved too limited to satisfy his hunger for political influence, he proceeded, in 1912, to buy up shares in one of Fleet Street's lesser newspapers, the *Daily Express,* which had been established twelve years earlier to compete with Northcliffe's *Daily Mail.*

Beaverbrook quickly found that newspaper ownership gave him much more potent political muscle than parliamentary office. He threw himself into building up the *Express,* and by the middle of the World War I he was not only in clamorous competition with Northcliffe at the newsstands, but was vying with him for full credit for the behind-the-scenes ouster of Prime Minister Asquith.

When Northcliffe died in 1922, the field was left to Beaverbrook to become England's most influential and, in many ways, invidious press baron. In 1918, he had started a Sunday version of the *Express.* In 1928, he acquired, for virtually nothing, London's *Evening Standard.* By 1935, his *Daily Express* forged well ahead of the *Daily Mail* in circulation; at more than two million daily sales, the *Express* now had the largest audience of any paper in the world.

Beaverbrook's method was an amalgam of formulas that had proved successful with other papers before. He championed conciseness and terseness; a lively gossipy writing style; and politics, money, and sex as his papers' chief subjects of coverage. With all that, though, he personally was somewhat of a prude and eschewed blatant sensationalism. Sex, for instance, was always more tittering than titillating in Beaverbrook's newspapers, and stories about freaks, witches, and savants generally were given short shrift. It was in newspaper layout and promotion that Beaverbrook's papers really shone, and in his savvy choice of editors over the years. All in all, the *Daily Express* and its Sunday version became models of the standard middlebrow newspaper in England.

Yet the often entertaining, eccentric Beaverbrook was widely feared and reviled in many quarters for his endless attempts, through his papers, to shape the future of England. An arch-conservative politically, and a man who went to increasingly outrageous extremes to malign those who disagreed with him, he was already on the way to being out of date and out of touch with the mainstream of postwar thinking when Rupert Murdoch went to visit him in 1953. Beaverbrook was in his mid-seventies that year and could muster little interest in the twenty-two-year-old Murdoch's plans for some tiny provincial paper in far-off Australia—even though Murdoch was the son of that country's most celebrated journalist. Beaverbrook had scant patience for his *own* son, Max Aitken, who'd been a much admired war hero ten years before but now, as heir apparent to the Beaverbrook dynasty, was forced to endure the humiliating, almost daily public word-lashings of his increasingly bilious and senile father.

After the briefest of hearings, Beaverbrook foisted his young visitor off on the editorial staff of the *Express*. Murdoch eventually landed in the care of Edward Pickering, the paper's night managing editor. Pickering assigned him to the far end of the subeditors' desk where, under the supervision of a senior copy man, he was given the task of rewriting idle, last-minute filler material taken from the various news wire services to which the *Express* subscribed. Murdoch's main challenge was to learn and master the *Express*'s famous filler style—short, "punchy" sentences sparked with wry turns of phrase, every sentence a new paragraph so that the most space was filled at the least typographical cost.

The impact on Murdoch was enormous. Here he was, actually installed in the mythic Fleet Street and working in the company of what was, in his inexperienced view, the most legendary corps of journalists—reporters and editors—in the world. His salary was a mere ten pounds (forty dollars) a week, but that didn't matter. He had plenty of private cash and was living very nicely at the posh Savoy Hotel nearby. The job was supposed to last only for a few weeks until he was given the okay by his mother to return to Australia. But once the okay came, he felt compelled to ignore it and stay on at the *Express*. "I was having an enormous amount of fun and learning a lot, too," he says.

It was more than that. For the first time in his life he was really on his own—out of the oppressive atmosphere of family and school and charged with carrying out a job that had nothing to do with his former universe or his tightly fixed place in it. He was exuberantly free of his father's humbling presence in his life. It was like being on a cruise ship, he told me, where one is not only physically but also spiritually transported from the routine and mundaneness of one's ordinary life.

Suddenly, Murdoch had second thoughts about returning to Melbourne. Why not a life, at least for now, on Fleet Street? He cabled his mother: I'm staying.

She cabled back: No you're not!

He cabled: Please?

She: It's too late. All arranged for you to go to Adelaide. Everything awaits your return. You wanted it. Now you must do it.

Murdoch complied. But as he left Fleet Street, he silently vowed to return someday.

Adelaide

Australia is roughly the size of the continental United States, yet its total population in 1953 was less than that of the state of New York. Occupying an entire continent of its own, plus the large satellite island of Tasmania, the nation is largely an arid surface wasteland ringed by stretches of fertile coastal plain. As a consequence, the great majority of continental Australia's population lives in the urban, suburban, and rural agricultural areas that by necessity evolved in those coastal regions.

The country is composed of five mainland states (Victoria, the smallest; New South Wales; Queensland; South Australia; and Western Australia), two major territories (the Northern Territory and the Federal Territory of Canberra, successor to Melbourne as the country's capital), and the offshore state of Tasmania.

Australia's system of government is more American in style than British. Its Federal Parliament is closer to America's Congress than it is to Britain's Parliament, consisting as it does of a separate House of Representatives and Senate. The Australian Supreme Court is similar in its function to that of the United States. The executive branch is headed by a prime minister and cabinet, and here, too, the form and methodology are more like those of Washington than London. One substantive difference is that Australia's government remains answerable to Britain's monarchy, at least in the technical and ceremonial senses. Thus, the British Crown maintains an Australian surrogate known as the Governor-General.

There is yet another difference. In Australia, voting is compulsory beginning at the age of eighteen. This, together with the small, relatively homogeneous and regionally concentrated population, produces a more intense national political consciousness than exists in the United States. The two principal political organisms are the mildly conservative-centrist Liberal Party and the left-leaning Labor Party, with the much smaller Country Party serving as the voice of the nation's more strident right-wing minority.

The five mainland states have their own internal governments, which are located in the respective state capitals—Sydney (New South Wales); Melbourne (Victoria); Brisbane (Queensland); Adelaide (South Australia); and Perth (Western Australia). The port city of Darwin on the north coast is the capital of the Northern Territory; Hobart is the capital of the offshore state of Tasmania.

Australia's economy was based originally on sheep-raising and wheat-growing, but during the twentieth century it has become much more rich, diversified, and industrialized. So, too, since the government revised its once highly restrictive immigration laws, has the population.

Nevertheless, Australia remains largely a nation of transplanted British values overlaid with a thick American influence. Despite its early progressive legislation in the matter of women's rights, its society is thoroughly masculine in its sensibility, national outlook, and manner. Toughness, physical courage, stoicism, and athleticism are prized self-perceptions; introspection and intellectual rumination are not. Australians as a whole see themselves as a "go-ahead" people, individualistic doers and achievers living on what is still a lonely global frontier. In some respects they are, but for the most part they are as herdlike in their manipulability and susceptibility to self-propaganda as any other highly organized society.

Adelaide, the capital of the state of South Australia, is the country's third largest city. Situated on the generally sunny south coast, it developed originally as the trading and shipping hub for the region's bountiful agricultural production. But by 1953, it had been transformed into the commercial gateway to Australia's rich inland minerals industry, which was centered on the large mining town of Broken Hill, nearly 300 miles to the northeast. Adelaide was a leafy, wealthy, refined city nearing 500,000 in population. Yet it incorporated many of the two-fisted, hard-drinking habits of an Outback ore camp. It was Australia's Chicago in small scale.

It was there that the twenty-two-year-old Rupert Murdoch

arrived late in 1953, ostensibly to represent his mother and sisters on the board of the Adelaide *News* and *Sunday Mail,* but really—in his own mind—to take charge.

The board was not like-minded. Put in place by Keith Murdoch before his death, most of its members had listened to him bewail his lack of confidence in his Oxford-student son's capabilities. They viewed his arrival as an aberration on Elisabeth Murdoch's part. What could the callow Rupert Murdoch contribute?

However, there were more pressing matters to consider. After Elisabeth Murdoch had refused to sell the Adelaide *News* and *Sunday Mail* to the Melbourne *Herald* group, the *Herald*-owned *Advertiser,* one of the city's other principal papers, announced that it intended to start its own Sunday paper to compete with the Murdoch *Sunday Mail,* as the daily *Advertiser* did with the *News.*

Some members of the *News* board were still perplexed by Elisabeth Murdoch's failure to sell out to the *Herald* in Adelaide, as she had done in Brisbane. The *News* and *Sunday Mail,* though profitable, were only marginally so despite the new-blood vigor that had been injected by the aggressive Rohan Rivett in his two years as editor. A circulation battle with the *Advertiser*'s new Sunday paper would only erase that margin and put the whole *News* organization back in the red, where it had been when Sir Keith had acquired it seven years before. Better now, proposed the same board members, to forestall a costly Sunday circulation war with the *Advertiser* by capitulating and selling the *News* and *Sunday Mail* to the *Herald* group.

Murdoch didn't know quite how to handle the board's polite indifference to him or the air of weary defeatism he encountered. Luckily, though, Rohan Rivett was on the scene, and it was he who pointed the way.

Rivett had enlivened the paper considerably in the two years since Sir Keith Murdoch brought him back from London to run it. He had remodeled it according to the Northcliffe formula, which the elder Murdoch had used so successfully to build up the *Herald* chain, but he'd been given a fairly free rein by Sir Keith in setting the paper's editorial tone and policy. As a result, on the basis of his leftist leanings, he had turned the *News* into a staunch mouthpiece of South Australian Labor Party politics, especially after Sir Keith's death.

Rivett's approach had offended a lot of old readers. But it

had brought in many new ones as well, since Adelaide was much more of an organized labor–oriented city than it had been before the war. The *News* now billed itself as "the people's paper."

Rivett's turn to the left, though, had also offended several key board members, which was another reason they wanted to get rid of the paper. Rivett had been fighting them bitterly during the year since Keith Murdoch's death, using as a defense his insistence that Sir Keith had not objected to the paper's change while he was alive. Indeed, he claimed, Sir Keith had approved of Rivett's transformation of the *News* and its Sunday edition, for he knew that it was the only way to increase circulation. Sir Keith was an experienced newspaperman and thus understood such things. Most of the board members were not.

It was true that the now-disaffected board members had gone along with the change while Keith Murdoch was alive. But after his death, his widow had in effect become the majority owner. Even after she refused to sell to the *Herald,* they had continued to importune Elisabeth Murdoch to agree to their wish to get rid of Rohan Rivett and the team of young left-wing editors and reporters he had assembled to produce the paper. On the theory that her husband would have wanted her to, she refused. She didn't particularly care for Rivett either, thinking him too much of a noisy, impetuous crusader, but her primary interest was in perpetuating what Keith Murdoch had started.

With Rupert Murdoch's arrival, Rivett saw a way to put an end to his struggle with the board and consolidate his editorial authority. After all, he had been a valued mentor to Murdoch just a few years before. He saw that Rupert's own once feverish left-wing sentiments had matured into a more thoughtful, pragmatic socialism. The younger Murdoch was no longer the wild-eyed, revolution-spouting quasi-Communist of his early Oxford days. Now he was a reasonably level-headed "thinker" who could write persuasive, pungent essays on social and economic justice and Australia's need to eradicate the divisions between its labor and ownership classes.

Rivett explained his problems to Murdoch and told him that if allowed to, the dissidents on the board would surely wreck the paper. Murdoch's role as a new board member would be ineffectual in preventing it, since he would have only one vote. What he needed was executive authority—in other words, to be in on the running of the paper. In other words, to have the title of publisher. With Rivett as editor and Murdoch as publisher, the two could run the paper as they saw fit, with no substantial interference from the board. At the same time, Rupert would be learning the business from top to bottom. All that was needed was his mother's cooperation in commanding the board to accept him as the new publisher.

Murdoch and Rivett went to Melbourne to confront Elisabeth Murdoch with the problem and urge their solution on her. She agreed and wrote a formal letter to the board, in her majority capacity, directing that Rupert be given the desired executive power.

Her command was carried out, and by the start of 1954, Murdoch was settled in the publisher's office of the Adelaide *News* and *Sunday Mail.* He was also made a vice president of News Limited, the parent company through which the two papers operated and which was controlled by Cruden Investments, Keith Murdoch's wholly owned investment vehicle and now the family's.

The appointments were a massive shot in the arm of Murdoch's still shaky self-confidence. "The Boy Publisher," as he soon came to be known around Adelaide, threw himself into the daily grind of getting out the *News* and *Sunday Mail* with an intensity that belied most people's previous perception of him as a rich man's indolent son. Almost immediately, Murdoch and Rivett found themselves plunged into battle with the *Advertiser*'s new Sunday paper.

Part of Murdoch's understanding with Rivett was that he would be allowed to write occasional reports and editorials, for he needed to learn as much about the journalistic side of newspapering as he did the business side—printing, distribution, promotion, advertising. He invoked that right within weeks.

The *Herald* had dispatched a last-minute letter to Elisabeth Murdoch implying that if she didn't agree to sell the *Sunday Mail,* the Sunday paper their *Advertiser* was about to launch would soon drive it out of business and cause News Limited dire losses. The letter was written in charitable but patronizing fashion, as if offering Keith Murdoch's widow an easy escape from what would otherwise be a painful financial experience.

She, for one, saw the missive as little more than a thinly veiled threat and was incensed that her husband's former company would approach her in such a manner.

Rivett saw it as a ploy on the part of the *Advertiser* to reduce the start-up expenses of its new paper. It would cost them far less to purchase the *Sunday Mail* and fold it into their own operation than to compete with it.

Rupert Murdoch saw it as both, but even more so as a priceless promotional opportunity for the *Sunday Mail.* One day, with Rivett's agreement, he printed the letter on the front page of the Adelaide *News* and accompanied it with a signed, mock-outraged editorial condemning the *Advertiser* and its parent *Herald* company for carrying on like monopolistic bullies.

The furor that followed was intense. Murdoch had broken the first rule of newspapering in Australia: Competing managements simply did not attack each other in print. It was a rule as old as Fleet Street itself, and it had been exported to Australia in all its rigid dignity.

The management of the *Advertiser* was outraged by Murdoch's breach. This was odd, since his stratagem showered as much free publicity on their nascent paper as it did on the *Sunday Mail.* Nevertheless the public enjoyed the public spat, and when the *Advertiser*'s new Sunday paper made its appearance, the war was joined.

In retrospect, Murdoch's impulsive ploy backfired, for the *Sunday Mail*'s new rival cut sharply into its circulation. The two papers fought it out fiercely for several years until business considerations intervened. Their continuing circulation-battle costs were causing each to lose money wholesale, and the News Limited board became alarmed at the way the *Sunday Mail*'s losses were draining the profits of the company's daily newspaper, the *News.* The board finally prevailed upon Murdoch and his mother to accept a truce offer put forth by the *Advertiser,* which was to unite the two Sunday papers under a single banner, with each company to own fifty percent.

Murdoch went along, but today he claims victory was still his. He maintained executive control over the combined paper, he says, and News Limited got the permanent printing contract, which enabled it to keep its presses going through the weekend rather than having to shut down. What's more, he had successfully fended off the ruthless predations of a much larger and wealthier organization. "Not bad for a twenty-four-year-old who was supposed to be a babe in the woods," he boasts.

The consensus of independent opinion among those who recall Murdoch's beginning years in Adelaide is that he performed competently, but that he takes altogether too much credit for himself.

"Today he never mentions Rivett," says one who was on the scene. "But if Rivett hadn't been there, the entire company would have gone down the drain. It was he who nursed Rupert through those early years, who kept the papers really going with his journalism while Rupert was thrashing around trying to learn the business side. Rivett was constantly rescuing Rupert from his mistakes."

Says another, "Though Murdoch was still a fresh-faced kid, he aged quickly. Not that he got old, but that he grew up fast, gained layers of business sophistication very rapidly. When he first came to Adelaide, he struck me as a bit of a softy—a young college idealist out of his element in the police-barracks atmosphere of a gritty newspaper like the *News*. But he flung himself in and got himself initiated real fast. I had to hand it to him.

"Only trouble was, after a year or so he'd gone to the other extreme, thought he knew it all. And that's when he started to get in trouble. He got abrasive and bossy, so that when he made a mistake, the people he'd rubbed the wrong way would jump all over him. This made him very defensive, feeling picked on. And so he'd lash out even stronger. Y'know how a person who's always on the defensive is. Always looking over his shoulder, always ready with an alibi. That's how he became. And his alibis began to stretch the truth, which is also what happens with guys who are always on the defensive."

Recalls another who worked on the *News*, "Rupert's time in Adelaide was really a shake-out period. It was where he learned all his permanent values about everyday business and newspapering. Adelaide had its fair share of business and political corruption. Much of it was in the city's old-line conservative establishment. Remember, Rupert was still presenting himself as a firebrand radical, against all the old-line traditions. Well, if the establishment could be corrupt, it was: 'Fight fire with fire.'

"The same for newspapers. All of Adelaide's other papers fiddled with the truth as if it were some sort of musical instrument. One could play any sort of tune one wanted.

"Say it rained for three hours yesterday. That was the truth—I mean, no one could deny it. Now one paper would come out and say, well, it was only a light mist and it failed to alleviate the drought, and the grapevines or whatever were still withering. Another would announce it as a deluge that threatened to wash away acres of grapes in a biblical-style flood. Another would treat it as yet a different kind of catastrophe, shouting that it had poured so hard that the grapes had been crushed—excuse the pun—by the weight and velocity of the raindrops.

"It was all to sell papers. The truth—the actual news, as it were—was merely a vehicle. The newspaper editors stepped in and drove it in any direction they saw fit, all for the purpose of getting readers. It was a child's game, really. The real news was subservient to the endless battle for circulation and revenue.

"That was the environment Murdoch broke his journalistic teeth on. Very quickly, he and Rohan Rivett were at odds. Rupert was the publisher of the *News* and naturally wanted to increase circulation. He saw what was going on around him, and he decided again: Fight fire with fire.

"Rivett, on the other hand, remained the purist. Oh, he was a crusader for all his humane causes, all right. But he did believe in honest journalism and resisted subverting the truth to advance his point of view. For instance, if some left-wing labor leader got caught with the old hand in the till, he'd report it with as much pizzazz as he would the crooked doings of a right-wing politico.

"So he and Rupert came to loggerheads fairly early on. Rupert, of course, wanted to fight fire with fire. Rohan wanted the *News* to maintain his sacred respect for the truth. He insisted on being Murdoch's conscience, and Rupert didn't like it."

Once the *Sunday Mail* merged with the *Advertiser*'s weekend paper, the *News* began to make a comfortable profit. But it failed to satisfy the taste for out-and-out circulation combat Murdoch had enjoyed during the *Mail-Advertiser* war.

By 1956, he was increasingly itchy to get rid of Rivett and take over the editorial side of the paper himself. But he knew that any attempt to do so would cause chaos among the News Limited board, which by then was squarely behind the paper's editor. And he needed the board's support for other purposes.

The other purposes had to do with Murdoch's growing frustration with his position. In his three years in Adelaide, he had gotten his hands thoroughly ink-stained in the *News*'s typesetting and printing rooms. He had repeatedly dirtied himself at the production desks working on layout. He had edited copy in the news pen and had pasted up photos, written headlines, and even gone out and covered stories himself. He had fought with union shop stewards, cajoled advertisers, argued with distributors, and jousted with Adelaide's political powers.

Murdoch believed he had fully learned the newspaper business, that his apprenticeship was well over. Technically, the *News* was his. But in reality it was not, since he remained unable to exercise control over its editorial direction. Until Rohan Rivett departed, Murdoch could not prove that he could run a newspaper in its totality. There was only one thing to do: Find another paper.

With the backing of his mother and sister, Murdoch had already proposed a program of expansion to the board of News Limited. Expansion, after all, was what his father had set out to achieve. Sir Keith's death had stymied that ambition, but there was no reason to consider it dead. Expansion was a natural condition of newspapering, Murdoch argued.

Look at the *Herald* organization in Melbourne, the Fairfax publishing conglomerate in Sydney, the King and Beaverbrook monoliths in London. Newspapering was like any other business: Expand or perish!

The board had responded "in its usually cautious, provincial manner," as Murdoch put it. "They were mostly small businessmen, lawyers, accountants," he added with distaste.

In other words, they did not share his youthful dream and were quite prepared to oppose any move to acquire another paper. Yet he judged that their resistance to an additional paper would be considerably less than to an attempt on his part to get rid of Rohan Rivett, especially if he could acquire one cheap. Quietly, without informing the board, he put out the word that News Limited was in the market.

The only paper available, Murdoch quickly learned, was a small, feeble weekend publication in distant Perth, on Australia's west coast, called the *Sunday Times*. Perth, a city of only 350,000, was almost 1,500 miles away from Adelaide by air—a six-hour flight on one of the country's internal airlines.

It seemed a dubious proposition. Nor was the price cheap, as it often is with a tired, failing paper. Yet Murdoch leaped at the chance to buy it.

After heated argument, he convinced the majority of the News Limited board to finance the purchase on bank borrowings collateralized by the combined assets of the *Sunday Times* and the

Adelaide *News*. He assured the board that he could turn the Perth paper around and quickly pay off the loans through its cash flow and operating profit.

That had become Murdoch's well-rehearsed business modus operandi. He hadn't yet been tested on its viability in the real-world newspaper marketplace, though. The Perth buy would be just such an acid test. The board realized that and decided it was worth the gamble, if only to prove the headstrong Murdoch wrong. When he failed, the banks at worst would foreclose only on the Perth assets, allowing News Limited to refinance the balance of the loans through Adelaide.

Murdoch, too, realized that it was a test. And he determined not to fail.

After a brief visit to Perth to study the situation, he replaced much of the stodgy *Sunday Times* staff with a small, handpicked cadre of young subeditors and publishing aides from the Adelaide *News*. Perth, isolated as it was on the country's lonely western rim, was arguably the most provincial and least cosmopolitan of Australia's major cities. Murdoch decided that its populace was starving for more news of the outside world, and a lot more local sensation and entertainment, than it was getting from the city's traditionally restrained press. "In a town like Perth, a Sunday paper should be ninety percent entertainment," he said.

Having handed that commission to his surrogates, Murdoch returned to Adelaide. But almost every Friday during the year that followed he was on a DC-3 or some other bumpy piston airliner bound for Perth. Once there, he usually found that his new *Sunday Times* staff had erred on the side of caution, preparing an edition of the paper that, although considerably more lively than anything else in town, was not lively enough for Murdoch's purposes. He would therefore rip apart half the paper and spend most of Saturday reorganizing it—ordering stories to be rewritten with more urgency, color, and exaggeration; thinking up sensational, blaring headlines; cleaning up the paper's layout; and dirtying its tone.

At first, Murdoch operated by the seat of his pants, relying mostly on the Beaverbrook-type journalism he had learned in London a few years before and combining that with his own ideas of what would attract the provincials of Perth without offending them. As time went on, he found that practically nothing he printed offended them. They were buying the paper in fast-increasing numbers, and it was almost as if they couldn't get enough of his saucy recipe. Accordingly, he spent his long weekly plane rides thinking up further forms of entertainment and titillation to put in the paper.

Thus was born in the mid-1950s what has since come to be known the world over as Murdochian journalism—the exaggerated story filled with invented quotes; the rewriting of cryptic, laconic news-service wire copy into lavishly sensationalized yarns; the eye-shattering, usually ungrammatical, irrelevant, and gratuitously blood-curdling headline ("Leper Rapes Virgin, Gives Birth to Monster Baby," read a typical early front page); endless pages of pap disguised as service and entertainment features ("Your Horoscope," "Your Favorite Psychic's Predictions," "How to Keep UFOs Out of Your Garden"); brisk, snappy, self-congratulatory editorials larded with boldface and underlinings, as though the reader had to be guided through the forest of verbiage; the insipid gossip column or two; the extensive space devoted to sports—all wrapped in cheap, smudgy tabloid form and promoted with the apocalyptic fervor and energy of Bible Belt evangelism.

In Perth, Murdoch also learned that as far as commercial appeal and circulation were concerned, what really mattered was not what was in the newspapers he published, but what was in the promotion of them.

"That has always been Rupert's real genius in the newspaper business," says a man who was hired in the early Adelaide years to work on the promotion of his papers and has since followed him around the world in the same capacity. "He always spent much more of his budget promoting his papers to the public than anyone else did. In Perth and Adelaide, it was posters and billboards and contests and giveaways and radio spots, many of which I thought up. Later, in Sydney and London, it was all those things plus television and lotteries. The promo formula was always the same as that for the papers themselves—loud, urgent, upbeat, trashy, and entertaining, and always pitched to the lowest common denominator. It promised a 'new' experience. Whether the papers delivered what the promos promised was another question. But as promos, they were usually good and almost always successful. To paraphrase your bloke Mencken, 'Murdoch could never go broke underestimating the intelligence of the Australian public.'"

The Stuart Affair

His turnaround of the Perth *Sunday Times* when he was still in his mid-twenties filled Murdoch with smug self-satisfaction and produced an increasingly cocky arrogance to go with it. It also broadened his horizons, and he began to move in several directions at once.

His success in Perth gave him growing credibility in Australia's banking community; significant lenders now started to approach him with offers of funds for further expansion. He immediately used his new importance to seize control of the board of News Limited, silence his boardroom opponents, and look about for further acquisition opportunities.

At the same time, fortified by his Perth experience, he went about tightening his grip on the Adelaide *News*. Perth had convinced him that the *News* could stand improvement in reader-appeal—more liveliness, better layout, a much greater entertainment factor. Thus, while at first careful not to impinge too blatantly on Rohan Rivett's editorial authority, Murdoch started to make suggestions for changes in layout and emphasis. Rivett agreed to some, declined others. This only made Murdoch more insistent, and the relationship between the two entered an openly quarrelsome phase.

Their differences heated to a boil over the issue of whether the back page of the *News* should be turned over to advertising. When Rivett had come to the paper, one of his major changes had been to make its back page the front page of the sports section, and to him the back page remained inviolate. Murdoch, though, now saw the page as a promising promotional device to lure advertisers and reduce expenses. He could charge enough for a full-page ad, or several divided ads, to offset a big piece of the paper's daily production costs.

The dispute between the two roiled for almost a year. For all his newfound authority, however, Murdoch still could not bring himself to try to impose his will directly on Rivett. So he resolved the matter in another fashion. When Rivett took his family to Europe during his annual month-long vacation, Murdoch quietly ordered the change made.

Rivett returned, and when confronted by the fait accompli, angrily threw in his resignation. Murdoch talked him out of it, at the same time convincing the editor that the back-page change was a necessary publishing decision dictated by the need to trim costs.

Balefully, Rivett withdrew his resignation and agreed to stay on. Nevertheless the relationship between the two was forever changed. Rivett, aside from once having been Murdoch's mentor, had also been his friend—practically his only friend during his early Oxford period. Rivett's wife had befriended him, too, and to their children he had long been "Uncle Rupert."

Now Murdoch was Rivett's boss, and the editor thereafter was never allowed to forget it. It was as though Rivett's capitulation on the back-page issue had uncovered an unforgivable weakness in his character. Murdoch's dwindling respect for him would finally resolve itself in contempt as he progressively usurped Rivett's function. The entire affair would have near-tragic consequences for the older man.

In the meantime, Murdoch exercised his third role in the company: the expansionist. And once again he jarred the board. Rather than add another newspaper to its holdings, he set out to acquire Adelaide's only television station.

The year was 1957. Television technology had only recently established itself in urban Australia. Programming was still crude and the number of TV sets limited. Nevertheless, having observed the developments of the previous decade in the United States, every Australian communications entrepreneur could see that ownership of a TV station would soon be akin to possessing, as one Commonwealth tycoon rhapsodized, "a license to print money."

As in America, Australia's established radio broadcasters seemed the logical choice for the award of television licenses by the government. Such awards—only one or two for each city at the start—were dispensed by the Australian Broadcasting Board, a government agency much like the Federal Communications Commission in the United States. The Broadcasting Board was largely a creature of the longtime conservative prime minister, Sir Robert Menzies, and his administration. Thus the process of awarding TV licenses was bound to be a highly politicized one.

The twenty-six-year-old Murdoch resolved that he was not to be left out of the coming commercial television boom simply because he was a relatively small newspaper publisher and had no broadcast credentials. His first ploy, a short time earlier, had been to buy a radio station in Broken Hill, the busy mining center northeast of Adelaide. Then, forming a separate News Limited television subsidiary—a lightly capitalized shell company—he applied for licenses in Adelaide and Perth. In the meantime, he used the Adelaide *News* and Perth *Sunday Times* to drum up public support for his applications. Both papers, with their left-wing slant, were normally sharply critical of the Menzies government. In 1957, they intensified their criticism, attacking the government for having repeatedly advanced the idea that experienced radio broadcasters were the only companies qualified to run the new TV stations.

Murdoch got the sole Adelaide license, but only after a long and bitter political fight in which Menzies himself tried to intercede with the Broadcasting Board to prevent the award. As it was, he did succeed in depriving Murdoch of a Perth license, and the two quickly switched from being mere polite adversaries to sworn enemies.

"Rupert," says an old friend, "was getting a reputation as a gut-fighter. And he was also getting known all over the country, not just in Adelaide. He was a newspaperman who was making a lot of news himself.

"He liked that. The board in Adelaide didn't, though. Nor, particularly, did his mother. She was used to a certain amount of controversy in her life from being married to Sir Keith. But Rupert was raising it to a new level. A lot of people liked him and what he was doing. But a lot already hated him. And she didn't know how to handle that except to try and tame Rupert down. It was as if she was saying: 'What is this monster I've created?' "

But there was another woman in Murdoch's life by then, for in March 1956 he had married Patricia Brooker, whom he'd met through the Rivetts. Today, Murdoch refuses to talk about that marriage, which in 1959 produced the first of his four children, a daughter named Prudence. But by most accounts of acquaintances of the period, it was a union doomed to fail.

Speculates one, "Rupert was inexperienced with women. Most Australian men have this 'Sheilah' mentality, what you Americans have taken to calling machismo. ["Sheilah" is Australian slang for "chick" or "broad."] Women have a very compartmentalized place, sex and service. Rupert was no different. He just plain neglected Pat, was much more happy with his mates at the races or in the pub when he had a minute's spare time. Well, Australian women as a rule are used to that. But it didn't sit well with Pat, especially because he always found time for his mother and sisters. She got fed up competing with them. But what really hexed the marriage was what happened with Rohan Rivett."

What happened with Rivett was viewed by many around him as Rupert's vilest deed up to that point in his life—the symbol of a poorly molded character and the harbinger of a more unpleasant Murdoch to come.

It was 1959. Adelaide's TV-9—the Murdoch station—had been launched and was beginning to pile up healthy advertising revenues along with promising profits. Murdoch had made a surprise and nearly successful bid to take over the Adelaide *Advertiser.* He had started a national *TV Guide*-type magazine. Leaving Pat Murdoch at home, pregnant with their daughter, he had made an extended trip to the United States and England to inspect television broadcast methods there and arrange for the purchase of Australian rights to several popular American network shows. And he was formulating his next major plan for News Limited—a move into the big-city newspaper markets of Melbourne and Sydney, where he could really make his mark in Australian journalism and enter the mainstream of the country's political life.

All these diversions had drawn Murdoch's attention away from the daily management of the Adelaide *News.* Rohan Rivett, in the meantime, was thrusting the paper into the middle of a bitter cause célèbre.

A year earlier, a transient carnival roustabout named Rupert Stuart had been tried and convicted in Adelaide for the savage murder of a nine-year-old girl. Sentenced to death, his appeal to the local supreme court had been denied, and a date was set for his execution.

Stuart was an aborigine, a "colored native," the Australian

equivalent of an American Indian. Australia's treatment of its aboriginal population had long been a bitter bone of contention between the country's generally conservative political establishment and its liberal and radical elements. The radicals grasped at the Stuart case as a symbol of the injustices normally inflicted on the aborigines by the establishment. After Stuart's appeal was rejected, they demanded a further investigation of the matter, claiming that his trial had been rigged by the authorities and that the confession he made had been coerced.

At the forefront of the clamor was Rohan Rivett, who among other things had crusaded for reform of Australia's attitude toward its "abos" since taking over as editor of the Adelaide *News* eight years before. Backed by Murdoch, who was preoccupied with his other business ventures but who still presented himself as a champion of Australia's oppressed and disenfranchised, Rivett threw the full resources of the *News* into the fray.

Soon the paper produced "witnesses" among Stuart's acquaintances who claimed that he could not have committed the murder. Each day the *News* featured "explosive" new stories tending to exonerate Stuart and attacking Adelaide's prosecutorial establishment for covering up its own sins in the investigation and trial. This provoked a further review of the case by the Privy Council, the state of South Australia's highest appeals court, but it, too, declined to change the outcome.

Rather than put an end to the matter, the Privy Council's decision further inflamed left-wing passions. Now Rivett and the *News* turned their criticism on the South Australia government itself. Led by Premier Thomas Playford—the doyen of the "White Knights," as Adelaide's conservative political leadership was known—state officials countered with attacks of their own. They condemned the "rabble-rousing of Rivett's radical rowdies on the *News*," in the words of one official statement, and made several sarcastic references to Murdoch, questioning his left-wing credentials and accusing him of using his newspaper to try to embarrass Playford for personal reasons.

Until then, Murdoch had left the fight largely to Rivett and his editorial staff. Now, publicly impugned by what he called "Playford's patsies," he plunged into the battle with journalistic guns blazing. He ordered Rivett to step up his editorial campaign for the formation of a special impartial commission to investigate the Stuart trial. He deployed a team of reporters to dig up dirt on the Playford administration. Privately, he dispatched a note to Playford—the equivalent of an American state governor—threatening to expose improprieties among his staff unless an impartial commission was immediately appointed.

In his further zeal to retaliate, Murdoch all but took over the editorial desk of the *News,* turning it into a grim command post in the escalating verbal war. He not only began rewriting his subeditors' rewrites of *News* reporters' stories, he also substituted his own editorials for those of Rivett, lacing them with his own brand of vitriol.

Rivett was more disturbed than pleased by Murdoch's intervention. By letting his publisher in, he had yielded still more of his editorial authority over his staff; his reporters and "subs" were now taking orders from Murdoch rather than from him.

Moreover, he saw Murdoch's sudden insertion of himself into the affair as more an act of self-aggrandizement and political power-playing than one of genuinely humanist concern for Stuart. For all his progressive posturing, Murdoch had never been a friend of the aborigines. Indeed, he often spoke of them in denigrating terms.

But Rivett knew that Murdoch was planning to buy a newspaper in Sydney, and he wanted to go along as its editor. So he deferred to Murdoch in the *News*'s handling of the mounting Stuart case furor.

Finally, the Playford administration named a special three-man commission to look into the charges that Stuart had been railroaded. But that simply refueled the controversy. Midway through the hearings, the lawyer for the convicted killer stormed out. He proclaimed that the commission, two of whose members were the trial judge and the judge who had presided over the rejection of Stuart's Privy Council appeal, was unfairly stacked and merely going through the motions.

Murdoch bannered the walkout in the next day's paper, writing a front-page headline that purported to be a quote straight from the disaffected lawyer's mouth: "These Commissioners Cannot Do the Job!" In addition, he approved the wording of a pair of crude street posters promoting that day's edition. Each contained further headlined statements, attributed in direct quotes to Stuart's attorney, that made it appear that the attorney had attacked the personal integrity and honesty of the commission members.

Under Australian law, such statements could be interpreted

as criminal libels. Stuart's lawyer promptly denied that he'd uttered the words the *News* attributed to him. The Playford administration erupted in a paroxysm of indignation. It accused the *News,* and Murdoch specifically, of concocting the quotes. Playford himself announced that the *News*'s headline and posters were "the gravest libel made against any judge in this state" and hinted that a libel action against Murdoch and the *News* would follow.

The next day, with Rivett away, Murdoch authored an unsigned front-page editorial in which he admitted the deception: "Mr. Shand did not use these words and the headline should never have been published and we regret that it was." He also apologized for the posters.

But he did not let it go at that. He went on in a wounded, sanctimonious tone to defend the paper, claiming that errors sometimes occur in the journalistic "fight . . . not only for justice to be done but for justice to appear to be done." And he finished with a rousing, self-righteous climax set in bold-face capitals: **WE MAINTAIN THIS STAND AND WILL CONTINUE, WITH PRIDE, TO FIGHT FOR THIS IDEA!**

The entire statement was the prototypical Murdoch approach to being caught in a trap of his own making: a slight bow to the truth, then a self-serving, propagandist excuse for having ignored or distorted it in the first place.

In the end, Murdoch was able to boast that the ruckus kicked up by the Adelaide *News* resulted in the commutation of Stuart's death sentence to a sentence of life imprisonment. Today, he says that he has no doubt, and had no doubt at the time, that the aborigine committed the murder, but that he is still sure the police fabricated evidence to get Stuart's conviction.

But the South Australia government brought a criminal libel indictment against the *News* and Rohan Rivett, who was arrested and released on bail. As publisher and editor, respectively, Murdoch and Rivett stood to go to prison if convicted.

At trial in 1960, they were eventually acquitted, but only after testimony by Rivett and Kenneth May, a former *News* political reporter who had become one of Murdoch's right-hand men on the paper's business side, made it clear that Murdoch had been the principal hand in the publications at issue. Murdoch himself refused to answer questions.

The testimony was given with Murdoch's approval, though. He'd learned that the government was not interested in sending the son of the illustrious Keith Murdoch to jail, but was intent only on giving him an object lesson. If he would take the brunt of the blame, the government would not press its case.

By 1960, Murdoch, immersed in his efforts to move into Sydney, was bored by the entire affair. Hence, he went along with the charade of the trial. Rivett did, too, but more reluctantly— much to the annoyance of his onetime protégé.

In Murdoch's account, Rivett had become "unhinged" by the clash, one moment fearing the possible consequences of the trial, the next, "almost hungering for a conviction so he could go to jail and become a martyr" for the cause of radical journalism. The way Murdoch's snap-judgment mind works, Rivett's vacillations betrayed a serious character weakness.

Whether real or imagined, they gave Murdoch the final excuse he needed to get rid of his former friend and mentor. A few weeks after their acquittal, he fired Rivett via a terse three-sentence letter delivered to his office. The letter was opened by the editor's secretary, who promptly broke down in tears. When Rivett got it, he cleaned out his desk and was gone in an hour.

According to the accounts of others, though, it was Murdoch who had become unhinged. Rivett had no wish to go to prison. But he was profoundly dismayed by Murdoch's complicity in what was essentially a trial that was no less rigged than the Stuart murder trial had been.

Rivett had originally been astounded by Murdoch's editorial admitting the false headlines and posters. He believed a newspaper must stand behind what it prints, that it should be willing to go to court to defend its integrity, and that Murdoch, without consulting him, had prematurely caved in to threats by the Playford administration. Notwithstanding Murdoch's editorial, a case had still been brought against them, and his admissions were now being used against them to prove the libels they stood accused of. Had it not been for Murdoch's apologia, the government would have had no real grounds to bring its case.

Rivett believed that having allowed himself to be sucked into the judicial system, Murdoch, as the publisher of the *News,* had a solemn duty to defend the paper—and themselves—against the charges, even at the risk of a guilty verdict. Despite his refusal to give testimony, Murdoch's posture during the trial had grown increasingly conciliatory toward the prosecutors.

When Rivett learned the reason—a tacit deal between Murdoch's lawyers and the Playford administration to wrap up the matter without convictions, in exchange for a post-trial editorial in the *News* reaffirming its faith in the judicial system it had so vehemently attacked—he was at first livid. Soon, though, he was persuaded to go along with the strategy, mostly by hints from Murdoch that it would be best to put the whole matter behind them so that they—Rivett included, or so he was led to believe—could proceed with Murdoch's planned takeover of a newspaper in Sydney.

Rivett, then, went along to go along, as it were, in the expectation that he'd soon be editing a paper in Sydney and making more money. It could fairly be said that by sacrificing his principles, he got what he deserved from Murdoch.

Yet friends of his insist that he had no choice but to accede to Murdoch's strategy, and that he deserved nothing of what he got. They hold that Murdoch was happy that Rivett had thrust the *News* into the Stuart case, for it had raised circulation by the thousands, but that when it came time for the Playford administration to exact retribution, Murdoch needed a scapegoat to absolve himself of his own blame with the board of News Limited, which had also been named as a defendant in the case.

Murdoch, they claim, killed two birds with one stone when he fired Rivett. In addition to solving his "Rivett problem," he also got himself off the hook with his board, in the process further cementing his authority. As a by-product, he established a new hard-and-fast policy for himself—no more editorial independence on any of his papers. Thenceforth, he would always be the boss of the news and editorial pages, and those he hired who later challenged that regency would do so at their own peril.

Rivett's dismissal was the next-to-last installment in the completion of Murdoch's business education. And at twenty-nine it marked the beginning of the end of his political radicalism, such as it remained. Thereafter, he would gradually metamorphose into a stringent right-winger.

The process started with Murdoch's invasion of Sydney. Late in 1958, he had used surplus earnings from News Limited to begin quietly buying shares in the Adelaide *Advertiser,* a plan hatched during his trip to the United States a few months earlier. Ron Boland was an editor who had been instrumental in the Perth *Sunday Times* success. He subsequently became the editor of the Adelaide *News* and accompanied Murdoch on the trip. According to him, Murdoch's scheme at the start was partly serious and partly motivated by his desire to shake up his father's successors at the *Herald* company in Melbourne, which still was the majority owner of the *Advertiser.*

"Ever since his father's death, the *Herald* people had been a thorn in Rupert's side," Boland said. "It was his secret dream to one day take over the *Herald* and clean house. In the meantime, whenever he could make trouble for them, he would."

Early in 1959, armed with a hefty line of bank credit supplied by Australia's recently established Commonwealth Bank, Murdoch made his move. Speaking for News Limited, he publicly offered to buy out the entire *Advertiser* company at a price well in excess of its current per-share market value.

The offer, coming just before the outbreak of the Stuart affair, shook establishment Adelaide to its foundations and provoked a fierce internecine fight within the *Advertiser*'s board. Given the size of the offer, some members lobbied for its acceptance on the ground that it represented too great a profit to the company's small shareholders to turn down. Others, especially those representing the Melbourne *Herald*'s 40 percent interest, refused to consider it, claiming that Murdoch would destroy the respected old paper. The *Herald* majority eventually prevailed, and Murdoch's bid was foiled.

But not without some expense. Murdoch's offer had made the *Advertiser*'s many non-*Herald* stockholders realize what their stock was really worth, which was considerably more per share than the price at which it is was being traded. Thereafter, they began to put organized pressure on the *Advertiser*'s management to improve the stock's performance. To counter the pressure, the board was forced to increase its annual dividends, thereby eating into the company's profitability and eroding its performance.

Murdoch thus had a victory of sorts. And he still had his hefty line of bank credit. But when he began to look at the prospect of moving into a Melbourne paper, the *Herald* group made it clear that they would leave no stone unturned in their resolve to thwart him there.

Murdoch had learned by then to pick his own fights. Nothing would have given him more pleasure than to go head to head against the rich, powerful *Herald* on its—and his—home turf. But given the current nationwide stink about his role in the Stuart affair, he realized the time was not yet ripe to advance on staid, conservative Melbourne. So he turned his acquisitive eyes on the more raffish Sydney.

Sydney

Australia's most populous city in 1960 at two million, and its most cosmopolitan, Sydney had a lucrative newspaper market long dominated by three rival dynasties headed respectively by the Fairfax, Packer, and Norton families.

The Fairfax Company owned the Sydney *Morning Herald* and evening *Sun*, along with their Sunday editions, and was operated by Rupert Henderson, widely considered the city's sharpest, toughest press baron.

The Packers had the *Daily Telegraph,* the *Morning Herald*'s principal competitor, and the *Sunday Telegraph.* Frank Packer, a rough-and-tumble ex-prizefighter, stood at the head of the *Telegraph* company.

Ezra Norton had inherited the Norton chain of low-grade tabloids in Sydney, Melbourne, and Brisbane, and by 1958 was intent on selling all three. Among them were the shoddy afternoon Sydney *Mirror* and its Sunday edition, each of which competed, after a fashion, with Fairfax's *Sun*.

Norton had told Fairfax's Henderson of his intention to sell. Henderson, afraid that Packer might buy the *Mirror*, slick it up, and thus go into competition with him in the afternoon as well as the morning, took it off Norton's hands himself, along with the Melbourne and Brisbane tabloids. Originally, he flirted with the idea of shutting down the sagging *Mirror,* but he feared a public outcry. So he kept it running, in effect competing with himself, albeit at a growing loss. Finally, early in 1960, he could bear the losses no longer and began to look for a buyer. His only exclusions were the Packer family, for obvious reasons, and the Melbourne *Herald,* to which he was loath to give an opening in Sydney.

Then along came Rupert Murdoch, himself looking for an opening. Murdoch had made his initial advance on Sydney by buying a string of suburban papers and a women's magazine from the Cumberland company, which was headquartered in Parramatta, a few miles north. He'd paid a million Australian pounds for the package—a high price, but a mere dent in his Commonwealth Bank credit reservoir.

Now, from his new base in Parramatta, he surveyed the Sydney scene. He knew Rupert Henderson as a friend of his father's and decided to call on him.

As a result of his visit, Murdoch agreed to buy the Sydney *Mirror* from the Fairfax organization, plus the two small ex-Norton tabloids in Melbourne and Brisbane, all to the consternation of Henderson's advisers. They had warned him against selling the poor-cousin *Mirror* to the "young troublemaker from Adelaide." Their grounds were that on the basis of his past record, Murdoch would cut advertising rates, make his own deals with the print unions, and upset the Sydney applecart in dozens of other ways to make the moribund paper competitive with the *Sun.* And besides, said Robert Falkingham, the Fairfax company's treasurer, Murdoch "has proved that he is not a man to honor his agreements."

When Murdoch was a student in England, his favorite newspaper had been London's tabloid *Daily Mirror,* the early twentieth-century invention of Lord Northcliffe. By 1950, the liberally illustrated *Mirror* was by far the biggest-selling paper in the world, the standard-bearer of the Fleet Street tradition of combining sex, violence, and sensationalism with uncomplicated political discourse and putting them into a package that could be read easily in a brief bus or subway ride. When Murdoch sought a temporary job after leaving Oxford in 1953, the *Mirror* had been his preferred choice. He had ended up at Beaverbrook's *Express* only because of his previous embarrassing encounter with Cecil King, the head of the *Mirror* company.

Nevertheless, the London *Daily Mirror* had remained close to his heart in the years that followed. He'd modeled his papers in Adelaide and Perth as much on it as on what he'd learned in his short stay with the *Express.* In fact, Murdoch told me, when he left London to start in Adelaide, his deepest ambition was to return one day as the owner of the *Mirror.* It was, then, a fulfilled prophecy of sorts that the newspaper that brought him into his first big-city market was called the *Mirror.* He promptly set out to remake it on the lines of its London namesake.

Murdoch recalled Douglas Brass, the Adelaide *News* correspondent in London, and named him editor of the Sydney *Mirror*—much in the fashion his father had summoned Rohan Rivett
nine years earlier and installed him at the Adelaide paper. Brass,
a New Zealander, was no Rivett, though. Aggressive and as
tough-talking as his name suggested, but far less ideological, he
also shared Murdoch's admiration for the *Mirror* in London and
was much more accepting of the fact that Murdoch would be the
ultimate framer of editorial policy and journalistic style.

Nearing thirty, Murdoch was fully formed in his character
and personality. His "proletarian" background enabled him to
retain a certain casual breeziness and camaraderie with his employees, whether they were high-placed editors, mid-level reporters, or the "ink-stained wretches" in the printing plant.

"He was a regular guy," says one. "He'd come into the *Mirror* almost every day and, though you knew he was the boss, he'd
get right in there with you like he was just another grunt. He'd
drink with us, go out and eat with us, have us round, joke about,
and so on.

"But he *was* the boss. His friendliness was all a bit calculated.
When he wanted something, he'd come put his arm round and
say—very quietly, at first—'Let's do it this way, eh?' Most of the
time you'd agree and do whatever it was he wanted.

"But if you resisted or disagreed, then it became more tense.
You could see him puffing up, going red, beginning to simmer.
He'd still be quiet, but he'd get like a schoolteacher with a way-
ward student—'You *will* do it this way, whether you like it or
not.'

"And then if you still refused, or if you somehow didn't get it
right, he'd begin to—well, not go loud, but go fussy and tongue-
clucking and exasperated. If you ever got to that point with him,
you were finished. I mean, from there on he wouldn't give you the
time of day, and he would enjoy your discomfort, your feeble efforts to make up to him."

"Once Rupert was in his position of power and appeared to
be on an endless track upward," says another, "it was general
bootlicking time all round. It became clear that he was *The Man,*
and it was either you were for him or against him. There was
endless jockeying for position in the tight little world he created.

"You could be a friend as well as an employee—in fact, he
encouraged that. But watch out if you goofed. He would shut you
out without a qualm, and once it was known you were shut out,

none of his other cronies would have anything to do with you. It was always a shock when it happened, because Rupert was usually so easygoing. Then he would explode, and you felt your whole world had shattered.

"He created a very subtle psychological hold on his people—the ones who remained loyal and in favor. If you were to do a real sharp investigation, you'd see there's not been a single individual that's come out of the Murdoch organization who's known as a significant journalist, someone who rose to the top of the field. They just don't exist. Anybody who stayed with Rupert committed himself to his philosophy, which is not about journalism, but about selling newspapers and getting noticed and making money and wielding power. Not that you can practice journalism without selling newspapers. But you can sell newspapers without practicing journalism, at least in the professional sense of that word. And that's what Rupert and his cohorts are all about, always have been."

Out of his Adelaide and Perth newspaper cadres Murdoch had formed a small, loyal circle of editorial cohorts who understood and agreed with his inflammatory journalistic style, and whom he could trust to carry it out under his constant goading and supervision. Led by Brass, they formed the nucleus of the new regime at the Sydney *Mirror*. Since Sydney was the closest of any Australian city to London in the intensity and grubbiness of its newspaper competition, there were few restraints placed on the new *Mirror*. The Packer and Fairfax groups, themselves cutthroat competitors for the city's large morning readership, had long before established cheap sensationalism and fact-bending as the principal standards for their papers. In order to grab the *Mirror*'s proper and profitable share of the afternoon market, which was dominated by the Fairfax *Sun*, Murdoch and his underlings simply had to outdo the Fairfaxes and Packers in that regard.

Outdo them they did. In two years, much to the embarrassed annoyance of Rupert Henderson, the *Mirror* began to challenge the *Sun*'s dominance. Henderson had fully expected Murdoch to fail with the *Mirror*, which was why he'd agreed to sell it to him over the protests of his closest associates in Fairfax. He'd believed that Murdoch lacked the financial wherewithal to save the paper, much less make it competitive with the *Sun*, whereas the Packer and Melbourne *Herald* organizations each would have had plenty of money and experience to pour into the task.

By selling to Murdoch, Henderson thought he had solved two problems at once. First, the sale would ensure that his *Sun* maintained its considerable dominance and profitability, even increase them once the neophyte Murdoch was forced to admit failure and fold the *Mirror*. Second, by arranging for Murdoch to be the one to close down the *Mirror*, Henderson would avoid having that public onus placed on him. He was almost right.

Although nominally Douglas Brass was the Sydney *Mirror*'s editorial boss, he was in reality no more than the ship's helmsman, taking his steering orders from the captain—Murdoch. That, at least, is the impression one gets from talking to several people who worked on the paper.

"Rupert was here almost every day in the beginning, in his shirtsleeves, tie off, shirt all smudged and fingers filthy with proof ink," recalls a former subeditor, "going over layout, stories, headlines, the lot. It was like 'bringing up baby,' with him the parent and Doug Brass the hired nanny. He was teaching Doug how to be his kind of editor, in the process doing all the work himself, then letting Doug try to duplicate his example, and then picking apart Doug's efforts."

The revival of the *Mirror*, although it took a few years, was by all accounts a remarkable feat. It was made all the more so by the fact that Murdoch was a newcomer to the Sydney newspaper wars and to behind-the-scenes power-brokers of the city's political and business establishment.

But his success as a newspaper businessman was again at the expense of his reputation as a journalist. The *Mirror* quickly became Sydney's most bizarrely sensationalist paper, almost a caricature of what the city was accustomed to in its already shoddy news reportage.

"The *Mirror* had to out-lie the liars, out-distort the distorters, out-shock the shockers," says a veteran of Sydney's newspaper world. "And it did. It raised the standards of Australian journalism to a new low, if you'll forgive the mixed locution."

A typical example of the paper's "inventive" approach, even when it came to what, by all measures, was serious news, occurred during its coverage of a civil war in nearby Dutch New Guinea in 1961. The Sydney *Sun* had a correspondent on the scene who was sending back vivid reports of the fighting, thus scooping the *Mirror* almost daily. Finally, editor Brass prevailed upon Murdoch to allow him to send *Mirror* reporter Brian Hogben to the scene.

After giving Hogben a reasonable time to arrive in New Guinea and organize his reportorial resources, Brass and his colleagues eagerly awaited his first dispatch. But nothing came— day after day, nothing. The *Sun,* in the meantime, continued to scoop the *Mirror* with its own eyewitness reports of the jungle fighting.

Frustrated at being beaten, and still hearing nothing from Hogben despite their repeated calls and cables to Hollandia, New Guinea's capital, the crew at the *Mirror* proceeded to concoct their own story—the sort of dispatch they imagined Hogben would send. Written in suitably purple and punched-up prose, and riddled with jungle-warfare clichés, it told a tale, among other things, of cannibals and shrunken heads. A few days later, with still no word from Hogben, Brass had the "dispatch" printed under Hogben's byline.*

Such was the "fun"—as one *Mirror* old-timer put it to me— of newspapering in the Murdoch fashion. "Nothing got printed straight from the reporter to the page. It all got cut up and rewritten to fit by the subs, the guys he and Brass trained to inject the slime and sleaze.

"It's really not fair to blame the reporters for what went into Rupert's papers. They knew no matter how hard they worked, no matter how accurate they tried to be when they were out on a story, whatever they wrote would be changed to fit whatever game Rupert and his editors had in mind.

"There were two kinds of reporters—those who got fed up and quit, and those who stopped worrying about accuracy and objectivity because they knew it would get them nowhere. Those were the guys, provided they were ambitious and ass-kissing enough, who went far in Murdoch's realm."

Murdoch, though, was not having much fun. Financially, the first two years of the *Mirror*'s existence were a touch-and-go proposition, and he came close more than once to tossing in the towel.

Too, his marriage was breaking up. Soon he and Patricia Murdoch were at each other's throats, with accusations of infidelity and other acrimonies, and consulting lawyers.

Nor was Murdoch's mother pleased with the course his career was taking. She had borne his journalistic excesses in Ade-

---

* Hogben soon surfaced and, despite his annoyance at the false report once he heard about it, eventually became a key editor in the Murdoch organization.

laide and Perth with reasonable equanimity. But Sydney was much closer to home in her eyes, and what Rupert was doing with the *Mirror*—and with the other two small papers he'd acquired with it in Melbourne and Brisbane—had become keenly embarrassing to her. Due to travel to England soon to be made a Dame of the British Empire by Queen Elizabeth, she found it difficult to restrain herself from publicly criticizing Rupert. The family name meant something, after all, and he was sullying it with his meanderings into the near-pornographic.

Finally, Murdoch was receiving a painful and expensive education from Sydney's trade union establishment. Australia had been one of the first nations in the world to accept and protect the rights of organized labor. Its union movement was not only a powerfully well-entrenched component of the country's society but was also reasonably respected. The newspaper guilds were particularly strong, and no big-city publisher could hope to survive without making constant accommodations to his labor force.

In Adelaide and Perth, Murdoch had dealt relatively easily with local print unions that were generally benign in their demands. But Sydney was a hotbed of labor militancy. Many unions, including some within the printing industry, were dominated by Communist ideologues and were even suspected of receiving their orders straight from Moscow.

Emboldened by his success in dealing with the unions in the south and west, when Murdoch took over the *Mirror* he declined to join the Sydney newspaper publishers' association, which existed primarily to present a common front against the unions. He told the other publishers that he could handle the *Mirror*'s unions by himself.

It was a brave but hubristic decision. Learning of it, the leaders of the *Mirror* work force realized that Murdoch would fail to get the support of the city's other papers if they mounted a strike for increased wages and other benefits—which is what they immediately threatened to do.

Murdoch's heavily financed purchase of the *Mirror* demanded that the paper continue publishing so that he would have sufficient cash flow to meet his loan-repayment obligations. To allow it to be shut down by a strike would be a mortal blow, not only to the *Mirror*, but to Murdoch's future standing with the Commonwealth Bank.

Thus cornered, Murdoch was forced to give in to the unions'

demands. As he later put it, "It was terribly expensive and took an enormous toll. It set us back by years in our efforts to make a go of the paper. It was the greatest lesson I ever learned. Publishers must stick together, and if one paper is struck, all must shut down."

The experience was the final installment of Murdoch's newspaper-business education, although he would not always hew to his "publishers must stick together" axiom. And it was yet another stimulus to his rapidly changing political outlook. He realized that as a businessman and publishing entrepreneur, he was a natural enemy of the militantly left-wing organizations—as militant as he had been ten years earlier—that would bleed him dry if given half a chance. "I had to admit it," he told me. "I was a bloody capitalist."

It was not just with the Fairfax group's *Sun* but also with the Packers' *Telegraph* that Murdoch eventually positioned the *Mirror* to compete. Though published in the morning, the *Telegraph* was essentially an all-day paper designed to vie both with Fairfax's *Morning Herald* and with its afternoon-evening *Sun*. Murdoch kept advancing the first-edition printing times of the *Mirror* until it, too, became practically an all-day paper

His other strategy was to market the *Mirror* heavily in Sydney's suburbs. There, by virtue of his earlier acquisition of the Cumberland group, he'd acquired a favorable distribution network and a large subscription list through which to promote the paper. This brought Murdoch the instant enmity of Frank Packer, whose *Telegraph* until then had more or less had the suburbs to itself.

The rich, aging Packer was one of the half-dozen most powerful men in Australia. An outspoken, ultraconservative political kingmaker and a coarse, ruthless, unprincipled business manipulator, he was the scourge of Sydney, at once reviled and feared, and to many an embarrassment. Enlisting the cooperation of Rupert Henderson, who now had his own reasons to resent Murdoch, Parker declared a circulation war on the *Mirror*, vowing to spend thousands of pounds a week until Murdoch was "sent back to Adelaide with his fookin' tail between his fookin' legs," as one of Packer's sons put it in a war-council meeting with Henderson.

Murdoch was not chased back to Adelaide. He fought the battle and, if he didn't win, he didn't lose, either. The *Mirror* survived, eventually to become profitable, and ten years later Murdoch would have the satisfaction of taking the *Telegraph* away from the Packer family.

The war took a further toll on Murdoch's journalistic reputation, though, or what there was left of it. In order to survive, according to Douglas Brass, "Rupert made the *Mirror* more and more lurid." As well, say Brass and others, he took to engaging in sharp, often unethical business practices to save the paper—practices, according to Murdoch today, that were commonplace among the likes of Packer and Henderson and that had to be pursued to survive in Sydney's mean-streets newspaper environment.

It all became too much for Brass finally, and he fell out with Murdoch. He says that he tried to tone down the *Mirror* once its place was established, but that by then Murdoch would have none of it.

"He was a great idealist once. It was wonderful working for him. But in the end, I feel he thought of me as a rather elderly annoyance." An unwelcome reminder of his onetime idealism, is the implication.

Another ex-*Mirror* man says, "The Rupert Murdoch you see today was really formed out of that two- or three-year period in Sydney when he went head-to-head with Packer. If he had any doubts up to then about trashy, untruthful journalism being the road to fame, power, and fortune, he lost them all then. But the real impact was Frank Packer himself. Packer became the role model for Rupert. He was rich, had enormous power, and had achieved his preeminence by being totally crass and ruthless. Those things spoke very strongly to Rupert, and he decided, whether he knew it or not, that he had to beat Packer at his own game.

"He never copied Packer's bombastic personality—he couldn't, because by nature Rupert's too secretive and self-contained. But in everything else—the striving for position and wealth and power over people's lives—Rupert in many respects is a carbon copy of Packer."

I asked Murdoch about Packer. Rather than the usual denunciations I was accustomed to hearing from him about people who'd caused him business and personal problems, I received a gentle, almost fondly remembered response: "An amusing rascal."

This was not surprising, since despite their continued bitter conflict on Sydney's newspaper front, the two became oddly aligned on a different media battleground—television. The Fairfax and Packer groups each owned one of Sydney's two television stations. The government planned to grant a license for a third station in the near future, and Murdoch already had a lobbyist in Canberra, the new Australian capital, working in his interests. Television stations throughout the country, most of them owned by newspaper companies, were allowed to use the airwaves to promote and advertise their papers. This was an opportunity the Fairfax and Packer groups had fully exploited via their Sydney stations, much to the detriment of the *Mirror.*

The license for the new Sydney channel was offered in late summer 1962, and Murdoch was at the forefront of eleven applicants. Once more, he had to face Australia's Broadcasting Control Board, which meant he again confronted a regulating panel heavily influenced by the wishes of conservative Prime Minister Robert Menzies, who was widely believed to be in the thrall of the all-powerful Frank Packer.

Needless to say, Murdoch did not get the license. But he had a contingency plan. The Fairfax-Packer monopoly of Sydney television had brought a small channel in Wollongong, a seaside town forty miles south of the city, to the brink of bankruptcy. The Wollongong station's transmitter was situated atop a hill overlooking the region. Though not very powerful, when pointed north it had enough reach to be received in Sydney, provided viewers' antennas were properly oriented.

The reason the Wollongong station, Channel 4, was nearly bankrupt was that the major American distributors that were the prime source of television programs in Australia would not sell their fare to Wollongong. Their primary customers in the Sydney area were Packer and Fairfax. Packer particularly had warned them that if they sold competing movies and kinescopes to any of Sydney's suburban stations, they would lose his much more lucrative business.

But Murdoch had his own connections in America, going back to the start-up of his Adelaide channel five years before. He put out word in the United States that he was prepared to pay far in excess of what Packer was paying for many popular American films and shows, provided he could have them exclusively for Adelaide—and Wollongong. When his offer was favorably received, he proceeded to purchase Wollongong's Channel 4.

Murdoch thereupon flew to Hollywood and New York to make good on his bid. "I went over to America and bought every new program from every network that was available," he said. "I spent very nearly three million dollars to get Australian rights."

Frank Packer was in the States at the same time on his own buying mission. When he discovered he was being outbid by Murdoch, he realized he'd been outfoxed—"Rupert's revenge for the newspaper war Packer had declared," one of Murdoch's lawyers said to me.

Murdoch went back to Sydney to gear up suburban Channel 4 for the coming season and do battle with the Packer and Fairfax channels in the city. "I was in Honolulu and he [Packer] was in New York. He rang me . . . and he said, 'Let's do a deal.' "

The deal was Packer's offer to sell Murdoch 25 percent of his Sydney station and the same percentage of the Packer channel in Melbourne. In exchange, Murdoch would be required to share most of his newly acquired programming with the two stations while keeping the rest for Wollongong. In that fashion, although the Packer-Fairfax television monopoly in Sydney would be broken, it would only be a crack, not a fissure, and all parties would benefit financially.

Murdoch accepted. The newspaper circulation war would go on, much of it now waged over the air. But for television, Murdoch and Packer had become business partners. Their deal in effect put Packer's imprimatur on Murdoch's presence in Sydney. And by virtue of it, Murdoch now possessed not only a lucrative newspaper and magazine fiefdom in Australia, but a television barony as well.

The Australian

Nineteen sixty-two was of major importance in Rupert Murdoch's life. During that year, he proved that he belonged in Sydney and, though barely into his thirties, could play the power game every bit as well as the veteran major leaguers of Australia's media, business, and political establishment. He proved, too, that he could trim his own political views to fit his entrepreneurial needs, a skill he would perfect in the years to come.

Moreover, Murdoch learned that his burgeoning empire was no longer some small informal family business. It had turned into a major corporation in which accountants and lawyers and dozens of other administrative types were as necessary to its management as his close circle of editors and promotional aides had been to its early growth. As a consequence, he was forced to devote much of his time in the years that immediately followed to reorganizing News Limited into a proper company befitting its new station and to finding executive managers, financial planners, tax experts, labor coordinators, and legal advisers to man the essential below-decks corporate machinery while he, figuratively, remained fastened to the flying bridge with his binoculars, bullhorn, and longtime yeomen.

It was during this period that Murdoch formed his second cadre of intimate aides—the trained and experienced business operators who would help build News Limited into a huge public company spanning three continents.

The most important impact of 1962 on Murdoch, though, was his trip to the United States to buy television programs. It was his third visit in five years. With each trip he became more impressed with the rich style, pace, and diversity of American life.

As far as he was concerned, the United States was light-years ahead of his own country in business competence and sophistication. America's cities and metropolitan regions, along with the multiplicity of its technology, made Australia seem like a waif, a stepchild in the family of industrialized nations.

The United States was at the height of its global power, wealth, and glamour in 1962, and Murdoch began to yearn to be part of it. The only visible Australians of note who were succeeding in America—making money, enjoying its diverse material benefits, dipping into its cornucopia of entertaining diversions—were tennis players. If young tennis players, why not a young newspaper and television mogul? If there were millions to be made in Australia, there were billions in the States.

The highlight of Murdoch's trip was a personal audience with John F. Kennedy in the White House. If anyone better symbolized the masculine glamour and accomplishment of early-1960s America, Murdoch could not imagine who it might be. Received by Kennedy as an important Australian newspaper publisher and television broadcaster, Murdoch, despite the tough-minded visiting journalist pose he assumed, practically melted in the glow of the President's natural charm.

"Rupert very rapidly changed his style of doing business, of conducting himself in general, after spending that time in the States," Bruce Rothwell, one of Murdoch's longtime editors, told me. "At least superficially. He came back even tougher, but quiet-tougher, calmer-tougher, smoother-tougher, his mind more organized with plans, a bit more commanding and imperious after all those years of winging it. I'd say he'd made up his mind to copy the style of lots of the American chief execs he'd met."

The chief executive who impressed Murdoch more than any was New York's Leonard Goldenson, the head of the American Broadcasting Company. He had gotten to know Goldenson on an earlier visit in 1958. At that time, Goldenson was turning the small, feisty ABC television network into a legitimate rival of the twin Goliaths, CBS and NBC. His method was to pursue "downmarket" programming, a combination of entertainment and news shows designed to appeal to the coarser tastes of the American public. ABC became known as the "schlock network" during the 1950s; but Goldenson's strategy worked, and by 1958, the ABC web had begun to erode the dominance of CBS and NBC.

Goldenson's approach to television in America was similar

to Murdoch's to newspapers in Australia. Murdoch was already planning to get into Australian television in a big way in 1958, and his ideas for that medium were the same as they'd been for his papers: downmarket programming. As a result, most of the shows he bought that year for his Adelaide station came from ABC. And he and Goldenson became fast business friends.

It turned into much more than just a business relationship, however. Goldenson was almost twenty years older than Murdoch. He was a cool, tough, decisive executive who played craftily on his role of underdog in the hotly competitive New York television arena, and he refused to be cowed by his much richer rivals or embarrassed by the many outraged criticisms of ABC's programming and promotional methods.

In time, Goldenson became Murdoch's newest mentor. On every one of his trips to the States after 1958, Murdoch did much of his business with ABC, and in 1962, it was Goldenson who persuaded Frank Packer to come to an accommodation with Murdoch over the Wollongong issue. It was, then, a large dose of Goldenson's business philosophy and style that many observers in Sydney perceived in the "changed" Murdoch of 1962.

Goldenson's Jewishness also had a significant impact on Murdoch. Until then, Murdoch had known few Jews well. Growing up in Australia, he'd been exposed to the routine anti-Semitism of that country's Christian-dominated society. At Oxford, the matter became more complicated. Murdoch was there at the time when Israel had just won its independence and was being besieged on all sides by its Arab enemies. For the most part, the English intelligentsia tilted heavily toward the Arabs in its sympathies, the result of centuries of ingrained anti-Jewish social feeling and of the long history of British colonial presence in the Arab world.

On the other hand, the young Murdoch was an avowed Socialist at Oxford. Israel had been the creation of the Zionist movement in early twentieth-century Europe. The nonreligious tenets of Zionism were nothing more than a form of political and economic socialism of the kind espoused by many of England's postwar intellectuals and academics. The Israel of the late 1940s and early 1950s was a rigorously Socialist society that subscribed to the British democratic-parliamentary system of self-governance. Thus, many British Socialists were duty-bound to pull for the "Jewish State." If Israel's existence didn't exactly eradicate the anti-Jewish prejudice that was as endemic in England as it was in Australia, it certainly ameliorated it in many quarters.

As a Socialist, Murdoch quickly came to admire and identify with Israel's struggle to establish itself. And he particularly became aware of how the struggle, so often one of violence, was exploding some of the anti-Semitic stereotypes he had grown up on—for example, that Jews were physical cowards. As for the stereotype of Jews being financially aggressive, brash, devious, cutthroat, pushy, and concerned only with making money—well, he certainly possessed many of those traits, too.

Leonard Goldenson finally helped Murdoch sort out his mixed feelings about Jews, though. As head of ABC, Goldenson was a major figure in New York's Jewish establishment. As well, he was an outspoken supporter of Israel, appearing frequently at fund-raising dinners and bond rallies and heading up various committees devoted to advancing the cause of Israel in the United States. He was, to put it in a phrase, a charter member of the so-called "Jewish Lobby" in America.

Murdoch could not like and model himself on Goldenson without liking his unabashed Jewishness. As elsewhere, anti-Semitism was still a powerful element in American business and social life, even in cosmopolitan New York. Yet Goldenson, like many of his ambitious New York counterparts, made no effort to disguise his Jewishness. If anything, they wore it on their sleeves, mostly out of their pride in Israel. In a place like New York, it was almost fashionable to be a Jew in the 1950s, especially if one's ambitions were focused on achieving a niche in the city's establishment. Jews were still excluded from high positions in many of the city's top banks, law firms, corporations, clubs, and other vital components of the New York power grid—as indeed they were in those of the other major cities of the United States— but they were no longer barred from weaving their own banks, law firms, corporations, and clubs tightly into the mesh.

This was the New York Rupert Murdoch encountered in the 1950s, and he was impressed especially by the no-nonsense energy and assertiveness of the "new" Jewish executive—not the smooth scions of the old-line, "Our Crowd," German-Jewish families that had assimilated generations before, but the upwardly thrusting sons of the ghettos of Eastern Europe. These Jewish businessmen and lawyers and bankers had started as outsiders, almost outcasts, and were now spitting and clawing their

way into the New York establishment. Murdoch, too, was a spit-
ting-and-clawing outsider in his own Australia, and it was easy
for him to identify with these New York Jewish counterparts.
When the time came for him to make his permanent move into
the United States fifteen years later, it was to them that he would
largely turn for support.

And they would respond eagerly, but not just because Murdoch represented a source of business. They felt they could
"trust" him on Israel. Leonard Goldenson had not let a meeting
with Murdoch go by during his first trips to New York without
giving him a dissertation about Israel and its importance in the
global scheme of things. He often likened Murdoch to an Israeli,
pointing out that Australians were the "Jews of the Orient." Israel
was a nation of Europeans in the middle of a distant Arab environment; Australia was a nation of Europeans in a distant
Asian environment. The similarities between the two were greater
than less. Religion and cultural orientation were less important
than the fact that each country was an "oasis of democracy"
within a vast, politically hostile world. Australia, Goldenson argued, had a great deal to learn from Israel.

Goldenson's personality and lectures thus had the effect of
sharpening Murdoch's sympathy toward Israel. As a result, his
Australian papers took on a decidedly pro-Israel tone during the
early 1960s—a fact that did not always please his surrogates in
the top editorial chairs. The eventual resignation of Douglas
Brass as editor of the Sydney *Mirror*, for instance, is said by some
in Murdoch's organization to have come about over that issue, although Brass himself has always insisted it was due to other dis-
agreements. Murdoch simply says, "When one of my editors tries
to prevent me from exercising my rightful domain over a paper,
he's gone."

But Goldenson's analyses about Israel and Australia had an
even more direct impact. Israel, a nation only since 1948, was as-
sertively and noisily out in the world, making a place for itself
through aggressive international trade and political arm-bending.
Australia, by contrast, was a long-indolent colossus. It seemed
content to remain a global backwater; satisfied forever to be
shaped by, rather than shape, international events; pleased to go
on enjoying whatever small share it could garner of the technological and economic ingenuity of other nations.

The conclusions Murdoch drew from these observations

were to turn him almost overnight into a fervent Australian nationalist, worrying not just about his own business, but about the business of Australia itself.

As he would later say in a speech in London:

> Australians are no longer content that their country will go on being inevitably, irreversibly, or without protest, a metal quarry for Japan, a pastoral lease for distant investors, a province for Madison Avenue, or a South Pacific windbreak for French nuclear scientists. . . . They are no longer content to be a pale echo of great and powerful friends, to be a secondhand society, a reflection of another hemisphere and sometimes another age. They are seeking a fresh, vigorous Australian identity of their own.

The speech was delivered in 1972, but it encapsulated ideas Murdoch had begun to form a dozen years earlier as a result of his trips to the United States.

To implement these ideas, he had determined to make himself a major force on the Australian political scene—not just the pesky gadfly he'd been up to then, but a figure of consequence who could, through his newspapers and television stations, shape Australia's future. His first order of business, as he saw it, was to get rid of the powerful, anachronistically conservative Menzies government, which had been entrenched since 1949 and remained blindly and zealously rigid in its guardianship of the nation's status quo.

"Australia was young," Murdoch said to me. "There was this great young generation coming of age, a lot of them the children of the postwar immigrants. They were looking for an identity, and they had nothing in common with the Old Guard, which had been running the country for so long. Yet they faced a future of more-of-the-same unless the Old Guard was ousted."

He set out to oust it, to become the champion of the new generation, of the "new Australia" he viewed as desperate to take its rightful place in the pantheon of major world powers.

"Rupert saw the nation as becoming the economic linchpin of the Asian South Pacific," says another of his editorial associates of the time. "He saw Japan making this great economic comeback in the north and said Australia had to be the Japan of the south. And even beyond that, the America of the Southern Hemisphere. That was his idealism at work, and I had no doubt that it was genuine, for Rupert was still capable of idealism in his early thirties. But as with all impassioned ideologues, the ends always justified the means with him. And there were always less idealistic, more nefarious currents of motivation running through him. I can remember some wild editorial conferences at Holt Street [the headquarters of the Sydney *Mirror*] where we all sat around thinking up ways to piss on Menzies and his claque. Rupert would practically salivate with revenge.

"Much of his contempt for the government was shaped by his desire for retaliation against Menzies and his boys for all the problems they'd caused him with the television licenses and such. Rupert glossed over those motives in public with a lot of idealistic posturing about the 'New Australia,' but in private it was pure retribution that drove him."

Whether driven by revenge or idealism, or by a combination of the two, the simple fact was that Murdoch and his newspapers lacked both the reach and the credibility in the early 1960s to have much effect on Australian political sentiment. His Adelaide paper still suffered from its sullied reputation stemming from the Stuart affair. His paper in Perth was far too distant from the center of power—the east coast Sydney-Canberra-Melbourne axis—to matter. His *Mirror* subsidiaries in Brisbane and Melbourne, each called the *Truth*, were little more than semipornographic rags masquerading as legitimate newspapers. And the *Mirror* itself, now the flagship of Murdoch's chain, was hardly more respected.

Only his television stations provided a potential platform for Murdoch's crusade against the incumbent government. Unfortunately for him, the government had placed severe restrictions on what could be broadcast over the airwaves, on the theory that television was too easy a medium by which to corrupt the public mind via partisan propaganda.

It soon became apparent that if Murdoch were to have the influence on the country that he desired, he would have to create a new national image as a responsible voice and a new forum through which to speak. Thus was born the newspaper known as the *Australian,* today proclaimed by many of his apologists as "the other side of Rupert Murdoch."

Murdoch's then-fifty-four-year-old mother had returned from her investiture in England in 1963, and said in effect, as she later told me, "Rupert, you must absolutely do *something* to rescue our name. All these horrid papers you're putting out—it just won't do. I don't care how much money you're making for the family, there must be a balance. You must publish something decent for a change."

Such pressure had been building for years. Since in a very strong sense he owed the position to which he had risen to his mother, Murdoch could not yet ignore her reprovals. Even his sister Helen was beginning to express embarrassment, and he owed her a lot, too. (Murdoch's two younger sisters, by then in their twenties and nominally principals in Cruden Investments— still the vehicle by which the family controlled News Limited— were content to remain in the background.)

Other sources of pressure were such figures as Douglas Brass, Kenneth May, Adrian Deamer, Ron Boland, "Curly" Bryden, and Frank Shaw, who had become primary lieutenants of "Murdoch's Mafia," a characterization made in a 1965 speech by a crony of Prime Minister Menzies. To one degree or another, all leaned to the left in their political sentiments. Each had grown increasingly frustrated over the fact that Murdoch's insistence on cheapening his papers had worked against their pet causes. Hundreds of thousands of people bought and read the papers each day. But for the most part they were not the kind of people who were interested in digesting editorials and columns of meaningful political and social criticism, no matter how easy to read. "Tits-and-bums," scandals, games, puzzles, advice to the lovelorn, horoscopes, sports, crime stories—those were the things most readers bought Murdoch's papers for.

Anna Murdoch, Rupert's second wife, also takes a large measure of credit for his decision to create the *Australian.* Born Anna Marie Torv in Scotland in 1944, she was the first offspring of an Estonian father who had fled that World War II–besieged Russo-Baltic state, landed in Scotland, and married the daughter of a family in the dry cleaning business. Ten years after Anna's birth, in 1954, the Torv family emigrated to Australia. Anna, a bright, serious, attractive blonde with a talent for writing and a terse style of speech, graduated from high school in Sydney and in 1962 got a job as a cub reporter on the Sydney *Mirror.*

"Mostly I wrote about going to parties and women's dresses," she says. "I think I would have become pretty good if I'd stuck at it, but at eighteen I was very nervous and unsure of myself. We had a system of cadetship—or apprenticeship as you'd call it here—and we ran a 'cadet' newspaper within the office to show what we could do. I first met Rupert when I was assigned to interview him for the paper. . . ."

The introduction came through Douglas Brass at a popular watering hole near the *Mirror*'s plant on Holt Street in Sydney's Surrey Hills district. Murdoch was still struggling through his bitter divorce from Pat. He was living on his own and was often seen at the pub, carousing with his employees.

"In those days I was doing everything to excess," he told me. "Drinking, smoking, gambling, whoring, you name it. I was wearing myself out with work and my various vices." I don't think he meant that he was actually employing the services of prostitutes; his use of the word "whoring" no doubt meant something like "chasing women."

Murdoch was profoundly smitten by the young Anna Torv. Anna has described herself to me as having been "somewhat of a hippie" at the time. A longtime friend recalls her as "a teenaged den mother, very much involved in causes, extremely idealistic, surrounded by young friends who she nurtured and fed, naive and inexperienced in many ways, with a pure, virginal air, yet stiff-spined and ambitious and extremely clever, giving off an aura of knowing much more about life and people than she really did."

Anna Torv was a Roman Catholic. According to another friend, "It was a close call whether she would end up a nun or a woman of the world. Had she not got involved with Rupert, it wouldn't have surprised me to see her in a convent eventually. She was very much a cloistered puritan in many ways. On the other hand, she was always wanting to be out in the world, solving its problems and helping people through their travails."

The anguish she perceived in Rupert Murdoch interested her enough to compel her to respond to his overtures, for she very quickly became involved in his life. It was an improbable union on the surface, once it became serious in 1964—the serene, self-effacing Anna Torv and the rambunctious, high-strung Murdoch, thirteen years her senior.

"Not at all," she says. "Rupert and I were very good for each other. We're alike in many ways, and we complemented one another. He taught me how to assert myself. And I taught him humility."

When Anna Murdoch talks privately today of her relationship with her husband, she does so with such touches of tart humor. Some friends call it bitter sarcasm. She and Murdoch are, nevertheless, a smoothly functioning public couple, and Anna vigorously defends him whenever his style, integrity, and character are attacked. She, like many others, points to the *Australian* as a symbol of people's mistaken views of him.

It was because of the pressures exerted on Murdoch in the early 1960s to publish a paper that would be worthy of his father's name that he resolved to launch the *Australian.* Australia had no national daily. Murdoch by then owned printing plants in Sydney, Melbourne, Brisbane, Adelaide, and Perth. In order to fulfill his need to have an impact on the Australian government and on the country's future, he determined that the paper should be headquartered in Canberra, the new and still raw capital city the government had built in the sierra separating East Coast Australia from its arid inland prairie. Canberra was 150 miles southeast of Sydney and 300 miles northeast of Melbourne. His plan was to have the paper made up and typeset in Canberra each day, then to fly the printing forms to each of his plants in the various outlying state capitals for printing and local distribution, with each regional edition to have its own advertising. In layout and context the paper would be "serious," that is, concerned almost exclusively with national and international politics and economics—a daily paper designed to appeal to the country's educated upper classes.

To run the editorial side of the *Australian,* Murdoch hired the mercurial Maxwell Newton away from the Fairfax group's *Financial Times* in Sydney. Newton later recalled his instructions. "Rupert and I met over a drink. He said to me, 'I've got where I am by some pretty tough, larrikin methods, but I've got there. And what I want to do now is produce a newspaper my father would have been proud of.' " ("Larrikin" is Australian slang for "disreputable.")

Even his enemies do not fault Murdoch's courage in creating the *Australian* in 1965, for such a paper was "indeed needed to lift the country out its global provincialism," according to one of them. They do, however—as do many others who are more sympathetic to him—bewail what he did with it. It was a money-losing proposition from the start. Still, he has kept it alive to this day, discarding editor after editor in the attempt to hit on a formula that will make it at least marginally profitable.

The first editor to go was Newton, who very quickly "became appalled by Rupert's interference.... Throughout the planning period Rupert was excellent," Newton told author Michael Leapman.

> I think he gets more fun out of planning things than actually the business of doing them. He's not very good at managing things....
>
> Rupert was excited and at the top of his form. He was happy. It was when we got started that he started to get unhappy because he was continually afraid that somebody—myself—was going to, as it were, take over.... Another thing of course was that while he had this great ability as managing director to get into the detail of the organization, he carried this to extraordinary lengths. The first four or five months, up until the time I left the organization, Rupert would quite often be seen down on the stone [the production editor's desk] making up the paper.... Very unnerving. This is the sort of work that should be done ... by a sub-editor earning about twenty-five pounds a week.*

It was not just this "mother-hen" aspect of Murdoch's nature that his people resented. (Richard Searby, his old schoolmate, likes to describe Murdoch as a "fidget" and attributes the antagonisms he creates primarily to that quality of his character. I have often seen Murdoch walk into shops in New York and fussily reorganize their newspaper and magazine displays so that his various publications are given the prominence he thinks they deserve.) It was also the imposition of his will on how the news the *Australian* reported should be slanted, and how its editorial and opinion columns should be pitched.

"He never really gave you a direct order at the start, though," says one ex-editor. "It was always in the form of a suggestion at first, very reasonably expressed. But if he thought you didn't follow it, he would soon be back with a repeat, this time not so reasonably put. It would go on this way until he got to the point where it was no longer suggestion or persuasion, but 'goddamnit, do what I say or you're fired!' "

The *Australian* almost totally preoccupied Murdoch between 1965 and 1968. But no matter what he did with it, he couldn't

---

* Michael Leapman, *Barefaced Cheek,* Hodder & Stoughton, London, 1983, p. 36.

seem to make it work in the fashion he'd envisioned. It became *too* respectable—a dry, abstract paper that was modestly popular with the nation's relatively small intellectual element but too staid to shake up the traditional lethargy of Australia. To Murdoch, it was almost prima facie proof of the futility of "decent" journalism.

Nevertheless, he would keep the paper going as a money-losing talisman of what he grew fond of calling his "essential dedication to quality." This was because his other papers, along with his television interests, had turned News Limited into a rich company indeed, and Murdoch himself into a millionaire. During that period he acquired a yacht, a vast upland sheep-and-cattle farm fifty miles from Canberra, further publishing properties in New Zealand and Hong Kong (*Asia* magazine), a new wife (Anna Torv and he were married in 1965), a second daughter (named after his mother), and a modicum of national respectability and political influence.

Had he remained in Australia, Murdoch might have matured into a cohesive force behind the nationalism and Australian self-pride he claimed so vigorously to favor. It is a measure of the shallowness of that political commitment that he didn't. Australia remained too slow, too provincial for him. As early as 1967, when he realized that the *Australian* was going to be nothing more than a *succès d'estime,* he began to think seriously of broadening his media network beyond the South Pacific. He thought particularly, of course, of England and America. And he thought back even more particularly to the vow he had made to himself in 1953—to return one day to London's Fleet Street.

MURDOCH

ENGLAND

News of the World

"It was a quiet Friday night," recalls a man who was a key Murdoch aide in Sydney. "Most of the staff had left, the offices were empty. I was on my way out. Rupert was still in his office, and as I passed his door he waved me in.

"I figured he wanted to talk to me about a circulation campaign we were working on. He was on the phone. As I eavesdropped on his end of the conversation, I could tell he was talking to someone in London. Well, it went on for ten or fifteen minutes. Then, when he rang off, he said to me, 'How'd you like to go to London?' I thought he was talking about a trip. I said I'd love to, but I wouldn't be able to get away till the following Monday at the earliest. He said, 'No, I mean how'd you like to move to London?' That's when I learned he was about to make his own move on England."

The time was mid-October 1968. The person Murdoch had been talking with in London was Stephen Gordon Catto—more properly, Lord Catto—a stocky forty-six-year-old partner in the leading British merchant banking firm of Morgan Grenfell. Catto, who inherited the Scottish title of Second Baron of Cairncatto, was a rising pillar of the British financial establishment and a principal force in the aggressive and increasingly controversial Morgan Grenfell.

Catto's association with Murdoch went back to the early sixties, when he had passed through Australia on business for the huge Hong Kong and Shanghai Bank Corporation, of which he was a director. At that time, Murdoch had decided to start quietly buying stock in England's IPC publishing conglomerate, Cecil King's organization. IPC still owned the London *Daily Mirror.*

Murdoch confided to Catto his love for the *Mirror* and said that he hoped to accumulate enough stock in IPC to one day get his hands on the paper. Catto, sensing a future source of lucrative business in Murdoch, agreed to act as his financial surrogate in London and use his position in "The City"—London's financial center—to pave the way for the Australian.

But Catto's phone call to Murdoch that late Friday night was not about IPC. It was about another opportunity that had suddenly arisen in Fleet Street. *News of the World,* England's most widely read and profitable Sunday newspaper, was for sale. Well, practically.

News of the World was the granddaddy of sordid Sunday journalism in Britain. As such, it was an institution among the country's poorest and least educated classes, and they revered it to the extent of six million copies in sales each week. Its formula was a mix of sexual titillation and feigned moral outrage. With explicit detail that was usually exaggerated, or else invented, it flooded its main "news" pages with graphic yarns about bestiality, criminality, prostitution, and the sexual antics of the upper classes. Then, with great editorial rectitude, it would bemoan the decline in the country's moral standards, all the while invoking the glories of the England that once was. It was a weekly peepshow and pulpit wrapped in a single slick package. For its efforts, the family that owned the paper for almost eighty years had become exceedingly wealthy.

In 1968, that family was headed by Sir William Carr. Chairman of *News of the World* and its largest stockholder, the fifty-six-year-old Carr suffered from debilitating circulatory problems and other physical ailments. During the previous few years, ignoring the new competition of television, he had let the paper drift to the point that its profits began to decline sharply. That had triggered a feud with his cousin, an eccentric scientist and inventor named Derek Jackson who owned the second largest block of shares in the company. Between them, they controlled 57 percent of *News of the World.*

A month before Catto's call to Murdoch, the disaffected Jackson had announced that he was selling his stake. Carr had tried to buy his cousin's shares at their stock market value but had been rebuffed when Jackson insisted on a price nearly twice that. Unable to meet Jackson's demand, Carr was forced to stand aside and watch aghast as Jackson, through his own merchant bankers, sought an outside buyer. If an outsider acquired Jackson's piece of *News of the World,* Carr, with only his 32 percent, could lose his iron grip on the company and all the luxurious perks that went with it.

News of the World's unsettled situation was no surprise to Murdoch when Catto phoned him. Catto had been keeping Murdoch informed about the events in London all week. What he told Murdoch that night was that Jackson had found a buyer for his 25 percent block of shares, that the buyer had been out in the market acquiring additional public shares to make a further inroad on William Carr's 32 percent holding, that Carr and his family were taking steps to resist, and that all of London was abuzz over what appeared to be shaping up as an out-and-out takeover battle.

Who was the buyer, Murdoch wanted to know.

"Maxwell," replied Catto over the long-distance line.

In 1968, forty-five-year-old Robert Maxwell was already a legend of sorts in England, albeit a tainted one. He was also something of a mystery man. Maxwell had been born Jan Hoch in 1923, the son of a peasant family in Czechoslovakia. Barely educated, he had made his way to England during World War II. He claimed to have learned to speak fluent English in six weeks and to have served in various British wartime military posts, reaching the rank of captain.

After the war, Jan Hoch changed his name to Ian Robert Maxwell and remained in Britain. Perceiving a postwar need for the publication of scientific information, he acquired a small publishing house in 1951 and built it over the next fifteen years into the highly profitable Pergamon Press, the country's largest scientific and technical publisher. A militant and outspoken, if eccentric, Socialist, and a shameless self-promoter, during the latter part of that period he was also elected to Parliament as a member of the British Labour Party—an office he still held in 1968.

Many of Maxwell's business dealings regularly came under attack, however. In 1968 and 1969, while he was trying to take over *News of the World,* he was also involved in negotiations to sell part of his Pergamon Press to the American financial wheeler-dealer Saul Steinberg. Steinberg would publicly accuse him of rigging Pergamon's profit statements, and a subsequent government investigation would support the charges. "Mr. Maxwell is not, in our opinion, a person who can be relied on to exercise proper stewardship of a publicly held company," concluded the official report. Which was another way of saying that Maxwell was a "white-collar crook," one of the milder epithets used to describe him by bankers, lawyers, and business leaders in London and elsewhere.

Maxwell alternately railed at such characterizations and shrugged them off. "I'm the man everyone loves to hate," he recently said. "I really have no time to worry or care what people say about me. And that infuriates my enemies. They see a man with the hide of a rhinoceros."

Maxwell has always struck me as a man who revels in making enemies, a man for whom waging pitched battle in the business, political, and social trenches is like an aphrodisiac. Rupert Murdoch, for as long as I've known him, has given the same impression. It might be seen as poetic justice, then, that the two, scarcely known to one another in 1968, both foreigners, both aspiring power brokers, would become bitter enemies and repeated combatants on the battleground of London's Fleet Street.

Lord Catto's second message to Murdoch was that Maxwell's bid for *News of the World,* at that time valued at twenty-six million British pounds, had run into a serious snag. Maxwell was an avowed ultra-left-winger. *News of the World* was an ultra-right-wing paper, notwithstanding its sensationalist character. The fit was all wrong, and not only the Carr family but the public and the government itself were beginning to raise a stink. A vacuum was rapidly forming. It might be a vacuum Murdoch could very profitably fill. Would Murdoch be interested, Catto asked?

Murdoch had already done a crash course on *News of the World*'s finances and profit picture. The paper was a cash cow, no doubt about that, and along with it would come a chain of provincial papers and a profitable printing subsidiary in northern England. He reflected wistfully for a moment on the stock in IPC that he had been methodically collecting. Then he put the *Mirror* out of his mind and said to Catto, "Yes."

Catto advised Murdoch to stand by for another call in an hour or so. When it came, near midnight Friday, Catto told Murdoch that he'd just talked with the financial representatives of William Carr and *News of the World* and that he'd suggested him as an ally in their efforts to ward off Maxwell. They had reacted positively, Catto said, and were off at that very moment testing the idea on Carr. It appeared there would be no immediate response, he added, but Murdoch should be prepared to fly to London late the following week.

Catto was wrong. There *was* an immediate response, and it came to him the next morning from Harry Sporborg of the Hambros merchant bank, Carr's and *News of the World*'s anti-takeover strategists. Maxwell, Sporborg had learned, would raise his bid on Monday to a price that might win him the company before anyone had a chance to head him off. He had talked to Carr about bringing in Murdoch with a friendly counterbid, and Carr was interested. But Murdoch must get to London immediately to confer with Carr about his role.

A few years before, Murdoch had parlayed his keenness for the wagering side of horse racing into an interest in owning and racing his own horses, an avocation his Sydney rival Frank Packer had long been noted for. Told by Catto on Friday night that he wouldn't be needed in England until the end of the following week, Murdoch flew south to Melbourne Saturday morning to attend the Caulfield Cup, the first of the major races of Australia's spring season. But he informed no one of his plans. When Catto phoned on Saturday to ask him to get to London by Monday, no one he spoke to knew where Murdoch was, not even Anna Murdoch.

Only through educated guesswork, and a public paging system, was Murdoch located at the Melbourne race course late Saturday afternoon. Receiving Catto's message, he phoned his wife in Sydney and asked her to check the international airline schedules. By the time he flew back from Melbourne there would be only one flight left for Europe, a Lufthansa plane to Germany. He told her to book him on the Lufthansa flight and meet him at the Sydney airport with his passport, a suitcase, and the sheaf of documents he'd collected on *News of the World* during the previous weeks.

The message Murdoch received from Catto in Melbourne had emphasized that his trip to London should be made in utmost secrecy so as not to alert Maxwell. The journey took almost a day and a half. When Murdoch arrived in London on Sunday, October 20, he didn't know quite what to expect. His initial impression was that he would simply be "stealing *News of the World* away from Maxwell," with the support of Sir William Carr. But when he was finally closeted in person with Catto Sunday night, he learned, much to his annoyance, that the process would not be so simple. Carr had no intention of accepting Murdoch as a full takeover substitute for Maxwell. He expected the Australian merely to purchase enough public voting shares in the *News of the World* company to make it impossible for Maxwell to acquire a majority.

"I was expected not as a white knight," Murdoch told me, "but as a Sancho Panza to Carr's Don Quixote."

Murdoch told Catto he hadn't come all that way to serve as Carr's buffer. If he fought Maxwell in the marketplace and won, he wanted full control of *News of the World.* Either way, Carr and his family would be out.

Not so fast, cautioned Catto, a master of merchant-banking intrigue. There were three problems to be surmounted. The first was to obtain Carr's acceptance of Murdoch as a savior. That done, the second, between them, was to defeat Maxwell. And once that was accomplished, the third was to reap the reward— full control. It had to be done in steps, though, Catto warned. Carr was on the verge of paranoia and must be coddled for now, made to believe that Murdoch was no more than a friendly samaritan with no ulterior motive. Where there's a will, said Catto, uttering one of his favorite clichés, there's a way.

The key to the forthcoming battle was the voting stock in *News of the World.* Maxwell already had a guaranteed 25 percent through his commitment to purchase Derek Jackson's holding. The Carr stake had been augmented by the shares owned by other members of Carr's family, who had hurriedly pledged their loyalty to Sir William after Maxwell's designs on the company had become known. That left 35 percent, or 3,360,000 publicly owned shares, to be fought over. Maxwell had already obtained some of those through his secret purchases on the London Stock Exchange at the end of the previous week, raising his ante to just over 30 pecent. All he needed was another 21 percent to capture full control.

However, Catto had started, also secretly, to buy shares on Morgan Grenfell's account in anticipation of Murdoch entering the fray. He had accumulated 3½ percent, he said, and pledged them to Murdoch. If Murdoch now proceeded to buy shares himself on the open market—also in secret, to keep the price from suddenly soaring—all he would need would be an additional 7½ percent. That, coupled with the 3½ percent Catto had acquired plus Carr's expanded 40 percent holding, would give the Carr-Murdoch faction 51 percent and leave Maxwell with no chance at a majority. The entire effort would cost Murdoch only a few million pounds.

Getting the money was no problem; Murdoch could easily finance the investment through News Limited assets and Australian bank loans. But he thought it an excessive amount for what he'd be receiving—a small slice of a decreasingly profitable newspaper and its subsidiaries. There had to be more in it for him.

Catto assured him there was—much more. Murdoch's alliance with Carr would be a foot in the door. The besieged proprietor would be so grateful that he'd agree to Murdoch's becoming managing director of *News of the World*. In fact, that would be their primary condition for joining in the battle to stop Maxwell. Murdoch might acquire only 11 percent of the company, but he must have the major say in how it was managed thereafter.

And then came Catto's trump card. Once Murdoch had the managing directorship, and after Maxwell was disposed of, he could increase his percentage of *News of the World* by ordering the issuance of a new block of shares in the name of News Limited—enough shares to match if not exceed Carr's personal authority. With that accomplished, he would then be in a position to shunt Carr to the sidelines and assume exclusive control of the company and the paper. By so doing, he would establish himself solidly on Fleet Street at a fraction of what it would have cost him had he continued to pursue his quest for the *Mirror*. And years ahead of time, too.

Murdoch marveled at Catto's ingenuity. He was used to the vicious hurly-burly of Australian business, to be sure. But there, though the style was cutthroat, its underhandedness was usually aboveboard—that is, "You knew everyone else was out to screw you, and vice versa, so everyone acted accordingly," as Murdoch once told me.*

London, however, was different, or so he'd thought. Like most outsiders, Murdoch had grown up on the legend of London as the cradle of gentlemanly conduct in business and financial af-

---

* Indeed, Murdoch was fairly fresh from having been "screwed" by Frank Packer. Through a series of financial machinations carried out by Packer, Murdoch's 25 percent ownership of the Sydney and Melbourne TV stations had suddenly shrunk to 10 percent.

fairs. Yes, Fleet Street had always seemed an exception; press lords like Northcliffe and Beaverbrook had been notorious for their tricky dealings. But The City was reputed to be pristine in its approach to business and finance. Yet here was Lord Catto, a principal in one of The City's most celebrated banks, proposing a strategy that bordered on the Machiavellian in its slyness—perhaps even on the deceptive and fraudulent, as Sir William Carr, its victim, would later claim.

There was nothing illegal about the plan, though—at least on its face—and Murdoch warmed to it instantly. The more he thought about *News of the World* as he leafed through that Sunday's edition, the more he thought: "What a way to break into Fleet Street!"

Their next task, Catto told him, was to meet with Carr and his advisers to see if the embattled proprietor would take the bait. He arranged a meeting for Tuesday morning at Carr's Belgravia townhouse. On Monday, he spent most of the afternoon drilling Murdoch on the negotiating posture he should take. Under the legal code, Catto could not conduct the discussion with Carr; he could only sit at Murdoch's side and advise.

The ailing and dyspeptic Carr did not exactly rise to the bait, but when it was thrust in front of him he had no choice but to bite. The meeting started early Tuesday morning. Murdoch knew no one but Catto. Barely were the introductions over when he blurted out his demands to Carr. He would buy enough market stock to put them, together, over the 50 percent mark. But in exchange, Carr would have to step down as chief executive (managing director) and hand the post over to him.

Carr was flabbergasted, not only by Murdoch's proposal but by his manner. (Murdoch concedes today that his style may have been abrupt; he blames it on a combination of nervousness and jet lag.) Impossible, Carr said.

Murdoch shrugged and stood up, as if ready to walk out. "Let Maxwell get it, then," he said aloud to the frowning Catto. "I'll go home."

The mention of Maxwell seemed to galvanize Carr out of the funk he was in. "He's an evil man, you know," he said to Murdoch.

"Well, I'm not an evil man," Murdoch replied. "I'm here to help you if you want it. But I don't like to waste time on dither."

"Sit down, Mr. Murdoch," Carr said after a moment. Suddenly, negotiations were under way.

In the end, a compromise was struck. Murdoch consented to purchase enough public shares in *News of the World* to give the Carr-Murdoch alliance 51 percent. Murdoch would be named not the sole chief executive, but joint managing director with Carr. In exchange, Carr agreed to the creation of a sufficient number of new shares in the company, issued to Murdoch, to give the Australian a holding equal to Carr's—40 percent. In exchange for that, Murdoch further agreed that a member of the Carr family, starting with Sir William himself, would remain chairman of the board of *News of the World* for the "foreseeable future," and that he would never try to increase his stockholding over that of Carr's so as to achieve majority control for himself.

The deal gave Murdoch considerably less than he'd expected going into the meeting. Only Lord Catto's whispered encouragement prodded him into accepting it. It was still a "foot in the door," Catto assured him. He could attend to the matter of Carr and his family later on.

Up to that point, Murdoch's presence in London, and his meeting with Carr, had remained a secret, although few knew who he was anyway. However, Maxwell had announced his new bid for public voting shares in *News of the World,* and the stock market price had begun to creep upward. The next day, Wednesday, Murdoch started buying in the market. Simultaneously, *News of the World* announced that he had joined with it to block Maxwell's takeover attempt. Maxwell, surprised, said to the press, "Who is Rupert Murdoch?" Much of Fleet Street asked the same question, and Thursday morning's papers were filled with quickly patched together stories about the little-known Australian interloper.

By Thursday afternoon, Murdoch was able to announce through a public relations man hired by Catto—John Addey— that he'd thus far acquired nearly 4 percent of *News of the World* stock in the name of News Limited, his principal Australian company. He also revealed some of the details of his pact with Carr, among them that new shares would be created in the *News of the World* company by merging two or three of his Australian subsidiaries into it, thereby giving him 40 percent to go with the Carr family's 40 percent.

This brought an immediate and heated protest from Maxwell to the London Stock Exchange's Takeover Panel, the stock market's self-regulatory arm. Maxwell accused Murdoch and Carr of violating various rules of the panel's Takeover Code. He pointed particularly to Rule 33, which held that public companies such as *News of the World* could only enlist allies to defeat takeover attempts if such schemes were "not prejudicial to the interests of the public shareholders at large," and to a correlative rule that stipulated against companies' buying their own shares to repel a takeover.

With Murdoch's Thursday announcements and Maxwell's public reaction, all of England knew that a tumultuous financial battle had been joined. Two weeks earlier, *News of the World* voting shares had been selling at a modest 28 shillings, or just under a pound and a half (the equivalent of about $3.50 in American currency).*

The week before, as rumors of Maxwell's plan spread, the price had risen by a shilling and a few pence as speculators started buying the stock. Then Maxwell had broadcast his first bid. In effect, it was a tender offer to buy public stock at 37½ shillings per share. At the start of the following week, he upped the offer to nearly 50 shillings, or 2½ pounds. By midweek, the market in *News of the World* stock had turned into a frenzy, which was further fed by the announcement of Murdoch's entry into the fray.

Murdoch wondered what he'd let himself in for. What had started in his view as a simple take-it-or-leave-it financial maneuver had turned overnight into a Napoleonic war. Besieged by batteries of Fleet Street reporters and photographers, he had to go into hiding, fleeing the Savoy Hotel for the private flat of a friend of Catto's.

But his troubles had just begun. On Friday, Maxwell's complaint to the Takeover Panel, coupled with the intensifying volatility of the market in *News of the World* shares, provoked the Stock Exchange into suspending all trading in the stock for two months. Murdoch was left with only his recently acquired 4 percent, Carr with his 40, and Maxwell with about 32. There was still no party with the needed 51 percent, and the whole issue of control was dropped into limbo until the end of December.

How would it be resolved? After the two-month cooling-off

---

* In 1968, the British pound contained 20 shillings, or 240 pence. In 1971, the currency system was "decimalized" in the fashion of the dollar. Thereafter, the pound consisted of 100 pence and the shilling was eliminated. This did not affect the relative value between pound and dollar, however.

period, by a vote of all existing shareholders up to the time of the
suspension of trading, the Takeover Panel ruled. The vote would
be held at a public shareholders' meeting on January 2, 1969.

With the order of battle thus radically altered, Murdoch had
two choices. He could simply forget about the entire matter,
withdraw to Australia, and let Carr and Maxwell fight it out between themselves at the shareholders' meeting two months hence.
Or he could wade further in and take on Maxwell himself at the
meeting.

"By then I didn't even consider the first choice," Murdoch
says today. He had very quickly come to despise the blustery, in-
sulting Maxwell. "He'd said some rather nasty things about me to
the press. And some nasty things about Australians in general. I
couldn't let him get away with that."

But Murdoch was motivated by more than vendetta. Although Carr insisted on holding him to their agreement of the
previous Tuesday, Murdoch could reasonably have invoked the
Stock Exchange's suspension of trading as having automatically
mooted their pact.

However, as Catto explained to him, the Stock Exchange's
mandating of the shareholders' meeting actually made the prospect of his winning *News of the World* all the brighter. If it was
Carr against Maxwell alone at the meeting, Maxwell would probably get enough votes, even with his smaller percentage, to oust
the sickly Carr from day-to-day management of the company.
But with Carr and Murdoch against Maxwell, Murdoch's presence could easily swing it to their side—on the argument that he
was an experienced and successful newspaper publisher, while
Maxwell was a newcomer to the business. The shareholders
would opt to go with experienced, rather than inexperienced, new
blood.

Also, they had two months in which to mount a publicity
campaign against Maxwell, pointing out not only his inexperi-
ence but his shady business reputation and his history of rampant
socialism. Would the conservative public shareowners of the
right-wing *News of the World* opt for a fiercely self-avowed left-
winger as their new leader—who could guess what he'd do to the
paper? Or would they prefer a political "independent" like Murdoch?

Murdoch reminded Catto that he himself had a rather well-
publicized left-wing history, at least in Australia.

That was *past* history, Catto said. It was clear that Rupert had sharply revised his political stance, was it not?

He'd be whatever he had to be to whip Maxwell, replied Murdoch. Actually, his political sensibilities were in a state of flux. "I still had a lot of liberal impulses working," he told me. "But I was also beginning to have conservative ideas."

Catto thus convinced Murdoch to press the fight for *News of the World* through the January shareholders' meeting. The suspension of trading and the ordering of the meeting had been blessings in disguise. True, they had delayed the outcome of the war. But they made its waging considerably cheaper. Not only would the public shareholders be likely to vote for Murdoch and Carr over Maxwell. When they had a chance to observe the young, healthy, energetic Murdoch acting on behalf of Carr, who in contrast would appear to them as old and enfeebled, they would be disposed to give Murdoch carte blanche to do whatever he wished with *News of the World.* Hence, when Murdoch later made his move to dispose of Carr, there would be little or no resistance. *News of the World* would be his in all ways.

A Frost Descends

The scenario played out as if custom-written, with one variation. Having decided to see the fight through, Murdoch became more daring than Catto. He informed Carr that his decision to proceed was contingent on Carr's agreement to drop the joint managing directorship arrangement reached at their initial meeting.

Carr, too, recognized the danger of going up against Maxwell at the crucial shareholders' meeting without the Australian at his side. He protested Murdoch's demand but without much conviction, as he knew it would be almost impossible to enforce the rest of their original agreement if Murdoch pulled out. Finally, he made the concession.

With that in hand, Murdoch readied himself for the shareholders' meeting. Much of his preparation was in the public relations arena. He mounted a private investigation of Maxwell's previous business dealings and personal life and handed the unfavorable findings over to John Addey, his press agent. Addey leaked them to selected newspapers in London, and although there was nothing about them that could be considered legally damning, enough negative innuendo about Maxwell got printed to raise serious questions about his integrity. Maxwell tried to fight back with leaks of his own about Murdoch, but most came down to little more than simple name-calling. "That wretched little moth-eaten kangaroo," was just one of the quotes attributed to Maxwell.

The other significant aspect of Murdoch's preparation was his tactic of stacking the shareholders' meeting in his and Carr's favor. A few days before the session, the Takeover Panel ruled that the only votes cast would be those represented by shares held

prior to Maxwell's first tender offer. This meant that Murdoch
could not vote his own 4 percent, but that Maxwell could tally the
25 percent commitment he had from Derek Jackson plus the additional 7 percent he'd acquired in the market prior to his first
public offering.

That made the ratio Carr's 40 percent against Maxwell's 32
percent at the start. Thus, ony 28 percent of the votes remained at
issue. If Murdoch-Carr could get 11 percent, they'd win.

But Maxwell had potent ammunition of his own—his last 50
shilling bid of October, which he said remained in effect. He
would promise to buy the shares of those who voted for him for
2½ pounds each. That represented an enormous profit to those
who held large blocks of shares purchased at less than 1½
pounds—institutional investors such as banks, insurance companies, and pension funds. Given the inevitable turmoil at *News
of the World* if Maxwell were to win, the institutions might well
be inclined to vote for him simply to take their profits and get out.
Murdoch and Catto had to preclude the possibility of Maxwell
getting more than 17 percent of the remaining votes. If he did, the
Murdoch-Carr alliance would fail to achieve the 51 percent it
needed to succeed.

"Maxwell accused us of stacking the meeting," Murdoch
said later, conceding that the accusation was at least "half-true"
but insisting that the tactic was not illegal. "I made sure that the
hall was full of our people. We didn't turn anyone away, but we
had our numbers there in case. . . ." One technique he used was to
persuade sympathetic stockholders who couldn't be at the meeting to sign over their shares temporarily to *News of the World*
staff underlings, who signed contracts promising to return them
once the meeting was over.

After all the heated preparation and intensive press coverage, the January 2 shareholders' meeting was an anticlimax.
Maxwell gave a long, bombastic speech to the more than 300
voters present. After attacking Murdoch and the management of
News of the World, he raised his offer to buy shares to 52 shillings
each. "If you support *News of the World*," he added, "your shares
will be worth today only 39 shillings, and tomorrow will begin
sinking from that." The implication was clear: they would be a
bunch of fools to go along with Carr and Murdoch.

Said an embittered member of the Carr family later, "Maxwell took the wrong approach. He flogged his obnoxious personality in front of everyone and then made it clear that he felt

nothing but contempt for anyone who would even consider not throwing their vote to him. On the other hand, Murdoch's contempt for us was totally masked by the deliberate modesty of his speech. He was visibly nervous and seemed almost out of his element. He said only a few words. He pointed mainly to his publishing record and suggested that under his and my uncle's leadership the company would thrive. He didn't mention Maxwell once.

"I say 'Murdoch's contempt' because clearly it was entirely calculated modesty on his part, a pose. He knew by then that the vote would go his way—Maxwell's tasteless desperation made it all the more obvious. So he was just cooling his heels, currying our favor until the vote became official and he could start to demonstrate his own contempt for all of us, and his treachery, by going back on his agreement with my uncle and cleaning us out."

The reference is to the fact that shortly after his overwhelming win, by 299 to 20, Murdoch began a concerted campaign to get rid of Carr and his top management associates.

"I had no choice," Murdoch says. "Once I got in there and saw how badly the organization was run, I had to clean house. Everything was dreadfully old-fashioned and stultified." In his mind, Carr was the symbol of *News of the World*'s musty outdatedness. "Yes, you hurt some feelings along the way, but you do what you must do. Remember, it was a public company. As the new chief executive, I had to answer to the shareholders."

Murdoch started by buying up many of the Derek Jackson shares that had gone begging after Maxwell's defeat. Together with the new shares issued to News Limited, he soon controlled more than 50 percent of the company. He informed Carr of this after the fact and then told the older man he would no longer be needed as chairman of the board. Murdoch intended to fill that position as well.

Murdoch held his breath to see how Carr would react. He anticipated a fight, a monumental lawsuit. But he also hoped that Carr might be so dispirited and distracted by his various ailments that he'd capitulate.

Although he first threatened to fight, Carr in the end did capitulate. In mid-June 1969, at the company's annual meeting, he resigned. Murdoch breathed a sigh of relief, took over the chairmanship, appointed several new directors, and turned his attention fully to reshaping *News of the World*.

Not as compliant was the paper's longtime editor, the hefty, colorful Stafford Somerfield. Somerfield had been with *News of the World* since just after the war, had run its editorial side for nearly fifteen years, and had been second only to Carr in the hierarchy of importance at the paper. Indeed, of the many daily and Sunday chief editors in London in 1969, none was more publicly identified with his paper than Somerfield was with *News of the World.* It mattered not that the paper was a journalistic travesty. That it was written for the lower classes, but from an upper-class point of view, gave Somerfield, as well as Carr, a certain cachet within the British establishment. They were seen as doing the country a public service, if only in the form of keeping the lower classes entertained and therefore distracted from any serious expressions of displeasure over their disadvantages.

To Murdoch, Somerfield was yet another glaring symbol of the paper's antiquated ways. Plus, he didn't like the man, finding him "a pompous ass who sucked up to the aristocracy and was much too complacent about his own self-importance."

Somerfield had to go, too. He had made his own disdain for Murdoch abundantly evident, and he'd let the new publisher know that he expected no interference with his running of the paper. That was something Murdoch could not abide—he *always* had the final editorial say. The only trouble was that Somerfield had a lucrative, ironclad, long-term contract with the *News of the World* company that made it impossible for Murdoch to fire him except at the cost of paying off the contract.

The British newspaper industry had a long tradition under which a proprietor—unless he was also its chief editor—dared not interfere with the day-to-day editorial policy and management of his paper. That was not to say the tradition was universally honored. Owners generally hired editors who were willing to carry out their employer's editorial mandates while maintaining the illusion of independence. Northcliffe and Beaverbrook—and to a lesser extent Cecil King—were notorious examples of newspaper owners who had held sway over the editorial slant and content of their journals. But no proprietor in recent Fleet Street history had taken the approach Murdoch did with his papers in Australia, which was to establish himself as the ultimate and absolute boss of the editorial side.

"As proprietor, I'm the one who in the end is responsible for the success or failure of my papers," he told a television interviewer in 1969, shortly after acquiring *News of the World.* "Since a paper's success or failure depends on its editorial approach, why shouldn't I interfere when I see a way to strengthen its approach? What am I supposed to do, sit idly by and watch a paper go down the drain, simply because I'm not supposed to interfere? Rubbish! That's the reason *News of the World* started to fade. There was no one there to trim the fat and wrench it out of its editorial complacency."

That was only one of many such statements Murdoch made about his intention to play a vigorous hands-on role in the editorial "revival" of *News of the World*. Some interlocutors replied by suggesting that his only proper task as proprietor was to find and hire an editor he could trust to carry out the needed improvements. "But I've already got an editor," Murdoch would say sourly, indicating Stafford Somerfield. "It's just a matter of acclimatizing him to my way of doing things."

Somerfield, though, was not the type to subject himself to such acclimatization. During the first few weeks after Murdoch's takeover, the two men eyed each other frostily, with Murdoch making frequent cracks about the indolence and smugness he perceived in Somerfield's staff and Somerfield haughtily complaining to others about the Australian's initial "lead-booted attempts to usurp my position."

The tension between the two began to bubble in March 1969 when Murdoch played his final card in forcing Sir William Carr—Somerfield's longtime friend as well as employer—out of the *News of the World* organization, stripping him of his chairmanship of several of the parent company's minor subsidiaries. Shortly thereafter, Murdoch ordered the firing of several of the paper's veteran columnists and reporters and their replacement by people handpicked by him. In April, he personally revised an advertising poster promoting a forthcoming edition of *News of the World*—the editor's responsibility—after it had been approved by Somerfield. He next ordered Somerfield to refrain from sending correspondents abroad without getting his permission first.

Somerfield says today that when he finally confronted Murdoch with his protests against such interference, Murdoch said, "I did not come all this way not to interfere! You can accept it or quit."

Clearly, Murdoch, at least to Somerfield, had embarked on a course designed to force the editor to resign. In that way, Murdoch would be rid of Somerfield without having to pay off his large contract. But Somerfield refused to be cowed so easily.

He demonstrated his resolve in May when he was vacationing in Spain. Murdoch took advantage of his absence to make wholesale changes in the layout of *News of the World* and to order the elimination of the editorial page, the principal forum of the paper's right-wing sermonizing. When Somerfield heard about it, he rushed back to London and countermanded Murdoch's order. Then he dashed off a furious letter to the paper's board of directors, which read in part:

> As Editor I am responsible for the newspaper and its contents. Whether present or absent, or whether indeed the Editor has knowledge of all the contents of the paper, his responsibility remains. . . . The Editor is the servant of the board and the managing director [Murdoch]. But this does not mean that the chief executive, acting independently of the board, can take the Editor's chair, seek to discharge his functions, or introduce fundamental editorial changes in the paper. . . .

As a new member of the *News of the World* board, Murdoch was one of the first to see Somerfield's missive. And as the company's new chief executive, he succeeded in blocking its dissemination to the rest of the board. After doing so, he summoned Somerfield to meet with him.

"At this interview," recalls Somerfield, Murdoch "held out the olive branch and asked me to continue, saying that he thought we could get on happily together. I agreed to carry on."

Somerfield believed he had made his point and that Murdoch would thereafter "behave." What he didn't reckon on was the notorious Christine Keeler, who six years earlier had been at the center of an at once disturbing and hilarious government scandal in England.

Keeler was the celebrated call girl whose simultaneous sexual liaisons with a Russian military attaché-spy and John Profumo, the British defense minister, had brought the Conservative government of Prime Minister Harold Macmillan to the brink of collapse in 1963. In 1964, *News of the World* had purchased Keeler's "memoirs" for nearly $75,000 and—in its inimitably panting style—published them in serialized form over several months. In the meantime Profumo, his career and personal life ruined, was forced to resign and had penitently announced that he would devote the rest of his life to good works among the poor. Thereafter, he disappeared into the slums of

East London, seldom to be heard from again, his apparent good intentions, along with his privacy, universally respected by the British press and public.

At the time of Somerfield's détente with Murdoch in the spring of 1969, the perennially hard-up Christine Keeler was circulating in Fleet Street a proposal for an updated and considerably more juicy version of her 1964 memoirs. Among the first to see the proposal was Somerfield, who had overseen the publication of the original.

Why not? he thought. *News of the World* had been struggling since Murdoch's takeover to drop another of its traditional journalistic blockbusters on England and reinvigorate its reputation as the country's liveliest weekly. Chances were that a rehash of Keeler's story would give the paper just the kind of circulation shot-in-the-arm the new proprietor had been lusting after with all the "improvements" he'd been trying to make. Murdoch had made it clear to Somerfield that he didn't wish to change the basic image of the paper but rather to make it more outrageous and controversial than it had been. Keeler's reworked memoirs might just be the answer. And if the strategy succeeded, Murdoch would no longer have any reason to doubt Somerfield's editorial wisdom or his right to sole hegemony over the editorial side of *News of the World*.

Accordingly, in July, Somerfield urged Murdoch to approve an extraordinary outlay of $50,000 to buy the "new" Keeler memoirs. The Australian was accustomed to paying no more than $10,000 for such serialization rights. Yet after reading a rough draft of Keeler's latest ghostwritten version of her life in high places, he gave Somerfield the go-ahead. He, too, saw the revival of the Keeler-Profumo story as a smart circulation-boosting ploy.

Boost circulation the memoirs certainly did when they were published in a series of weekly installments beginning later in the summer of 1969. Independently audited figures showed that between July and December of that year, the average weekly sale of *News of the World* rose by nearly 300,000 copies over that of the same period in 1968, for a circulation of more than six million copies a week.

But at the same time, the wrath of upper- and middle-crust England tumbled down on Murdoch's head. That he had dared so crudely to revive the Keeler-Profumo affair, exposing the genuinely repentant and rehabilitated Profumo to a fresh round of humiliating publicity, outraged the British establishment and propelled it into a storm of public denunciation of Murdoch. Even the Press Council—Fleet Street's self-governing watch-dog—condemned the series. And London's main commercial television channel refused to run ads promoting it.

Murdoch's initial reaction to the furor he and Somerfield had created was to take full responsibility for the decision to buy and print the memoirs, deny that it was journalism far beyond the norm of Fleet Street sleaze, and boast that it was a terrific business move. "People can sneer as much as they like," he told a television interviewer, "but I'll take the 250,000 extra copies we're going to sell any day."

But very soon he began to suspect he'd been had by Stafford Somerfield. "I couldn't discount the possibility that Somerfield very cleverly laid a trap for me," Murdoch later told me. "That letter he'd written to the board in the spring was in reality an attempt on his part to get me to sack him so that I'd have to pay off his contract in full. But I didn't sack him—I accommodated his complaints and tried to get on with him. He was disappointed with that, so he talked me into going with the Keeler business, knowing full well it would kick up a row and get me in hot water and knowing full well that I'd then be forced to get rid of him.

"The son of a bitch led me down the primrose path. I had no way of knowing what a stink publishing Keeler would create. I was too new to the scene. But he knew—and I believe now that that was his plan: to embarrass me and ultimately get his contract paid off so he could go off and play with his bloody dogs."

That was Murdoch talking to me fourteen years after the fact. To some degree, he might have been right. For, once the controversy erupted, Somerfield reacted even more arrogantly than Murdoch did, thereby intensifying the public criticism of his boss. But for Murdoch to claim in retrospect that he had no idea that the series would trigger the public furor it did, because he was still a relative stranger to England, is disingenuous at best. In a memo he wrote to Somerfield on July 22, 1969, agreeing to buy the new Keeler memoirs, he made it very clear that he was aware of the possible consequences of printing them and insisted that they be sufficiently sanitized to prevent any backlash damage to *News of the World.*

It was this concern that prompted Murdoch personally to defend the series in public once the critical tempest erupted, whereas he might otherwise have remained silent. Suddenly, he feared that after the series reached its end, public disgust with *News of the World* would be so great that the paper would not only lose the additional circulation it had garnered, but much more beyond that. What's more, Murdoch was by then in the midst of trying to acquire a daily paper to go along with *News of the World,* and he believed that the mounting attacks on his journalistic judgment could foil his plans.

As it turned out, Murdoch need not have worried about wholesale public abandonment of *News of the World.* On the contrary, the experience further proved his contention that the more tawdry, "lively," and sensationalist a newspaper was, the more readers it would have and the more profits it would generate. This seemed even truer in England than Australia, since in England almost every Fleet Street paper had national distribution and thus a much broader market.

Nor did Murdoch have real cause for concern regarding his plans to pick up a London daily. For no matter the public outcry over the Keeler memoirs, and no matter his ongoing problems with Stafford Somerfield, he had demonstrated that he knew how to run and improve the balance sheet of a major British newspaper organization. That was all that concerned the bankers, brokers, and big-business traders of London, few of whom in any event read such papers as *News of the World.* For all they cared, Murdoch could have been the proprietor of a chain of fast-food emporiums. So long as he knew how to turn his product into major money, he would get all the help he needed from them.

But Murdoch did suffer a genuine personal anxiety as a result of the Keeler imbroglio, and that had to do with the matter of his and his wife's social acceptance. By then settled in a comfortable house on a fashionable London square with Anna and their year-old daughter Elisabeth, Murdoch had for all practical purposes emigrated to England. The middle and upper social classes of London were famous for their snobbery and inhospitability toward "ordinary" Australians. True, the wealthy Murdoch was no ordinary Australian. Yet the reputation for obsessively fetid journalism that had preceded him, and its firsthand confirmation with the Keeler series, made him seem very much the kind of Aussie most Londoners took sanctimonious pleasure in peering down their noses at.

Murdoch professes to this day to have cared "not a whit"

about being accepted socially in England in 1969. In fact, he has often expressed a deep contempt for most British social institutions and traditions.

Anna Murdoch, though, did care. Four years of marriage to Rupert had produced in her a deep perplexity about many things vital to her—about her husband, whom she perceived as a complex but fundamentally endearing man; about the viciously negative public reactions Rupert often left in his wake wherever he traveled; about the dubious virtues of Rupert's combative business and salacious journalistic creeds, which troubled her Roman Catholic sensibility and her feminine sense of proportion; and above all about her own increasingly visible role in the entire Murdochian scheme of things.

When Anna first arrived in London, before the Keeler memoirs were serialized, she was sought out eagerly by the press and gave a number of interviews in which she came across for the most part as little more than the attractive, dutiful, and not very bright young wife of Fleet Street's startling new press phenomenon. Although happy to be identified as Mrs. Rupert Murdoch, she was not content to be portrayed simply as her husband's domestic helpmeet and housekeeper. She was in fact highly intelligent, articulate, and assertive, if not aggressive, and she had deepening ambitions for herself as a writer and "communicator," as she once put it.

Nor was she pleased when newspaper articles later appeared, based on the interviews she had given, that slyly hinted that she owed her glamorous station in life to the fact that she had "married her boss." She had been through that sort of catty innuendo in the Australian press, of course—particularly that sector of the press controlled by Rupert's competitors. But she was hoping for a clean slate in England, to be assessed in her own light rather than in the reflected glow of Rupert's, and she was sorely disappointed to find herself pictured at best as an obeisant housewife, at worst as a gold digger.

Anna had managed at least partially to inure herself against the criticisms of Rupert that regularly reached her ears. But only partially. She knew her husband better than anyone, and she still clung to the hope that she could persuade the world that he was not the ogre that so much of it perceived him to be. Such persuasion had been beyond her power in Australia; by the time they married, his soiled reputation had been irretrievably cemented there.

But England represented a fresh start in Anna's mind. She had deliberately shaped many of the interviews to focus mostly on Rupert rather than herself—on his virtues as a husband and father, on his modest tastes, his simple pleasures, his humble domesticity. She believed she had made effective headway in helping to create a benevolent view of Rupert in London. But then came the Keeler fiasco!

Yet Anna still would not give up. And so, when an invitation came for Murdoch to appear on a popular British television talk show hosted by the ubiquitous David Frost—an invitation engineered by Murdoch's public relations man, John Addey—Anna practically dragged him into the studio.

The ground rules were simple, or so the Murdochs thought. Murdoch was to sit down to a long, friendly televised chat with Frost so that he could explain to the nation his "entirely sensible" rationale for printing the new Keeler memoirs and belie any fears that he lacked respect for British traditions of fair play, decency, and privacy. He would base his defense on the claim that although everyone knew much of what had happened in 1963, Christine Keeler's coming forward with additional "facts" in 1969 had made her story newsworthy once more. That the now-virtuous and widely admired John Profumo had to have his past political misdeeds and sexual peccadillos graphically raked over again was an unfortunate by-product of a contemporary news event but could not be helped.

"What would you have me do," Murdoch intended to ask, "suppress important news in order to spare the man further embarrassment?" He would lecture Frost—most amiably, to be sure—on the perils of withholding news for the sake of protecting people in high places. He would then turn and look directly into the camera. "Is that what the British people want from their newspapers?"

The whole performance would be a public relations gem, Addey assured Murdoch. Moreover, he could use the interview not just to justify the Keeler memoirs, but to lay out for the English public his entire publishing philosophy—his by then well-honed dogma that newspapers, to be viable, must give the majority of the public what it wants: brevity, liveliness, entertainment, and a few daily sensual kicks to brighten its day.

"What's wrong with using a newspaper to make people feel happy and upbeat?" Murdoch was fond of saying in response to his critics. The trouble was that whenever he said it, it was usually with a serious, almost mournful face, and a smirk was never far from his lips.

Under John Addey's guidance, and as Anna Murdoch looked on, the reluctant Rupert spent most of the day before the interview preparing for his appearance. Addey was optimistic. Although Murdoch was not an accomplished public speaker and had the annoying habit of appending a frequent interrogative "Yes?" or "Eh?" to the end of his sentences, Addey was certain that Frost would put him at ease. Frost prided himself on being a journalist, Addey told his client. But beyond that, he was an entertainer who cared desperately about producing a lively and interesting show. He had a knack for "bringing out" his interview guests, no matter how unpracticed they were before the camera. Rupert would be fine. "Just be yourself," Addey advised, "like you are now."

As Addey had suggested, David Frost was a curious amalgam of television journalist and entertainer. Having built his career as the medium's foremost satirist of serious news, he had done much to blur the distinctions between the two fields. In a way, he was not much different from Rupert Murdoch. Each exploited the public events of the day in terms of entertainment rather than information and analysis. Each depended on trivialization, exaggeration, and distortion for their effects. The only real dissimilarity between the two was that Murdoch's form of journalism was narrowly low-brow entertainment, whereas Frost's was designed to appeal to a more sophisticated audience.

Like Murdoch, Frost liked to think himself capable of meaningful journalism when the time called for it. Murdoch's publication of the Keeler memoirs was such an occasion, and when it was proposed that Murdoch appear on his show, Frost decided to turn it into a major news event in its own right. He did so, however, without telling John Addey what he had in mind. As far as Murdoch's PR man was concerned, his client's appearance was to be nothing more than an affable chat between the two men. Frost could be expected to ask a few challenging questions, of course, but Addey—and therefore Murdoch—expected the whole tone of the interview to be amicable and deferential.

Murdoch "walked straight into a trap," as he later put it to me. A few hours before he arrived at the studios, and unbeknown to him, Frost had taped a quick interview with one of England's leading Roman Catholic clerics, Terence Cardinal Heenan, who was an outspoken advocate of the good works John Profumo had been performing among the poor of London's East End. The Cardinal used the opportunity to decry Murdoch's "shocking cynicism and commercial greed" in republishing Keeler, thereby "unforgivably smearing" Profumo at a time when the ex–defense minister had "paid his debt to society" and was "doing God's merciful work" better than "any layman I have known."

Under Frost's deliberately sycophantic questioning, Heenan righteously added that many of the "poor unfortunates whose lives Mr. Profumo is so selflessly trying to improve" were surely readers of *News of the World*. "I think [Murdoch] . . . profoundly wrong in raking up the past of this excellent man and putting it in the homes of the people whom he is now trying to help."

David Frost's sense of news as theater was unerring, if not always pleasant for those he focused on in his "serious-news" mode. Airtime for the Frost-Murdoch live interview had arrived. As Murdoch waited offstage for Frost to introduce him to the packed studio audience, he quickly sensed he was in trouble. Frost larded his introduction with subtly snide references to Murdoch's reputation as an Australian publisher who would stop at nothing to sell papers. By the time his introduction ended, the more than two hundred people in the audience had been worked into a feverish anti-Murdoch pitch.

John Addey, sitting in the audience, was shocked and appalled. Murdoch, as he made his entrance onto the set, could barely control himself. Anna Murdoch, sitting before a monitor in the "green room," shriveled in angry despair.

Thereafter, it was all downhill for Murdoch. Although he later accused Frost of having tricked and sandbagged him, most of the blame for his pathetic performance rested with him alone. Frost assumed a superior and coldly adversarial tone as he began his questions, concentrating on the propriety of the Keeler memoirs. At first, Murdoch tried to be polite and reasonable, but his suppressed rage merely translated those qualities into an impression of extreme, furtive discomfort. He began to perspire, fidget, and stumble defensively over his words, unable to disarm either Frost or the studio audience. He gave the impression of a man caught in a monumental lie, and the more he stumbled about in his efforts to deflect the contradictions Frost pointed out, the more hapless he grew.

At a point early in the proceeding, Frost suspended his in-

quisition to play the taped interview with Cardinal Heenan. Then
he asked Murdoch if he had any reply to Heenan's remarks.
Murdoch expressed his indignation over Frost's "cheap shot."
Like a courtroom prosecutor, Frost gazed knowingly at the audience, then into the camera, as if to ask: "Should Mr. Murdoch be
sitting here complaining of cheap shots after what he has done to
Mr. Profumo?" The studio audience hooted in delight.

Murdoch's worst moment occurred when, after a further
skewering by Frost, he came back with a snide rejoinder about
libel. His riposte elicited another in a series of loud cheers from
John Addey in the audience. Frost snickered, "Your PR man's
doing a wonderful job over there. He's made more noise than the
other two hundred and thirty people put together. Still, that's
what he's paid for, isn't it?"

Suddenly made aware that Murdoch's only studio supporter
was a paid flack, the rest of the audience howled and hissed as
Murdoch further reddened.

The rest of the interview dissolved into a plain-and-nasty
bickering session between Frost and Murdoch. Frost coolly maintained his air of moral superiority while continuing to goad Murdoch, and Murdoch dug himself deeper and deeper into his defensive hole, his confusion, frustration, and fury exposed to the
view of the entire nation.

Frost ended the show with another sarcastic reference to
John Addey, who had continued to support Murdoch noisily
from his seat in the audience. "Your PR man's going mad again.
Your PR man is the only person who's applauded. You must give
him a raise." If anything, the humiliated Murdoch was ready to
fire him.

When Frost signed off, Murdoch stalked from the set. He
was met by Anna, who was every bit as livid as he. As they started
toward the studio exit, Frost, high on the knowledge that he had
just pulled off one of his better shows, caught up and put out a
conciliatory hand, inviting them for drinks in his "hospitality
room." Before Murdoch could respond, Anna answered for both
of them. "No, thank you," she said icily, "we've had enough of
your hospitality."

And as the Murdochs and Addey swept out of the building,
Murdoch vowed to exact revenge on Frost.

In a manner of speaking, not long afterward he would do
just that.

The Sun *Also Rises*

At the time of the Frost show, however, Murdoch had more urgent business at hand. One of his principal concerns when he took over *News of the World* was the fact that the paper published only once a week—on Sunday. As a consequence, its large-volume printing plant, along with the plant's big unionized labor force, lay idle for the rest of the week. Almost immediately after his takeover, he began to ponder a daily version of the paper. The idea made eminent business sense, since a successful daily could produce an enormous amount of additional revenue at a relatively modest additional cost. The only question was: With what other papers would such a daily compete?

London's journalistic scene was a smorgasbord of long-established daily newspapers, most of them published in the morning. There was the august *Times,* its modest circulation and tenuous profitability offset by its reputation as the nation's "newspaper of record." There were the *Daily Telegraph* and the *Guardian,* serious papers published for the country's educated classes, and the *Financial Times,* England's equivalent of *The Wall Street Journal.* There were the *Daily Mail* and *Daily Express,* raucously middlebrow papers that competed fiercely with each other, the first owned by IPC, the second the flagship of the Beaverbrook organization. And then there was the enormously popular *Daily Mirror,* the paradigm of lowbrow daily tabloids in England. In its formidable wake the *Mirror* trailed several gamely competing papers of similar style. Among them was the *Sun,* also owned by IPC.

Every market in daily morning journalism was amply covered, if not cornered. To which one a new Murdoch daily should address itself was clear, however. *News of the World*'s principal weekend competition came from the *Mirror* organization's two sensationalist Sunday papers. Given *News of the World*'s own journalistic orientation, it was only natural that a daily version compete with the *Daily Mirror.*

But could it be done successfully? The *Mirror* had a vast, well-entrenched, intensely loyal blue-collar following that went back for generations. Lately, though, like *News of the World* under the Carr-Somerfield management during the early 1960s, its daily circulation dominance had shown signs of weakening. Some attributed this to the fact that IPC was attempting to give the paper a more serious, "upmarket" image; others to the theory that the *Mirror*'s traditional older readership was beginning to die off, while the younger segment of the market—the "under-forty" generation—was being wooed away from newspapers by television.

Whatever the case, Murdoch grew increasingly certain in 1969 that a daily tabloid of his own, printed on the otherwise idle *News of the World* presses, had an excellent chance of succeeding. All it would take would be a paper that beat the *Mirror* at its own game—highlighting and sensationalizing the banal, the bizarre, the morbid, the sleazy. Given his successes in Australia based on the same formula, and given his cadre of editors and writers, which was by then smoothly expert in implementing, promoting, and expanding the formula, Murdoch had little doubt that such a paper, edited to appeal to the younger generation, would carve out a profitable niche for itself in the wild and woolly British daily tabloid market.

The only question remaining, then, was whether to create a daily from scratch or acquire an existing paper and use it as a starting point. By pursuing the latter course, Murdoch would at least obtain an established circulation base by which to soften the initial cost of going daily, as well as a distribution network. By beginning from scratch, he would be forced to spend as much if not more money.

Murdoch first explored the acquisition route. Buying the *Mirror* itself was out of the question, of course. IPC would not voluntarily part with its leading cash earner, and a takeover attempt would be inordinately—impossibly—messy and costly. He looked into the *Daily Sketch,* one of the *Mirror*'s weaker money-losing competitors, but concluded that its debts would be too much of a liability. By mid-summer 1969, he was convinced that his only realistic option was to start fresh. But then came an unexpected development.

In 1961, Cecil King's *Daily Mirror* organization, prior to its transformation into IPC, had fattened its publishing stable by acquiring the *Sunday People*, then the main weekend competition of *News of the World*, and the *Daily Herald.* The *Herald*, for a while London's best-selling daily in the 1930s, had sagged badly since then, due mainly to its outmoded left-wing, trade-union slant. Circulation continued to drop under its new ownership. Finally, in 1965, the *Mirror* company shut down the *Herald* and created a different semitabloid in its place. The new paper, called the *Sun,* was launched amid great fanfare about its being devoted to the interests of the affluent younger generation that at the time seemed to be revolutionizing London's cultural life—the frenetic, freewheeling generation of the Beatles, the miniskirt, and the disco.

The swinging London of the sixties cared little about reading newspapers, however, and the *Sun*, born of such great hopes and edited by its own distinctly new generation of "go-go" journalists, fared no better than its predecessor. Five years later, its circulation had fallen almost by half, and its more than $30 million in cumulative losses had become a serious drain on IPC's profitability. By mid-summer 1969, Hugh Cudlipp, the longtime editorial director of the *Mirror* organization, decided to sell the *Sun*, or failing that, to give it away to anyone willing to assume its debts. And failing that, simply to shut it down for good and swallow its losses. That option was the least desirable, however, since it might arouse the ire of the various newspaper unions against other *Mirror* papers.

News of Cudlipp's decision reached Robert Maxwell before it did Rupert Murdoch. Maxwell, still smarting over his last-minute loss of *News of the World* and still aching to establish himself in Fleet Street, quickly came forward with an offer for the *Sun*. His proposal was to take over the paper virtually for nothing, return it to its former life as a pro-labor chronicle, reduce its daily circulation aspirations to about 500,000, and run it on a shoestring with a much shrunken editorial and printing staff. In no way would it endeavor to compete with the *Daily Mirror*, he promised.

That suited Cudlipp and his board, but not the large, unionized work force that had been putting out the *Sun*. When details of the Cudlipp-Maxwell negotiations reached the paper's rank and file in the late July, all sorts of protest erupted. *Sun*'s union stewards made it clear that they would not sit still for such a deal, meaning as it did a drastic reduction in jobs. Maxwell, the self-appointed champion of the labor movement in England since the time of his first campaign for election to Parliament, was now condemned as the movement's foremost pariah. The *Sun*'s unions issued a veiled but clear ultimatum to Cudlipp: we will not accept Maxwell as a buyer; if you turn the *Sun* over to him, watch out for the rest of your paper.

But what else are we to do? Cudlipp asked. Our only alternative is to shut down the paper.

Find another buyer, the union leaders replied.

Who? queried Cudlipp.

The Aussie.

The man who first advanced Murdoch's name to Cudlipp was Richard Briginshaw, the head of the *Sun*'s largest union, and he knew whereof he spoke.

When Murdoch had learned of Maxwell's offer early in August, the effect had been like a carrot dropped in the path of a hungry rabbit. Although the *Sun*'s circulation had dropped to about 800,000 by then, it could provide just the base Murdoch needed, along with *News of the World*'s six-plus million weekend readers, to launch a successful daily. Moreover, he discovered, IPC was willing practically to give away the paper to Maxwell. As contemptuous of the uncouth Maxwell as anyone in Fleet Street, and eager to exact a measure of revenge for his "kangaroo" slurs of the year before, Murdoch could not resist another bout with the Czech-born "captain."

The only impediment to contesting Maxwell for the *Sun* lay in the question—should he win—of integrating that paper's work force into that of *News of the World*, which was dominated by a different group of unions. Murdoch had already antagonized the *News of the World* locals in his efforts to counter the extensive featherbedding and redundant "manning" that were endemic in the British newspaper industry. That, along with his increasingly quoted perorations against "the bleeding of British industrial initiative by the trade unions," had made Murdoch appear as much a public enemy of labor as the most ardent right-wing members of Parliament. Would he be any more acceptable to the *Sun*'s unions than Maxwell, especially when his own bid for the *Sun* would be contingent on more than modest labor reductions?

Before challenging Maxwell, Murdoch decided to get the answer directly by seeking out Richard Briginshaw, the *Sun*'s chief union leader. Informed that Briginshaw was vacationing in Italy, he immediately flew to Rome and tracked him down.

Briginshaw was a tough, hard-bitten veteran of London's labor strife, yet a realistic man who could see through the superficial passions and rhetoric of a work crisis to strike the kind of compromises that would have long-term benefits both for his rank and file and for himself. He was already on record as being irrevocably against Maxwell's proposal for the *Sun*. But the alternative—IPC's closure of the paper—was no more favorable. Either way, many jobs would be lost and his union would be seriously weakened. He was interested to hear what Murdoch had to say.

Murdoch had plenty to say. His career in Australia had been a constant round of hard negotiations with the newspaper unions there, and he boasted that he was held in high regard by Australian labor—an assertion that would have been angrily disputed by more than one labor leader in Sydney. He pointed also to his personal history, going back to his Oxford years, of sympathy toward labor causes.

But as a newspaper owner, he, too, was forced to be realistic and pragmatic, he argued. If he were to take over the *Sun*, he could not guarantee the jobs of the paper's entire work force. He would have to move the paper into the *News of the World*'s plant. To take the *Sun*'s entire printing staff with it would mean a financially intolerable duplication of labor from the very start—paying two, often three or more men to do the job a single man could easily handle. Such a burden would surely destroy any chance of reviving the *Sun* and turning it into the success Murdoch envisioned.

On the other hand, if he were allowed by the unions to produce the paper mostly with his existing *News of the World* workers, once its success was assured and its circulation began to grow, it would require a constantly expanding work force to maintain the pace of its growth. In that event, Murdoch promised, he would see to it that Briginshaw's constituents were the first ones hired. In the short run, some jobs would be lost. But in the long run, the unions Briginshaw represented stood to benefit.

"After all," said Murdoch, "my purpose here is to create jobs, not to destroy them."

Briginshaw accepted Murdoch's logic and quickly phoned Hugh Cudlipp to let him know that the Australian would be a better choice than Maxwell to take over the *Sun*. "Fine," said Cudlipp, "but we're in the midst of talks with Maxwell at this very moment. We can't shift horses in midstream. To let Murdoch come in now would be a breach of our duty to Maxwell to conduct good-faith discussions."

"What would you need?" asked Briginshaw.

"Maxwell has to be convinced that he has no chance of winning your people's approval. Once that's clear, he'll be forced to bow out. Then we can talk to Murdoch, if he's interested."

"Don't you worry," said Briginshaw, "he's more than interested. He wants the *Sun*. And don't worry either about Maxwell. We'll have him out of the picture in no time."

"No time" proved to be less than two weeks. At the start of September, after Briginshaw returned from Italy, he announced publicly that his union—the major union at the *Sun*—had decided irrevocably against Maxwell and his plans for the paper. Privately, Briginshaw told reporters that he was expecting Murdoch to enter the picture. In response to the resulting queries, Murdoch said that he hadn't yet talked to Cudlipp or anyone else at IPC, but that he intended to do so the next day.

That wasn't quite true. Murdoch had already talked to several people at IPC about the condition and prospects of the *Sun*. One was a promotional executive named Bert Hardy, who had been with the *Mirror* organization for twenty years and had played a major role in the management of the *Sun* after it was created out of the old *Herald* in 1964. Another was a veteran *Mirror* news executive, Alex McKay, who had once worked for Murdoch's father. They, too, had commended Murdoch to Hugh Cudlipp, and through them a meeting was scheduled between the two.

Cudlipp, the recent successor to Cecil King as chairman of IPC, was an irascible man who liked neither Murdoch nor his reputation. "There will always be someone around to scrape the bottom of the barrel," he had been quoted as saying about the Australian during the controversy over the Keeler memoirs. Too, the *Sun* was Cudlipp's personal baby—he had overseen its planning and launching in 1964 and had wet-nursed it through its subsequent five years of failing health. What if Murdoch turned it around and made a success of it? Should he manage to do so, it would be a profound embarrassment to Cudlipp, a glaringly negative reflection on his own newspaper savvy.

And then there was the matter of Murdoch's true intentions to be resolved. Surely if he got the *Sun* he would try to transform it into a direct rival of the *Mirror,* Cudlipp's leading paper. What wisdom was there, and what prudent corporate judgment, in handing over the *Sun* to a man who would inevitably use it to draw away readers from the *Mirror*?

To Cudlipp, those factors constituted the downside of any deal. Nevertheless, the upside had more compelling features. One derived from Cudlipp's fear that by shutting down the *Sun,* thereby bringing about the loss of nearly two thousand unionized jobs within IPC, he would trigger a bitter labor backlash against the rest of the huge corporation's publications. He was almost without a choice in the matter. He had to allow the *Sun* to stay alive, even at the cost of putting it in the hands of a competitor. The expense of such competition would be markedly less than that of an IPC–wide labor rebellion.

Beyond that, Cudlipp believed he knew the newspaper business better than anyone. If he'd been unable to make the *Sun* work, certainly no one else could—not even the upstart Murdoch. The fact that *News of the World* had increased its circulation by a few hundred thousand since its acquisition by Murdoch was no sign that the Australian possessed any special newspaper genius, for *News of the World* had been a going concern when Murdoch took it over. The *Sun,* on the other hand, had been a regular money-loser since its inception.

The likelihood was that Murdoch wouldn't be able to turn it around. What better way to put the Australian in financial distress than to unload the *Sun* on him and then watch him vainly pour millions into it as it spun further and further down the drain? Most if not all of those millions would come out of *News of the World* profits, thus weakening that paper's position, too, and strengthening those of its principal rivals—IPC's *Sunday Mirror* and *Sunday People.*

The upside outweighed the downside in Cudlipp's careful calculations, and in short order he agreed to the sale of the *Sun* to Murdoch.

"Sale?" Murdoch protested at their first meeting. "You were willing to give it away to Maxwell."

"That was a different set of circumstances," retorted Cudlipp. "His plan was to remove the paper from competition with the *Mirror*. You, I have no doubt, intend to compete."

Even at that, the price was the relatively modest equivalent of $1.5 million, with only $120,000 payable at the start; the balance was to be paid out of profits, if any, over the next six years. As it turned out, Murdoch's purchase was "the steal of the century," as one of his chief executives later boasted. Under Murdoch's guidance, the *Sun* was soon to become the greatest success story in Fleet Street history and his financial launching pad to America.

Murdoch says that he was fully aware of Cudlipp's strategy in letting him buy the *Sun*. When he first arrived in London to take over *News of the World*, Fleet Street had withheld judgment on him, and some trade pundits had even praised him in print as representing an injection of "vital new blood" into the stale and unexciting British newspaper industry.

But the honeymoon had been short-lived. Murdoch's intensifying feud with Stafford Somerfield, the details of which Somerfield did not hesitate to broadcast to his many Fleet Street cronies on other papers, his transparently phony defenses of his publication of the Keeler memoirs, and his public humiliation by David Frost—all had soured much of the London press establishment on him. In addition, he had taken to publicly criticizing British journalism in general as "dull," "trite," "long-winded," and "incestuous," among other characterizations, saying on one occasion that "papers here are written and edited for the benefit of each other instead of the public."

Finally, in his brief year in London, Murdoch had exacerbated the long-standing tension between Fleet Street management and labor. It was a time when new mechanical and electronic technologies were being introduced to make newspaper production more efficient and economical. Murdoch, though still professing to be a political liberal and backer of the progressive labor movement, was warning anyone who would listen that radical changes would have to be made in "the human mechanics" of newspaper production if the industry was to survive.

By that, of course, he meant the replacement of human labor by the imminent new generation of machines and computers for typesetting and printing, the heart and soul of the production process. He even extended his dire prognostications to the editorial side of the business, claiming that the new technologies would markedly reduce the white-collar work force needed to assemble a newspaper—reporters, editors, makeup men, proofreaders, and other such "unionized clericals."

Murdoch was speaking truths no one on Fleet Street wanted to hear—the unions because such talk made them nervous, defensive, and bellicose; the owners and managers because excessive union edginess invariably resulted in further inflammations of their in-house labor problems.

"When I got the *Sun,* I was pretty much persona non grata in Fleet Street," Murdoch says. "A lot of people were looking forward to my failing with it, Cudlipp and his IPC pals included, I'm sure. So I determined not to fail. It was as simple as that."

Well, not as simple as that. The eventual financial success of the *Sun* in the face of all odds against it crowned Murdoch's career as a genius of the pop-newspaper field. It also cemented his reputation as a brilliant international business and financial manager. At the same time, however, it increasingly drenched him in a self-perpetuating odor of moral and ethical disrepute.

Murdoch's plan for the *Sun,* a "broadsheet" paper under IPC, was simple: to transform it into a tabloid in the fashion of the *Daily Mirror,* fill it with the kind of simplistic, sensationalized sleaze that had worked so well for him in Australia, and then "promote the hell out of it."

At the beginning it appeared the paper would be a disaster. Between September and November 1969, Murdoch put together an editorial staff composed of his experienced Australian newspaper operatives, leftovers from the old *Sun,* and new recruits from other British tabloids. Nominally in charge was Larry Lamb, a hard-drinking forty-year-old Yorkshire-born veteran of the *Mirror* organization whom Murdoch had taken on as the *Sun*'s chief day-to-day editor.

But Murdoch was really in charge. The ambitious Lamb, along with his London-born deputy editor, Bernard Shrimsley, had been hired principally to ensure that the new *Sun* maintained a clearly British style and point of view while the paper became accustomed to Murdoch's Australian formula and its many non-British techniques.

The first issue was scheduled for November 17, 1969. John Addey arranged a large inaugural party at the *News of the World* printing plant in Bouverie Street, just off Fleet Street, where Anna Murdoch was due to push the button that would start the presses rolling. He had invited scores of potential advertisers, politicians, and other London luminaries to witness the launch. Few showed up. Many of the no-shows were at a rival party thrown by Hugh Cudlipp at the *Daily Mirror* plant a few blocks away.

That inauspicious beginning was compounded by the fact that when Anna Murdoch ceremoniously punched the button to start the presses, nothing happened. It took hours to fix the mechanical glitch, and when the machines finally thundered to life, the paper was well behind schedule.

What emerged was hardly more encouraging. The first edition came out looking like the product of a couple of schoolboys operating a crude home printing press. Pages were smeared, photos were grainy and blurred, the text was liberally peppered with typographical errors, and the layout was pedestrian. A few copies were smuggled over to the Cudlipp party. As Cudlipp flipped through the paper, he yelled triumphantly to Lee Howard, the editor of the *Daily Mirror*, "Lee, we've got nothing to worry about!"

"The Chickens Come Home . . ."

Cudlipp would live to eat his words, as would every other Fleet Street expert who inspected the *Sun*'s first few issues and smugly predicted the paper's doom. The consensus was that the lower-class British public, more sophisticated than that of Australia, would roundly reject the usual Murdoch mix of misleadingly sensationalized headlines and turgid, mock-urgent writing.

The verdict was dead wrong. Investing much more heavily to advertise and promote the paper than he had to start it, Murdoch clearly struck a responsive chord in the British psyche. Within a year, circulation was approaching the two-million mark, more than double that of the *Sun*'s last year under Cudlipp. With that new base, Murdoch then embarked on a full-scale circulation war with the *Daily Mirror,* forcing the *Mirror* to abandon its previous years' efforts to upgrade its appeal and to begin imitating the *Sun*.

The crucial breakthrough in the battle occurred late in 1970. The standard British tabloid was composed of four fundamental parts. They were the front page, which featured one or more headlined "news" stories; the third page, which was also known as the "cheesecake page" for its assortment of photos of scantily clad female "models" and beach frolickers; the two center pages—"the spread"—which were generally devoted to some unusually morbid feature; and the back page, which introduced an extensive sports section.

According to Graham King, who had moved permanently with Murdoch from Sydney to London to handle much of the promotion of the *Sun* and *News of the World*, what happened to give the *Sun* its great breakthrough "was one of those things that always seem to come about through inspired accident.

"One of our photographers had been on holiday in the south of France snapping pictures of that new phenomenon known as topless beaches. He came back and showed his pictures around the *Sun*. Although the conventional London tabloid had always featured a lot of flesh on Page Three—bathing beauties, starlets, that sort of thing—no one had ever dared picture naked breasts.

"Well, Rupert wasn't around, and I don't even think Larry Lamb was. Shrimsley was putting out the paper that day, and he decided that the topless beach pictures were A-one news. So, without asking anybody, he snuck one into the third page—a photo of this bare-bosomed beach girl in St. Tropez.

"The impact was just enormous. The edition sold out like it was printed on gold leaf. There was a hue and cry, of course. But the point was that the paper flew off the newsstands. When Rupert heard about it, he said, 'Let's do it again' a few days later. So we did—another topless beauty. The same result. The taboo had been broken, and from then on it was bare boobs every day on Page Three. And the *Sun* really took off."

Murdoch declined to take credit for the idea, but once it became a daily feature of the *Sun* he defended it as intrepidly as he did every other aspect of his journalistic formula. "What harm is there in bringing a little innocent cheer to people's breakfast tables?" was one of his retorts to critics. "I mean, it's all done tastefully. They're not the kind of poses you see in the hard-core men's magazines."

Everyone from church groups to women's organizations to the newspaper establishment itself came down on him, however. The harm, they insisted, was that it violated moral precepts, exploited women, imperiled the innocence of children, and further cheapened journalistic standards.

"Hypocritical rubbish," exclaimed Murdoch, privately reveling in the controversy. "If it's so objectionable, why are so many more people buying the *Sun*, tens of thousands of women included? I answer to no one but the public. They tell me what they want, and I give it to them. If the public didn't want nudes, I wouldn't go on publishing them. Go complain to the public, not to me."

Says Anthony Philips, a British media analyst, "By that time, it had to be clear to anyone with half a brain that Rupert Murdoch's principal interest in life was not in journalism as such but in the business of publishing, solely for profit, what passed for newspapers. For him to call himself a journalist, or even a genuine newspaper publisher, was an abomination. Implicit in those vocations are an adherence to certain minimal standards of truth and accuracy. He repeatedly sneered at such standards. He was not the first in Fleet Street to do so, but he made fewer bones about it. He was obsessed solely with selling newspapers, making money, and carving out a very substantial personal power niche for himself in England, as he'd done in Australia.

"All well and good. But the ultimate hypocrite was him. Rather than come out and say in plain words what he was doing, he hid behind unctuous statements about how he was making the news more intelligible and readable. That was the real rubbish. He was not dealing in news, he was dealing in cheap fantasy. And all his top editors and writers were so beholden to him for their jobs that they went along, all the while claiming they were genuine, humble journalists—that highfalutin' word."

Sex and violence, together with the bizarre and the occult, had from the start been the cornerstones of the Murdoch formula. All those factors had been central to the success of British tabloid journalism, too. With the *Sun* and *News of the World,* however, Murdoch and his cohorts simply refined and concentrated the Fleet Street tradition, transforming a style of publishing that had always hidden behind coyness and innuendo into one that was direct and graphic. Predictably, the public ate it up.

But it was almost as if Murdoch and his formula's other chief advocates were ordained by some higher power to pay personally for their exploitation of the British public's baser tastes. The "day of atonement," as one sermonizing London churchman would later call it, came not long after the launch of the new *Sun.*

Unbeknown to Murdoch, two impoverished immigrant brothers had seen several of his appearances on television and read some of the press interviews with Anna Murdoch. In early December 1969, they concocted a scheme designed to enrich themselves vastly. Their plan was to kidnap Anna Murdoch and hold her for ransom—a crime they conceived, except for its prospective victim, straight from the gruesome and sensationalized kidnap stories they had pored over in *News of the World,* the *Sun,* and other such papers.

The brothers—Hosein by name—learned that Anna Murdoch tended to travel around London during the day in her husband's chauffeured Rolls-Royce. They tailed the car for a few days. After establishing a pattern, they set a day early in January 1970 to carry out their plan. What they could not anticipate was the mordant twist of fate that would befall them.

By early January, the Murdochs had gone to Australia for an extended visit. Murdoch had turned his Rolls—a company car— and its driver over to his top executives at *News of the World* for their use in his absence. Among those executives was Alex McKay, the former IPC operative who had become one of Murdoch's closest aides after the *Sun* takeover.

On the day of the kidnapping, McKay unwittingly reserved the Rolls for the use of his own wife, Muriel, who needed it for a shopping expedition in London's West End. By such happenstance was set in motion a train of events that would end in brutal tragedy, not for the Murdochs, as intended, but for the McKays.

Having picked up the trail of the Murdoch Rolls as it tooled about London with a single woman in the back seat—the pattern they had established a month earlier—the Hosein brothers waylaid the car at a light, quietly forced their way in at gunpoint, seized the woman they were sure the infinitely wealthy Rupert Murdoch would pay anything to recover, and made off with her.

Had Muriel McKay had the presence of mind to agree with her captors' insistence that she was Anna Murdoch, she might have survived her ordeal. But after much heated protest on her part, which evidently included waving her driver's license and credit cards in their faces, she convinced them that she was who she claimed to be—"the wife of a nobody," as the brothers' prosecutor later put it—and that they had made a monumentally dumb mistake.

Had the kidnappers had the presence of mind to admit their boner, chalk it up to bad luck, and let their captive go, they would probably not be behind bars today. Instead, whether out of panic or pique, they murdered Muriel McKay and dumped her body where it was bound to be discovered. The two men, talkative types, were eventually found as well. After being tried, they were jailed.

The grim episode took Rupert Murdoch sharply aback, Anna considerably more so when she learned that she had been the real target—not to mention Alex McKay. But it did nothing to alter Murdoch's view of the wisdom of his apparently crime-inciting publishing formula or of the mental capacity of the audience it was primarily directed to.* Nor did it seem to modify McKay's advocacy of Murdochian journalism. McKay went on to become one of Murdoch's chief apologists and a top-level, highly paid executive and director of the worldwide Murdoch media complex.

Murdoch, hiring a full-time bodyguard to protect his family, was content to write off the episode as an unfortunate social accident. It was no accident, though, that the large majority of the British public remained ignorant of its connections. Except for early reports of Muriel McKay's mysterious disappearance, Murdoch's papers gave the incident—a crime that would otherwise have been right down their alley—scant coverage. The rest of the press, invoking a curious form of professional courtesy, followed suit. The usual sensationalist bannering of ugly news did not operate when such news personally affected the barons of Fleet Street and their families.

If anything, the McKay murder further steeled Murdoch's determination to solidify his grip on his British press fiefdom and to do so in his own unimpeded fashion. Just prior to his departure for Australia in December, he had given a dinner for Stafford Somerfield at which he indicated to all present that he and the longtime *News of the World* editor had settled their differences and would thenceforth be working together harmoniously. When Murdoch returned in February, however, practically the first thing he did was call Somerfield into his office and, finally, fire him.

Murdoch believed that the "harmony" he'd established in December meant that Somerfield would comply with his future orders as to the paper's editorial side. Somerfield, on the other hand, took harmony to mean that Murdoch would refrain from issuing further editorial edicts.

While Murdoch was in Australia, Somerfield had gone around Fleet Street boasting to his friends about how he had forced his new proprietor to capitulate in their battle over editorial autonomy. It didn't take long for word of Somerfield's self-encomiums to reach Murdoch in Sydney. By then well aware of

---

* A 1974 survey in the industrial north of England—one of the *Sun*'s and *News of the World*'s primary markets—would show that every time an article on wife-beating appeared in either paper, the incidence of wife-beating complaints to the police rose sharply in the days that followed.

the snide, back-biting side of Somerfield's personality, he had no reason to doubt the stories. Upon his return, he resolved to get rid of the recalcitrant editor once and for all, no matter that he'd be required to pay off Somerfield's contract.

The payoff was expensive—the equivalent of nearly $200,-000. But to Murdoch it was worth it, for finally he achieved full editorial dominion over both the *Sun* and *News of the World*. The editor he installed in Somerfield's place, although a longtime member of the *News of the World* staff, made it clear to Murdoch that he was willing to be considerably more compliant than Somerfield.

The two papers marched forward, then, with Murdoch as their de facto editor-in-chief, further reshaping their form and content. As in the *Sun,* soon a parade of nubile nudes became a staple of *News of the World*, along with a regular menu of highly distorted "news" stories and questionable "features," all wrapped in a package of misleading, fake-urgent headlines and treacly prose "that could only be described as puke-making," to use one Fleet Street veteran's phrase.

When the National Union of Journalists—the reporters' and editors' guild—censured him in June 1970 for debasing the standards of British journalism, Murdoch shot back with the claim that since his methods had saved a dying paper, thereby preserving hundreds of NUJ jobs, the union should thank him, rather than criticize him.

Much of what he said in his defense was supportable. His journalistic techniques not only saved but created jobs. And they appeared to provide a large portion of the British reading public with what it wanted. Yet much of what was asserted by way of complaint about Murdoch's papers was even more supportable. That the new *Sun* and *News of the World* blatantly appealed to and exploited the most prurient of public tastes, and regularly violated the simplest canons of journalistic ethics, was readily apparent. As time went on and the Murdochian formula became more solidly rooted at the two papers, both would frequently be exposed in the practice of distorted coverage. Although other British papers were sometimes guilty of the same sins, none pursued such a course with the assiduousness and cynical frequency that Murdoch's did.

Newspapers, went the anti-Murdoch argument—even the cheapest tabloids—were in the nature of a public trust. Every paper had a duty to reflect public values and standards, to be sure. But beyond that, newspapers were also morally obliged to try to elevate those values and standards through a policy of adherence to as much truth and accuracy in their news and feature pages as possible. Admittedly, Fleet Street, especially its tabloids, did not always pursue that policy. But Murdoch's press seemed unilaterally to have rejected the policy outright and established a new one in its place, one proclaiming that it was perfectly acceptable to lie to the public, both to attract its attention and to manipulate its moods, passions, and opinions.

Notwithstanding Murdoch's many public rationales for his papers' behavior, almost every word out of his mouth appeared to confirm the critics' charges. Words like "lively," "breezy," "trenchant," and "entertaining" remained the prime ingredients of the apologetic gruel he regularly served up. These were juxtaposed with "dull," "stale," and "long-winded," which he used to describe the journalism of the rest of Fleet Street. As such words tripped distastefully off his tongue, it grew clear that he equated truth, accuracy, fairness, and comprehensiveness in newspapers with somnolence and prolixity, and that liveliness and entertainment were their antidotes. But the records of the *Sun* and *News of the World* as he'd refashioned them, along with those of practically all his Australian papers, demonstrably proved that the distortion of facts, whether in the reporting of genuine news events or in the incessant self-promotion to which the papers devoted so much of their space, constituted in his mind their basic liveliness and entertainment. In other words, Murdoch's sense of journalistic duty and relevance depended almost solely on factual invention and banal, vacuous sensationalism.

Once Murdochian journalism became a fixture on Fleet Street in 1970, the *Sun*'s main daily rivals were forced to go radically downmarket in their style and content in an attempt to counter the *Sun*'s rapidly expanding commercial appeal. The same was true for *News of the World*'s Sunday competitors. Led by Murdoch, tabloid journalism in Britain became more trivial and retrograde than ever—colorful and rowdy, but built on a foundation of sand. It was like "professional" wrestling, a sham version of the real thing.

To be fair to Murdoch, his one attempt at quality journalism—the *Australian*—had been a continuing financial failure for six years, although that may have been due to nothing more than his own inability to understand such journalism and its markets. Also, London was saturated with high- and mid-quality newspapers. Having determined to publish a daily paper to make the *News of the World* plant more economical, and having settled on the only paper readily available, from a business point of view he probably had no option but to travel the low road with the *Sun*; it was his only realistic chance of turning it around and making it profitable. Still, such an explanation exactly pinpointed Murdoch's real priorities, which had always been focused much more rapaciously on the financial aspects of journalism than its ideals.

In Murdoch's 1970 business theology, a newspaper functioned exclusively as a servant of the corporate balance sheet. It was nothing more than a product to be marketed at a cheap price to the greatest number of people possible, like a toaster or an alarm clock. As with many a purveyor of cheap, low-quality mass-market goods, Murdoch was forced to invent an entire mythology about how his products enhanced people's lives. Although many purchased his products, few bought the mythology, not even the scores of newspapermen who put their professional scruples aside in exchange for the salaries Murdoch paid for their fealty, men who otherwise would have been ashamed to be identified with his brand of journalism. As more than one has said to me, "I help put out Rupert's junk, but you wouldn't catch me reading it."

The more intensely his journalistic practices were attacked, the more desperately Murdoch sought the public's approval of them with defenses that were as meretricious as his papers themselves. Eventually, it became clear that his work would never bring him the personal and professional esteem he yearned for. So he decided to raise the ante. If he couldn't earn esteem, he'd get power. One way or another, he would win the respect he believed he deserved.

In 1970, Murdoch was, as he recently said to me, "in the process of redefining myself politically." This meant that having long since outgrown the radicalism of his youth, he was even shedding the residual liberalism that had borne him through the 1960s. He found himself suspended temporarily in a personal political limbo, devoid of certitude, dogma, and conviction. In fact, as he further described it to me, "I tended to be more on the conservative side when I was in England, more in the liberal camp when in Australia." Much of that was attributable to Murdoch's disillusionment with the labor movement in Britain—in many respects the trade unions acted more greedily and corruptly than their traditional corporate adversaries. Much, too, had to do with the murder of Muriel McKay, which Murdoch blamed on the liberal immigration policies of the recent Labour-dominated governments of Britain.

Under Prime Minister Harold Wilson in the 1960s, the Labour Party had had its second major postwar stint at the nation's helm. In Murdoch's view—and it was certainly not unique to him—the ramifications were beginning to appear far worse for the future of England than those produced by the Conservative Party government that had preceded it, the government that had fallen in large part because of the 1963 Profumo-Keeler scandal. Although Murdoch still halfheartedly supported Labour in its efforts during the 1970 elections to remain in power, he was not disappointed when it was ousted.

But he was hardly happy with what replaced it—a government that stood for what he contemptuously viewed as "the tired old Tory outlook, hopelessly outdated and with nothing new or workable to offer." Britain had plunged into an abyss of political and economic stagnation, Murdoch was convinced. Something radically new was needed to reanimate the country and help solve its major woes, most of which he now believed were caused by the past sixty years of government encroachment on individual and corporate enterprise and of massive Socialist welfarism. Murdoch didn't yet know what that "something" might be, exactly. But whatever it turned out to be, it had to include a major revision of encrusted political, economic, and social practices. And whatever it was, through his two London newspapers he fully intended to be in its vanguard.

In the meantime, Murdoch attended to business. Late in 1970, making good on his threat to David Frost of the year before, he bought a majority holding in the London Weekend Television organization from Britain's General Electric Company and several smaller shareholders. (Frost was one of the founders, owners, and directors of LWT, and it was through LWT that Murdoch's interview by Frost had been broadcast.) LWT had grown enormously bloated in the five years since its formation. Never a financial success, by 1970, it was sinking fast under the burden of its huge payroll and bank debt and was on the verge of collapse. That General Electric, its most prominent major owner, was willing to abandon ship was the clearest sign of all that the company was doomed. The best that could be hoped for, agreed the majority of its board, was a merger with another British broadcaster, Thames Television. When Murdoch acquired GE's holding, talks toward that end were well underway, even though it was doubtful that Britain's Independent Television Authority—the government commission that regulated TV ownership and programming—would permit such a move.

In Murdoch's view, LWT's problems stemmed directly from its highbrow approach to television programming. Licensed to broadcast only between Friday and Sunday evenings, a period of the week in which surveys showed that the majority of the British public craved light entertainment, it had persisted in presenting a schedule overloaded with serious and sophisticated fare. And with its reputation for quality programming, LWT had developed an idealistic, smug, and redundant staff of highly paid managers and producers. Murdoch believed that if he could pump some "really commercial thinking" into LWT, just as he'd done with his newspapers, he could save it.

The Television Authority's rules made it impossible for any single stockholder to gain effective control of a commercial broadcasting company. Murdoch therefore had no hope of taking over LWT in an ownership sense. But his acquisition of GE's share gave him a key seat on the board. By then, the Television Authority had vetoed a merger with Thames Television. The rest of LWT's board began to look upon Murdoch as the only other chance for survival. Murdoch was quickly able to persuade the board to put him in full executive charge of the company's reorganization. Even David Frost, a 5 percent owner and a major voice on the board, deferred to him. Murdoch was consistently cool to Frost during their time together at LWT, and Frost would eventually be forced out.

Murdoch moved fast. For the first time in his career he was running a business entity that was not his own. In a year-long virtuoso performance he demonstrated—to what was essentially a group of outsiders—why he was so skilled at curing financially crippled media companies. He spent most of 1971 ruthlessly paring LWT's production staff and facilities to the bone, reorganizing its management, sales, and financial arms, and reordering its programming policies. He did not, as many had feared, impose the lowest-common-denominator approach of his newspapers on

LWT's programming. But he did take it considerably downmarket, and by doing so proved his argument that regular highbrow broadcasting had no place in commercial television.

LWT was soon on the path to profitability. Murdoch recruited John Freeman, a well-known English journalist who had just finished a stint as Britain's ambassador to the United States, to take over the day-to-day running of the company in mid-1971. Nevertheless, he remained behind the scenes as Freeman's *éminence grise* for some time thereafter. For his part, Freeman began to advise Murdoch on business opportunities in the United States.

The United States: Murdoch had been thinking more and more about the United States. On his trips two or three times a year back and forth to Australia, he had usually traveled by way of New York and California. He'd become more of a fan than ever of the American way of life. Through Leonard Goldenson and others, he had vastly expanded his contacts in New York's financial, legal, and media establishment. Despite his success in England—despite even his stellar managerial performance with LWT—he was still viewed as a pariah by much of London's cultural and social hierarchy. Anna Murdoch, then pregnant with their second child, was growing increasingly restive in the face of constant social snubs, as was he—their only real friends after three years were the members of Murdoch's Australian Mafia who had followed them to London in 1969. Anna was eager to break out of that insular circle. Too, she was still unsettled, even fearful, in the aftermath of Muriel McKay's murder.

But it was Murdoch's growing dissatisfaction with the economic and political climate of England that most prompted his thoughts of expanding to the United States. The *Sun* and *News of the World* continued to pour high monthly operating profits into his newly created British holding company, which he had incorporated as News International Ltd. and taken public through a limited stock offering. News International was majority-owned by News Limited, Murdoch's Australian holding company—itself majority-owned by Cruden Investments. It had as its principal subsidiaries the *Sun, News of the World*, and Murdoch's share of LWT, along with the printing, paper, and provincial English newspaper properties he'd inherited through his purchase of *News of the World*. News International was piling up cash in 1972, cash that had to be invested quickly to avoid Britain's punishing corporate tax rates. Moreover, News International had been given an almost unlimited line of credit by a consortium of British banks organized by Lord Catto, a key member of the News International board.

Tapping those resources, Murdoch, in early 1972, made a run on the nonvoting stock of the financially troubled Beaverbrook organization, publishers of London's *Daily Express, Sunday Express,* and *Evening Standard.* He soon accumulated about 20 percent of the shares, an investment of about $7 million.

The move created a loud stir in Fleet Steet when it was revealed in April, with dozens of Murdoch's critics objecting to what they perceived to be his monopolistic aspirations. In fact, the purchase was little more than a tactic on his part to protect some of News International's mounting profits from the tax collector. Plus, it was a gesture made "to rattle the establishment," as Murdoch later characterized it to me. At that time, "I was really looking for a major investment in America."

A Foot in the Door

The one thing the United States did not have in 1973—had never had—was a nationally distributed daily newspaper in the fashion of Murdoch's *Australian* or the *Sun* and other such dailies in England. The advent of automated printing and satellite communications had made the prospect of such a paper technically and economically feasible. The question remained: Was it economically realistic?

No, Murdoch was assured during each of his trips through the States in the early seventies. America, though not that much larger than Australia, was demographically much more diverse and regionally more varied. Such a paper would never sell. Major urban dailies, centered in metropolitan hubs from Boston and New York to Los Angeles and Seattle, dominated their regional markets in terms of national and local news. A "serious" national daily, except perhaps for the initial novelty of it, would be ignored.

Who said serious? Murdoch replied. He pointed to the New York *Daily News*, a metropolitan tabloid that had the nation's largest local circulation. Then he displayed a copy of his London *Sun*. What about a combination of the *News* and the *Sun* on a national level? "Emphasis on crime and scandal and pretty girls, the kind of stuff that happens in one place but never gets reported in others, with plenty of photos, sports, celebrity gossip, and features?" as he once put it to me.

The United States already had such a national tabloid, Murdoch was told, although it could be hardly characterized as a newspaper. Called the *National Enquirer,* it sold in the millions, but it was a weekly.

Murdoch was already well acquainted with the Florida-based *Enquirer*. Though American-owned, it was edited and written for the most part by a staff of grizzled British tabloid experts. It was an Americanized clone, practically, of Murdoch's *Sun*. If anything distinguished it, it was the fact that—thanks to the more liberal American libel and privacy laws—it could distort stories with much greater impunity than the *Sun* could. And it did.

Murdoch was not persuaded that America would resist a new national daily. His tabloid formula had proven to have great mass appeal in Australia and England, and the still-rising sales of the *Enquirer* demonstrated each week that a huge American market existed for such journalism.

Not even the costs of starting up discouraged him. The only major hurdle was distribution. It would be easy enough to assemble each day's paper at a central location—say, New York—and have it printed by satellite at various plants around the country for overnight regional and local distribution. The problem was: who would distribute it?

The existing newspaper proprietorships in the country's major cities would not look kindly upon the introduction of a national daily into their markets. Murdoch was warned that they would do everything they could to discourage the paper's distribution through conventional outlets. Such actions would be in violation of various antimonopoly and restraint-of-trade laws, perhaps, but it might take years, and millions of dollars in litigation costs, to get that question resolved.

And then there was the inevitable union problem. Murdoch's original notion was to produce and distribute his projected paper with nonunion labor, then use the money he saved to promote it heavily on television around the country. Would the print unions in America's major cities stand for a nonunion paper competing with the papers they produced? Definitely not, and the local unions could be even more disruptive of distribution than the ownerships for which they worked.

Still, Murdoch was not so much discouraged as diverted from his 1972 idea for a national paper in the United States. Suddenly his attention and presence were drawn back to Australia.

The occasion was the news that Frank Packer and his sons had decided to divest themselves of their Sydney newspapers—the daily *Telegraph* and its Sunday edition—in order to concentrate on their more profitable Australian television and magazine interests. The Fairfax organization, Murdoch's primary afternoon competitor in Sydney, was said to be sniffing around the *Telegraph*, eager to take it off the Packers' hands and then merge it with its morning *Herald.* Murdoch felt compelled to rush back and do some sniffing on his own.

The result was that he quickly outmaneuvered the Fairfax group. In a complicated but lightning deal, he acquired the *Telegraph* papers for News Limited at a price of $17.5 million. That figure, though excessive relative to the *Telegraph*'s actual market value, was eminently reasonable to Murdoch when viewed in the light of what he got. What he got, free and clear of debt, was Sydney's second leading morning paper to go along with his by then best-selling afternoon *Mirror.* Now he would be competitive with Fairfax in the morning as well as in the afternoon. If he could succeed in getting the *Telegraph* to overtake the Fairfax *Herald* in circulation, as he had done in pushing the *Mirror* past the Fairfax *Sun* a few years earlier, he would be the undisputed press king of all Australia.

During the previous three years, Murdoch had run his Australian domain largely by telephone and Telex from London, with only an occasional quick visit to Sydney to make hands-on adjustments. His most troublesome property remained the *Australian.* The year before, he had returned to preside over a wholesale revamping of the money-losing paper, firing its latest editor, Adrian Deamer, muting its serious left-wing editorial tone and slant, and "de-dignifying" its style and content.

The *Australian* had collected a small but intensely devoted national readership in its seven years of existence and sold about 140,000 copies a day. Murdoch's alterations caused a furor in that narrow circle, most of which was comprised of the country's left-leaning intellectual class. Many of its traditional buyers actually boycotted the paper after Murdoch fired Deamer, and it would take years for its circulation to recover.

In altering the *Australian,* however, Murdoch was driven by motives other than simply to stem its financial losses. Those motives related to his statement to me that by 1971 he tended increasingly toward conservative values when in England, while in Australia he remained "more in the liberal camp." By "liberal" he meant that although he was no longer the militant radical of his youth, and although he was more cynical than ever about politics and politicians, he still supported much of the Labor Party creed in Australia as against that of the ruling conservative establishment.

During the late 1960s, just prior to his migration to London, Murdoch, through his various papers, had been instrumental in boosting the national prestige of Edward Gough Whitlam, the leader of the Australian Labor Party. "It wasn't that Gough Whitlam was the answer," Murdoch told me. "But he was all there was at the time."

In return, Whitlam had listened to Murdoch's private suggestions—usually made during weekends at Murdoch's farm near Canberra—on Labor Party policy. In 1971, a national election was in the offing for the following year. Murdoch determined at all costs to get the fifty-five-year-old Whitlam elected as prime minister and a Labor government installed. His primary vehicle would be the *Australian.*

But during Murdoch's time in England, the *Australian,* under Adrian Deamer, had drifted far to the left and had become as contemptuous of the Labor Party's moderate leftism as it had been of the ruling establishment coalition's "archaic conservatism." Deamer had no more tolerance for Whitlam than he did for the incumbent prime minister, conservative Billy McMahon. And he had turned the paper into a virtual propaganda sheet against the United States and its prosecution of the war in Vietnam.

To exploit the *Australian* in the fashion he intended, Murdoch had no choice but to oust Deamer and give the paper a less sober, more popular style and tone. In Deamer's place he inserted Bruce Rothwell, who once described himself to me as "Rupert's handyman." Rothwell, though politically much to the right of the fence-straddling Murdoch, could be trusted to do his boss's bidding. For his part, Rothwell hoped to use his new position to pull Murdoch over to his side of the ideological fence. Both got their wishes.

The revamped *Australian,* together with Murdoch's other papers, operating under his personal editorial direction, played a crucial role in the election of Whitlam as the country's new prime minister in 1972. Indeed there was a great deal of truth to Murdoch's later published boast that "We single-handedly put the present government in office."

It was Murdoch's first full-scale attempt to use his power as a major newspaper publisher to influence the outcome of a national political campaign. In doing so, he withheld no ammunition from his armory of resources. Complaints about the blatant pro-Whitlam bias of his papers' election coverage were countless. Even a few of his own reporters, despite their acceptance of Murdochian distortion in other journalistic pursuits, publicly bristled at the manner in which their dispatches from the hustings were grossly twisted by Murdoch's editors, and sometimes by Murdoch himself, to favor Whitlam and disparage conservative candidates. Murdoch used not only their editorial and opinion columns, but devoted his papers' news pages as well to advancing Whitlam's fortunes, often crudely so.

The success of Murdoch's 1972 political effort was, for him, heady. It was even more enthralling, evidently, than the tens of millions of dollars he was raking in each year in profits from his media empire. This was reflected in the tag line of Murdoch's remark, two years later, about having "single-handedly put the present government in office." By then he believed he'd been betrayed by Whitlam. He added, "But now we're not happy with them, and if they don't straighten up we'll bloody well get rid of them."

Murdoch would indeed get rid of Whitlam, again using the *Australian* and his other papers, along with his extensive personal influence on the Australian political scene, to achieve the prime minister's ouster. In the meantime, he returned his attention to his ideas for the United States.

Not that he yet had a definite plan. By the beginning of 1973, Murdoch had all but abandoned the notion of introducing himself to America with a national tabloid daily. On the other hand, a weekly, in the style of the *National Enquirer*, seemed an increasingly promising alternative.

Given his track record, he had no reason to doubt that he could beat the *Enquirer* at its own game. The top editorial and financial aides he brought over from London and Sydney to study the prospect concurred. Accordingly, he put together a skeleton staff in New York and ordered them to begin working out the logistics. Their target date for a first issue was January 1974.

"The whole idea," says one of them today, "was to imitate the *Enquirer* but exceed its bad taste. We figured that if so many Americans were willing to pay a quarter for its level of shlock, they would be happy to fork out thirty or thirty-five cents for

what we'd have to offer. And the way we'd get them hooked
would be to flog the thing all over the TV here. You know, late-
night commercials tucked in between the 'magic vegetable slicer'
and 'join the army now' spots that were the staples of the post-
midnight hours. That's where the bulk of the *Enquirer*'s audience
was—all those millions of weirdos who stayed up all night
watching the telly."

But Murdoch was not content to have just a "weirdo" constituency in America. The first full-scale exercise of his political
muscle the year before, and his similar more recent excursions
into the British political arena via the *Sun* in London, had given
him a pleasant taste of the inherent power he possessed as a newspaper publisher. It went far beyond just money, far beyond the
firm grip he held over his own business empire and the lives of
the thousand or so people who worked for him. It was a new and
much loftier level of power, a potential to manipulate and control
politicians and to reshape the social, cultural, and economic
values of millions of people.

Fifteen years earlier, in Adelaide, Murdoch had tried in a
modest way to utilize that power during his fight with the local
government over the Stuart case. But then he had been a minor
publisher in a provincial city. Because of that, he had failed. The
memory of that failure and the intimidation he'd succumbed to
still rankled. Now, however, he was becoming a major world figure with the resources to spread his worldview to the United
States, to add his political voice in a significant way to the most
powerful political entity on earth.

He would not achieve that goal with a seamier version of the
National Enquirer, though, Murdoch realized. Nor had he yet
formed a clear-cut and consistent new worldview to replace the
fast-fading one of his younger years. He remained astride the fence
with respect to the vital political and economic issues of the day,
his residual visceral Socialist idealism still locked in silent war
with his burgeoning conservative and reactionary impulses. It
would take a major business crisis to break the impasse.

That crisis came in 1973 as Murdoch solidified his plans for
his first newspaper venture in the United States. During his
scouting visits the year before—the year of Richard Nixon's landslide reelection to the White House—he had returned to Washington and even had a visit with Nixon and several of his top
aides, a reprise of his 1962 meeting with John Kennedy. As

personalities, Murdoch and Nixon had much in common. Each was secretive, evasive, cold, ruthless, awkward, calculating, and power-conscious.

Murdoch was impressed with Nixon. Until then uncertain about the wisdom of America's pursuit of the Vietnam War and about Nixon's escalations of it, after his experience in Washington he became a Nixon enthusiast, a fact that soon began to evince itself in his main British and Australian newspapers.

Early in 1973, shortly after the election of Edward Gough Whitlam and the Labor Party in Australia, the Australian maritime unions, in protest against the renewed bombing in Vietnam, organized a nationwide ban on the servicing of all American ships entering Australian ports. When the Nixon Administration denounced the boycott and demanded its immediate end, the new Whitlam government, which had been supported by the unions, refused to intervene.

This enraged Murdoch, not least because at the time he was talking to several important banking firms in New York in anticipation of financing his publishing plans and felt he could not afford a sudden wave of anti-Australian sentiment in America. Moreover, having been sold in Washington on the efficacy of the bombing, he became convinced that the strike in Australia was a plot on the part of the unions to embarrass not only the United States, but the Australian government as well. He was further infuriated when several key members of Whitlam's cabinet issued statements sympathetic to the boycott.

Aware that Murdoch and his papers had been instrumental in the Whitlam government's ascension to power the year before, members of Nixon's State Department called on him to persuade Whitlam to put an end to the boycott. Murdoch tried but failed. Whitlam rejected his repeated personal demands on the ground that it would be inappropriate for a Labor government to quash the strike, notwithstanding the fact that it was being orchestrated by the unions' extreme left-wing elements. The boycott had the Australian public's approval. For his government to take a blatantly antilabor stand so early in its existence would wreck its chances of succeeding, Whitlam insisted.

Murdoch felt both betrayed and embarrassed—betrayed by Whitlam's refusal to do his bidding and embarrassed that the refusal had damaged his standing with the Nixon Administration. He reacted by ordering Bruce Rothwell and the editors of his other Australian papers to condemn Whitlam in print and formally withdraw their support of him and his government.

To a certain extent the tactic worked. Whitlam began to put behind-the-scenes pressure on the strikers through the Australian Trade Unions Council, and within a matter of days the boycott was called off. Although he took no public credit for this result, neither did Murdoch reject the expressions of gratitude sent privately to him by higher-ups in the Nixon Administration. His embarrassment was salved. He would not, however, forget Gough Whitlam's obstinacy.

Nor would he remain much longer on the political fence. The episode undermined the last vestige of Murdoch's liberal impulses. And because he gained considerable status by it in the high councils of the Nixon government, it thrust him firmly in the direction of the hard-nosed American political conservatism symbolized by Nixon.

By mid-1973, Murdoch was beginning to feel at home in the United States. Much to the satisfaction of Anna Murdoch, who had given birth to their second child, a son, and was pregnant with another, he had decided to move himself and the family to New York while he supervised the creation of the *National Star,* as his forthcoming *Enquirer*-like weekly was to be called. But then, that summer, came the Watergate extravaganza, the nationally televised Ervin Committee investigation of the White House's role in the notorious Watergate break-in of the year before.

Murdoch was at once fascinated and astonished by Watergate. In his view, the affair constituted a perverse abuse of the American news media's power. He believed that the liberal press—television, too—had blown up a run-of-the-mill dirty political trick into an hysteria-drenched scandal solely to get even with Nixon for the multitude of sins it ascribed to him, not the least of which was his support of his press-baiting Vice President, Spiro Agnew. Watching much of America revel in the Administration's increasing discomfort and paralysis during the summer of 1973, Murdoch became convinced that the liberal media had gone out of control, that for the sake of satisfying their own narrow craving for revenge they were irreparably damaging the United States' power and influence in the rest of the free world, a status that had already been seriously eroded by the same media's role in distorting the nation's purpose and role in Vietnam. As a

citizen of a country on the fringe of politically turbulent Southeast Asia, Murdoch was fearful of the consequences for Australia
of an outright American capitulation in Indochina.

To him, then, the Watergate hearings, and more particularly
the American news media's role in them, were reckless, irrespon-
sible, and self-defeating. Murdoch had no doubt that Richard
Nixon was as devious and unsavory as America by then perceived
him to be. But such was the necessary nature of politicians and
statesmen in the real world of ruthless international power struggle. Whatever Nixon's role in Watergate, by seeking to protect his
presidency from exposure and embarrassment he was acting
properly and, ultimately, in the national interest—indeed, in the
interest of the entire free world. To allow his Administration to be
crippled by the sort of petty, everyday scandal that was a staple of
the rough-and-tumble politics of Australia, he would have abandoned his realpolitik obligations to the country's various free-
world alliances, including those with Australia and England. To
Murdoch, Nixon was not just President of the United States; symbolically he was the president of Australia as well.

"The American press might get their pleasure in successfully
crucifying Nixon," Murdoch angrily told a friend at the time,
"but the last laugh could be on them. See how they like it when
the Commies take over the West."

Murdoch's abhorrence of the media's role in Watergate was
exceeded only by his contempt for that of the leaders of the Democratic Party in Washington. Again, in his view the Democrats'
instigation of the congressional investigations was simply a matter of revenge for the party's national humiliation in the previous
year's presidential election.

"The Democrats as presently constituted are finished in this
country and they know it," Murdoch exclaimed to the same
friend. "But they can't admit it. They can't admit that the old Socialist New Deal ideas they still cling to are no longer workable.
Instead of trying to break out of their ideological stagnation, they
spend their time lambasting Nixon over this Watergate thing. . . .
If anything brings about the downfall of this country, it'll be the
Democrats acting in league with the press."

The 1973 Watergate events, then, drove Murdoch once and
for all into the right-wing camp. Once he was firmly settled there,
everything that happened thereafter merely confirmed his newfound convictions. The debacle of the Vietnam War's conclusion,

the impeachment movement against Nixon, his subsequent resignation, the wildly inflationary aftermath of the 1973 Arab-Israeli
war—those and other such demoralizing developments were in
his mind largely due to the perfidy of the arrogantly liberal
American press and of a naive, anachronistic Democratic Party.

America had to be saved from itself, if only to preserve the
political freedom and economic independence of the rest of the
democratic world. Murdoch had no hope or wish of ever becoming an elected political voice in the United States. Yet he had at
his fingertips the potential of an even greater source of influence
and power than political office—an international media conglomerate of his own.* He could not expect to wield much direct influence through his soon-to-appear *National Star,* a paper designed
to appeal almost exclusively to the country's under-educated
"drone class," as one commentator described its readership after
the *Star* made its debut. But if he could get his hands on an important daily paper . . . !

It was then that Murdoch shook off any lingering doubts he
had about invading mainstream daily journalism in the United
States. A national daily, launched from scratch, still loomed as
too expensive and difficult a proposition; it would take years to
get started. His only option was to step in with a big-city paper,
which meant he would have to acquire one.

In 1973, the newspaper business in America was in profound
disarray. During the previous fifteen years, a succession of crippling strikes in various cities, a sharp rise in labor and newsprint
costs throughout the country, and rising competition from television had driven scores of major papers out of business or into
tenuous mergers. Independent newspapers in every major city
were sorely stung by the depression, and even the big chains like
Gannett, Hearst, Knight-Ridder, and Newhouse were forced to
close papers and retrench.

The shakeout was by no means over. Several financially

---

* By 1973, Murdoch's press empire consisted of eighty newspapers and
eleven magazines in Australia, Great Britain, and New Zealand and was
augmented by his extensive television and radio properties in the first two
countries. Many of those papers were smaller suburban and exurban publications inherited through his acquisitions of big-city papers. Through News
Limited in Australia and News International in England, he also controlled
a profitable network of independent printing, paper, and shipping companies.

strapped big-city papers remained in business, still struggling to avoid collapse but too dispirited to prevent it. The newspaper business was not considered a growth industry in 1973, and there were few investors interested in rescuing ailing and technologically outmoded properties.

Among the most enfeebled of the big-city journals was *The Washington Star*. With *The Washington Post*, it was one of only two major dailies remaining in the nation's capital. But the *Post*, having prospered enormously as a result of its role in exposing the Watergate break-in, had robbed the *Star* of much of what was left of its circulation. The *Star* seemed a perfect opportunity for Murdoch, and he seriously contemplated buying it in the early fall of 1973. He had just committed nearly $8 million to the start-up of his new weekly, however, and he found the asking price of $35 million too steep.

Inquiries into other ailing metropolitan papers around the country produced the same results. Not only were the proposed purchase prices exorbitant, but Murdoch would have been forced to pour in additional millions just to keep them afloat. Even to a risk-taker like him, such a prospect was not appealing. Despite his aspirations, experience, and business confidence, he concluded that he didn't know enough yet about the idiosyncrasies of the daily-newspaper scene in America to save a near-terminally ill paper. What he needed, he decided, was a reasonably healthy paper he could, at modest cost, take over and practice on. No such moderately priced property existed in any major U.S. city. But Murdoch discovered one in a smaller metropolis. The place was San Antonio, Texas.

Today, San Antonio is larger than such "major" American cities as San Francisco, New Orleans, Miami, Denver, Atlanta, and Boston. In 1973, though, it had a population of well under one million. Its newspaper scene was dominated by the Hearst-owned afternoon *Light* and a morning paper called the *Express*, the property of the much smaller Harte-Hanks chain. Harte-Hanks also published an afternoon paper, the *San Antonio News*, which competed with but had only half the circulation of Hearst's *Light*. Between them, however, the *Express* and the *News* had a combined daily circulation of about 140,000, as compared to the *Light*'s 120,000, and returned a marginal profit to Harte-Hanks. Nevertheless, the company was not averse to selling them. When Rupert Murdoch heard about that in September from his friend

John Newcombe, the Australian tennis star who was then involved in the development of a "tennis ranch" near San Antonio, he flew to Texas to have a look.

Murdoch liked what he saw. Although nearly half its population was Mexican, in its fast-growing but still rough-hewn character San Antonio reminded him of several of Australia's regional cities. And when he examined Hearst's *Light,* a paper that owed its popularity to its emphasis on San Antonio's extensive crime and violence, he was convinced that he could successfully challenge it with his own tried-and-tested formula. Indeed, he thought, San Antonio, a blue-collar city, was ripe for a much greater dose of Murdoch's brand of journalism than even the *Light* provided. The city's local television news shows reinforced Murdoch's certainty. They were more graphic than contemporary Hollywood horror movies in their obsessive coverage of crime and violence.

Murdoch quickly offered to buy the morning *Express* and afternoon *News* from Harte-Hanks. Within a month, a deal was concluded, although he was forced again to abandon his usual practice of "paying peanuts" for his new acquisitions. The two papers cost him nearly $20 million, much more than they were intrinsically worth. America was about to have its introduction to Murdochian journalism.

Killer Bees

Murdoch spent most of late 1973 and early 1974 shuttling back and forth between New York and Texas while he supervised the organization of the *National Star* and the reorganization of the *San Antonio Express* and *News,* along with their combined Sunday edition. The relatively sedate morning *Express* he left alone for the time being, since it was turning a modest profit at a daily circulation of 80,000. It was the equally staid afternoon *News* that had been losing money and circulation in competition with the more vivid Hearst *Light,* and it was to the *News* that he devoted most of his energies.

Murdoch imported a crew of editors and subeditors from his *Mirror-Telegraph* organization in Sydney to help him revamp the *San Antonio News.* Within days of his takeover, an entirely different paper began to appear, one based on the usual formula—an amalgam of crude, misleading headlines, lurid and usually distorted sex and crime stories, exotic pictures, mindlessly trivial features, contests, puzzles and comics, large doses of self-promotion and self-congratulation, beefed-up sports coverage, and heated denigrations of its principal rival, the *Light.* Murdoch's approach demonstrated what would become his standard operating procedure in America as elsewhere. When he acquired a profitable publication, he would merely fine-tune it, with most of his efforts directed to reducing its costs to make its circulation and advertising more profitable. When he took over a marginal or money-losing paper, on the other hand, he would completely revamp it according to his Anglo-Australian formula to pump up its circulation.

But in San Antonio, he encountered a new factor. Circulation plays a markedly different role in American newspapering than it does in England and Australia. The costs of increasing paid circulation are considerably greater here than there. As a rule, profitable American papers obtain only about 25 percent of their gross revenues through circulation. The other 75 percent comes through the sale of advertising space, and such sales are the principal, if not only, source of profit. In America, newspaper circulation wars are, at bottom, wars for the advertiser's dollar.

Murdoch was right: San Antonio *was* ready for a considerably more garish form of daily print journalism than it had been getting. Within two years, the circulation of the *News* rose from about 60,000 to more than 75,000. But there occurred no corresponding decrease in the readership of the *Light*, which had the bulk of the city's upscale advertising. In other words, the *News* did not take away any of the *Light*'s readers; it merely added 15,000 readers at the low end of San Antonio's economic spectrum, people who couldn't afford to buy the kind of products and services that were the staple of free-spending local retail advertisers. Thus, the *News* enjoyed no appreciable gain in advertising revenue. Meanwhile its own advertising and promotional costs, expended in its efforts to raise circulation, actually increased its losses.

All told, Murdoch's first venture into American daily pop-journalism proved a failure. Only the continuing profitability of his other San Antonio paper, the morning *Express*, enabled him to continue testing his formula on the *News*. Finally, when it became clear after three years that the formula wasn't working, he began to modulate the *News*'s more bizarre excesses. Gradually it settled for being a pale imitation of the *Light*.

But the American journalistic community had had its first taste of Murdochian newspapering and was, if not repulsed, bemused by it. In a certain light, his efforts in San Antonio were admirable, especially his aggressive promotion of the *News* on local television and his slanting of the paper to appeal to younger readers. Murdoch had said over and over again that television was turning the youth of the English-speaking world into "newspaper illiterates" and that his great journalistic purpose in life was to get them accustomed to reading newspapers. Who in the newspaper business could quarrel with such a high-minded mission?

But the means he employed clashed jarringly with the ends he proposed. First, if newspapers had any advantage over television journalism, it was in their ability to provide much greater depth and perspective to the flow of events in the world. Yet the Murdoch formula's terse, truncated style, its biased and obsessive emphasis on the sensational aspects of every piece of news it "reported," its daffily mordant concentration on trivia, and its blatant exploitation of readers' presumed fears and anxieties seemed to go television one worse—no, many times worse.

Okay, many American journalists concluded, so Murdoch was a cynical hypocrite, a newspaperman simply trying to make money by beating television at its own game. There was nothing essentially wrong with that.

It quickly became clear that there *was* something wrong with Murdoch's "crusade," however. Not even television journalism consciously and consistently presented news from such a single-minded, opinionated point of view. And as time went on in San Antonio, it became increasingly evident that the distortion of reality was the fundamental animating element of Murdochian journalism. That impression was powerfully and more widely reinforced early in 1974, when the first issue of his *National Star* rolled off the presses.

For all its prepublication hype, the tabloid *Star* was a bitter disappointment to all but the most gullibly mindless in America when it made its initial appearance in February. Murdoch had brought a battery of top *Sun* editors, including Larry Lamb, from London to New York to help him launch the weekly paper and had hired a few experienced New York tabloid editors and reporters to give it an "American tone." He had signed up the huge Ted Bates advertising agency to promote the weekly and had committed $5 million toward its subsequent first year's promotion. He had invested another $2 million in the logistics of printing and distributing the paper. In a series of prepublication interviews with the New York press, Murdoch declared that his new national publication was really a magazine—a "weekly news magazine" designed to compete with *Time* and *Newsweek* at the upper end of its circulation scale and with the enormously prosperous *TV Guide* in the middle. Little mention was made of the *National Enquirer* and its several extant competitors. His start-up circulation goal was targeted at one million a week, Murdoch said, reminding his interviewers that the paper's initial distribution would be limited to the northeastern quadrant of the United States.

Murdoch took advantage of the interviews to air some of his

opinions about American journalism, both of the newspaper and magazine variety. Generally, he held a dim view of it. Most daily and Sunday papers were "achingly dull" in layout, reportage, and writing, as were the news weeklies, monthlies, and Sunday supplements. American journalists—editors and reporters—were for the most part "elitist" snobs who practiced their craft not for the noble purpose of informing the public but solely to impress each other. American readers were being woefully shortchanged. The in-depth style of journalism prominent here—long, tedious stories packed with bushels of extraneous, meaningless facts and written in plodding or self-consciously literary style; the countless "opinion" columns; and the thoughtful, reasoned approach to editorials—was a "waste of the reader's time." Even "the feature stuff" and the sports were done badly—too many columnists expounding views that "no one really cares about." Murdoch's purpose with his forthcoming *National Star*, obviously, was to breathe some "life" into the moribund corpus of American print journalism.

To say that Murdoch's blanket criticisms of American newspapering and his equally outspoken defenses of his own journalistic practices (although he could not be made to admit to distortion) did not go down well in New York is to understate the case. No doubt some of the sneering contempt with which the *Star* was greeted by the rest of the Eastern press when it first appeared in February 1974 was attributable to Murdoch's "overbearing cheekiness," as a paper in London described his performance in the United States at the time.

But then, as one of his ex-deputies suggested to me, "Perhaps Rupert was simply doing it deliberately and calculatedly to stir up controversy. He thrives on controversy, y'know. He was spending millions to get the *Star* going, but he was afraid with all that, it still wouldn't be noticed. So he started to spout off about how terrible things were here, just to get it, and himself, better noticed."

Whatever the case, the *Star*, when it first appeared, was truly a dreadul piece of work, even for a paper that had no greater goal than to muscle its way into the *National Enquirer*'s domain. "Welcome to the Star, Folks" and "Let Us Make You a Star" were two of a frenetic hodgepodge of front-page headlines that also included "How to Make Millions," "How to be a Super Shopper," "Kung Fu," "$4 Dinner for Four," "The Ten Faces of

Richard Nixon," and "Exclusive Interview with TV's Prince Charming." Inside, principal stories included "His Kisses Kept Me Awake All Night," "Tattoos Could Save Your Pet," "I've Let Hundreds Die, Says Mercy Doctor," and a piece built around the breathless assertion: "If all the Chinese jumped up and down in unison, the vibrations would cause a tidal wave that could engulf America."

What the *Star* most resembled was the *National Enquirer* in its former "I Ate My Baby" days. The only significant difference between it and Murdoch's London *Sun* and *News of the World* was the absence of bared, thrusting female breasts. Indeed, the paper was—and has since remained—a potpourri of Fleet Street tabloidism, notwithstanding Murdoch's attempt to give it an American tone. A spread headlined "The Miracle Makers" could have been lifted straight from *News of the World,* and the "Letters to the Editor" page—letters from readers in the first issue?—even had British spellings.

The paper's crowning glory was an article that had been published earlier in Murdoch's *San Antonio News* under the headline "Killer Bees Head North." It utilized one of the favorite techniques of Murdochian journalism, arousing alarm in readers on the thinnest of pretexts.

The story was based on a single legitimate fact. In South America, as in many parts of agricultural North America, honey-bees are commercially bred and sold for the purpose of crop polli-nation. Years before, a wild African strain of honeybee had been brought across the South Atlantic by boat to Brazil, where it col-onized with the common domestic honeybee. The result was the emergence of a new type of Brazilian hybrid that came to be known as the "Africanized bee." As swarms of Africanized bees proliferated throughout central South America, they began to display an aggressiveness never before seen in the native variety and an occasional en masse tendency to attack animals and humans without apparent provocation.

Under its "Killer Bees Head North" banner, this is how Murdoch's *Star* began its story:

> Ferocious swarms of man-killing bees are buzzing their way toward North America.
>
> They have already smashed their way through Brazil, Para-guay, Uruguay, Argentina, Bolivia and Peru.

But don't panic. It may take ten to 14 years before the bees hit the U. S. . . .

The piece went on—in a style Murdoch liked to call "breezy," "zesty," "lively," and "fun"—to paint the monstrous threat the "deadly bees" would pose after they made their way up through Central America and Mexico, albeit not for another "ten to 14 years."

It was a vintage Murdoch "news story." The only trouble was that in several significant details it was fantasy. True, the bees could kill when they attacked in great numbers. But so could ordinary bees. The killing was strictly a result of the victim's being poisoned by more bee toxin than his or her system could handle. Yet the *Star* had it that each individual Africanized bee's sting was fatal.

Moreover, the "ferocious swarms" were not "buzzing their way" toward the United States in 1974. Nor had they "already smashed" their way through all the countries cited. It was possible that a few Africanized bees might eventually be transported inadvertently to North America in the hold of a ship or cargo plane.* But bee experts in the United States firmly discounted any threat to humans beyond that posed by native American bees. The Africanized bees' reputation, they said, had been totally exaggerated in South America. "If the people who wrote that story believed it, then they're the victims of their own gullibility," said Howel Daly, professor of entomology at the University of California.

Although he soon abandoned his comparisons to *Time* and *Newsweek,* Murdoch would not yield in his insistence that his new *National Star* was a worthwhile weekly. "Papers and magazines in this country are written to please Madison Avenue and the friends of the publishers," he repeated, answering the barrage of criticism the *National Star* received in the wake of its first issue. "They've lost touch with the desires of the reading public."

The statement assumed that the American public desired to be inundated and conned by mass-trash journalism. It assumed

---

* Indeed, evidence of a colony of South American Africanized bees was found near Bakersfield, California, in mid-1985. The bees had traveled there, it was surmised, in a crate of oil-field machinery that had been shipped from Brazil the year before. There were no reports of any attacks on humans.

the truth of the old saw about a sucker being born every minute. It assumed that Murdoch was another of those entrepreneurs who would earn a fortune by never underestimating the tastes of the American public.

To a certain extent he was right, of course—the previous success of the *National Enquirer* and its imitative offshoots had demonstrated the truth of those assumptions. But as a piece of journalism the *National Star* was infinitely worse than even the *Enquirer.* Which is not to say it was more sensationalist or outrageous. Oddly, it was less so; it was almost subdued in comparison to the *Enquirer.* In that respect, Murdoch, given his reputation for journalistic daring, had erred on the side of caution. The *Star* contained little in the way of scandal, whether real or imagined. And its layout—narrow columns, small type, scores of choppily abbreviated stories, a confusing welter of boldface headlines, a jumble of boxes and graphics—suggested an earthquake in the composing room. It had none of the visual slickness of the *Enquirer.* Its turgid prose left much to be desired, too. Endlessly straining for urgency, it was torpid and stale, the same handful of "flash" words used over and over again to try to incite readers' imaginations.

So, despite the obvious market for such papers and Murdoch's $5 million promotional campaign, which was much more arresting and professional than the product it pushed, there was a very real possibility that the *Star* would be a bust. But Murdoch made it clear that he was in the race for the long haul. "We have no intention of failing," he said when the notion was raised. "The only question is how great a success we'll have." He added, with much conviction, "I don't see how anyone can say the *Star* is tacky."

Time would prove that he'd have a considerable success, although it would take several radical and expensive adjustments in the paper's approach and format to put it in genuine competition with the *National Enquirer.* Today, the celebrity-gossip and advice-to-the-lovelorn-oriented *Star* (the "*National*" was dropped several years ago) is the financial linchpin of News America, Inc., the American holding company Murdoch formed to operate the *Star* and his San Antonio papers. It grosses in excess of $135 million a year on sales averaging about four million copies a week. Since the paper is a relatively low-cost operation, its annual profits exceed those of any other Murdoch publication in America.

They not only enable him to live exceedingly well in the United States, they have also been a key financial springboard for his massive expansion of News America.

The large majority of the *Star*'s readership—like the *Enquirer*'s—is said by market analysts to be made up of under-educated American women from the late teens to mid-fifties. In a sense, then, Murdoch owes his American fortunes to women, whereas in England and Australia his riches have derived mainly from the appeal of his chief pop-papers to men—bare bosoms and behinds, heavy sports coverage, sex-and-violence, and so on.

It is a compelling contrast, and it explains in large part why Murdoch has so far resisted employing, in the United States, his most notorious foreign circulation ploy—naked females—to solve his daily papers' struggles. Notwithstanding the fact that pictures of nude women are commonplace on newsstands throughout the country, often arranged in the most salacious poses, he is mortally afraid of offending his principal constituency, the *Star*'s female readership. Were the *Star* to fall, so, too, would the financial underpinning of his American expansion. Should the *Star*'s circulation ever threaten to fall, however, Murdoch seems fully prepared to start printing photo spreads of naked men, à la *Playgirl* magazine. This was an idea I once jokingly suggested to him and was surprised to hear him, in all seriousness, affirm.

In 1974, then, Murdoch staked his reputation as a new publisher in America on two papers that were bound to sully it. He roundly rejected criticism as the rantings of journalistic snobs and elitists who were motivated solely by envy over his ability to make huge amounts of money in a field filled with failures. He had heard all the criticisms before, in Australia and Britain, and was impervious to them. "The bottom line in this business is to make money," he explained. "If those who attack me had their way, there would be no newspapers."

The picture that emerged from the extensive discussion by and about Murdoch seemed clear. Although he continued to portray himself as an altruistic journalist who was forced by circumstances also to be a businessman, his words, together with his first two American publications themselves, made it evident that his real vocation was business and that journalism was merely its excuse. He boasted of his executive powers just as readily as he did of his journalistic expertise. He touted his ability to lead a large international corporation, to cut costs and maximize profits, to hire and fire managers and financial controllers, to wend his way through the corridors of high finance. Since his journalistic ethics and integrity had long been subjects of dispute, the new picture developing before the public's eyes naturally called into question Murdoch's ethics and integrity as a businessman. No one doubted that he was daring, opportunistic, and decisive. But there was little to dispel the image of personal ruthlessness and cutthroat determination that emerged from press interviews with Murdoch's former employees and foreign business adversaries. Given the questionable values at the heart of most of his journalism, did these values carry over into his other business life?

To a certain extent, the question had been answered the year before Murdoch's arrival in the United States, although few Americans knew about it. The answer was not in his favor.

In 1972, one of Murdoch's *News of the World* marketing subsidiaries in England had arranged to print and sell a dictionary in twenty-seven looseleaf weekly installments. The idea, heavily promoted in Murdoch's London papers, was for readers to purchase each new installment of the dictionary at the same time they bought their *News of the World*. Also pushed was a binder in which the consumer could enclose the twenty-seven sections once they were all collected. The entire package was priced at about twenty-five dollars. The beauty of it was, however, that its buyers would only have to put out ninety cents a week. Not only that, but the dictionary was a "genuine Webster." Or so Murdoch's promotion claimed.

By way of background, in the nineteenth century, an American, Noah Webster, had compiled a monumental dictionary of the English language that became the standard of all such reference works. Even in England the name "Webster" is to dictionaries as "Hoover" is to vacuum cleaners. Of course, Webster's original work had to be updated and expanded from time to time. By the early 1970s, its true descendant was A. Merriam-Webster's *Third International Dictionary*, which contained about 450,000 entries and sold in Britain in two illustrated volumes for the equivalent of seventy-eight dollars.

However, in 1931, Routledge and Kegan Paul Ltd., a British publishing house, had put out its own dictionary compiled and edited by Henry Wyld, a professor of English at Oxford. In 1972, Routledge still published this unrevised, unillustrated one-volume work under the title *Universal English Dictionary*. It sold for the equivalent of $12.50 and contained around 200,000 entries, although many of them were out of date.

In 1967, Routledge had licensed the American publication rights in the Wyld dictionary to a New York marketing company. A few years later, that company relicensed the book to Admacroft Ltd., one of Murdoch's *News of the World* marketing subsidiaries. When Murdoch decided to put it out in cheap illustrated installment form in 1972, it suddenly acquired the title of *Webster's Universal Dictionary*. It is not unreasonable to assume that this phony appellation was meant to induce *News of the World* readers into believing that they were getting, for only twenty-five dollars, a dictionary that normally sold for seventy-eight dollars in hardcover—the standard Merriam-Webster.

It did not take long for the subterfuge to be exposed. Several knowledgeable buyers of the first few Murdoch installments complained that the Admacroft "Webster" had no relation to the Merriam-Webster work, but was obviously a clumsily revised and illustrated regurgitation of the archaic Wyld dictionary of Routledge and Kegan Paul—which, by the way, could still be bought in bookstores, in one bound volume, for half of what Murdoch was charging for his weekly-installment version. According to a promotional blurb for the Murdoch edition, the dictionary contained "The newest words in Science, Technology, Politics and History—even modern-day slang language." But in most respects it remained true to the outdated 1931 Wyld text, including references to "the Great War" and the numerous errors that appeared in the original.

When challenged on the propriety of its "Webster" dictionary, a Murdoch spokesman replied that an "English scholar," whom he declined to name, had revised Admacroft's serialized newsstand edition. Murdoch's company was merely distributing the dictionary "on behalf of" the American licensors and was not responsible for its errors and idiosyncrasies. As for the use of "Webster" in the title, it was pointed out that there was no copyright in the name. In other words, anyone could put together a lexicography and call it a "Webster's dictionary."

The entire episode became fast-forgotten history in England. Murdoch says that he was unaware of the details surrounding Admacroft's acquisition and promotion of the dictionary—"I was running a big company with dozens of subsidiaries, and I didn't always know what was going on at the lower levels." Such a disclaimer is plausible, as any chief executive of a major multiproduct corporation will agree. But it must be weighed against the fact that, at the time, Murdoch was intimately involved with the day-to-day running of *News of the World* and the *Sun*, especially with their circulation promotions, and against the fact that later in his career he would personally be involved in other questionable campaigns designed to increase the readership of his various papers.

Publishers' circulation promotions and marketing campaigns are basically business schemes, not journalism, despite the fact that they might be carried out under the guise of the latter. Murdoch the businessman, then, appeared to be as crafty in that role as he was in his role as a journalist. As the editorial commander-in-chief of his journalistic empire, he was certainly not personally aware in advance of every untruth and distortion that appeared in his dozens of far-flung papers each day. Yet he had created a journalistic modus operandi for all his papers—the Murdoch formula—under which distortions and exaggerations in the dissemination of news were not only encouraged but were practically mandatory.

A similar modus was likely to have been grafted onto the operation of the business side of Murdoch's papers. Time would prove this to be true; for example, he constantly exaggerated his papers' circulation figures. So even if Murdoch *was* personally in the dark about the details of the deceptive dictionary promotion, he could not avoid direct responsibility for it by hiding behind exclamations of ignorance.

The Webster affair seemed like such a cheap, petty scam— why would a huge, rich organization like Murdoch's get involved in it? The answer: for the same reason it regularly got involved in cheap, petty journalistic scams—force of habit, aided and abetted by a public, in England and Australia, gullible enough to support and reinforce the habit.

In expanding his newspaper empire to the United States, Murdoch was betting that he could get away with such scams in America, too, that the American public was as seduceable as that of Britain and his homeland. Although he would have to struggle a bit more vigorously to win the bet, win it he would.

Sex in Government

The Keeler affair. The Frost show humiliation. The McKay murder. The Somerfield firing. The repeated condemnations of the *Sun* and *News of the World* by members of the British establishment. These and other events had turned Murdoch into a national cause célèbre in England. "The Dirty Digger" and "Murdoch of the Mammaries" were just two of the nicknames the rest of the media had pinned on him. If he was not officially persona non grata in London by 1973, unofficially he and his family had become social outcasts.

Murdoch claimed not to care. His only social interests were those that related to his business, and in Fleet Street and The City he was, if not liked, at least respected for his financial acumen.

But Anna, his wife, did care. Although she was not a gregarious woman, the growing wave of social snubs she was encountering had begun to depress her, as did the prospect of her children growing up in such a hostile environment. She had attempted to ease her gloom and increasing sense of isolation by embarking on writing projects—short stories, a novel. It was to be "my therapy," she said. But the sustained pursuit of the writer's craft is itself a somewhat gloom-filled and isolating activity. Also, her husband tended to dismiss her beginning efforts as worthless. "His criticism was much too devastating," she recalled recently. "I tried him once with a short story of mine and what he said was so mortifying that I couldn't touch it again."

Although Anna would have preferred to return to Australia, America at least represented a new beginning, New York a place "where one could be a bit more anonymous." If either of them had any lingering doubts about their decision to resettle in the

United States, they were erased by a further imbroglio triggered by Murdoch in London in 1973.

A favorite tactic of Murdochian journalism is to attack rival newspapers in print for the very sins—factual distortion and invention—that Murdoch's papers are regularly accused of committing. The tactic is partly a circulation ploy based on the theory that there is nothing the reading public enjoys more than a nasty word-brawl between competing newspapers. But it has another purpose, too, which is that "the best defense is a good offense." By often and loudly pointing out the journalistic transgressions and failings of other news organizations, Murdoch and his corps of editors believe that they can divert the critical spotlight from shining too brightly on them.

The technique is very much a function of Murdoch's character, as I got to know it over ten years. In his personal dealings, whether in the social or business realm, he is quick to try to duck blame for the questionable or untoward things he does or is accused of doing. The trait seems to be a deeply ingrained habit, a reflex. It usually manifests itself in an often obscenity-filled diatribe against whoever his absent adversary of the moment is. The diatribe focuses not on the point at issue, his own conduct, but on the alleged wrongs, stupidities, and character defects of the other person. Not infrequently, his denunciations are also laden with promises of retribution.

Murdoch can be very convincing when he engages in such self-defense. This is mainly because, despite the profanity and fury that permeate his language, he keeps his voice tightly controlled, almost mournful, and never allows it to rant. It's as if he is saying, "Well, as much as I hate to do it, I guess I have no choice but finally to tell the truth about so-and-so"—his latest enemy. One finds oneself listening to a confidential tale about the treacherous actions, motives, and human failings of Murdoch's adversary, or of the person who put him in an adversarial position with others. Suddenly, the offensive deeds of the adversary, not those of Murdoch, become the issue, and Murdoch emerges as the victim of the other's venality.

It was this trait—a combination of shifting blame and exacting revenge—that brought about Murdoch's departing shot on London in 1973. Had a newspaper practicing typical Murdochian journalism covered the event, it might have headlined it: "Furor over Murdoch Involvement with Prostitute."

Little had changed in London since the time, ten years before, of the Christine Keeler–John Profumo sex-and-spy scandal. Hundreds of expensive call girls continued to operate openly throughout the more elegant neighborhoods of the city, either as members of organized rings or as solo practitioners. And among their regular clientele remained the high-and-mighty of the British establishment.

In 1973, one of the better-known and more appreciated solo practitioners in that tony underworld was Norma Levy (née Mary Russell), an Irish-born prostitute in her mid-twenties whose career "on the game" was being managed by her husband Colin Levy, a petty crook. Among those who appreciated Norma was Viscount Antony Lambton, the Sixth Earl of Durham. At the time, Lord Lambton, forty-one, was Under Secretary of State for the British Ministry of Defense and a shining public symbol of British wealth, refinement, and respectability.

In 1973, Colin Levy found himself short of money. Aware that one of Norma's patrons was the celebrated Lord Lambton, he decided to solve his problem with a bit of blackmail. Camera in hand, he lay in wait outside Norma's bedroom during Lambton's next visit to their flat. At the appropriate time, at a signal from Norma, he burst into the room. With flashbulbs popping in his face, the stunned Lambton was frozen on film, *in flagrante delicto*, for posterity.

The fruits the Levys anticipated from their harvest of snapshots failed to ripen. Lambton refused to cough up the money Colin Levy demanded. Instead, recalling the disaster that had befallen John Profumo ten years before when Profumo tried to cover up his own sexual misadventures, Lambton spilled the story to Scotland Yard and urged that the Levys be prosecuted for attempted blackmail. Suddenly Colin and Norma Levy found themselves threatened with arrest.

Murdoch's *News of the World* had long been known for its willingness to pay generous sums of money to ordinary citizens who had sensational stories to tell. The paper employed a pair of subeditors whose jobs were to take down such stories and then put them into the appropriate *News of the World* language. The more documentation a "tattler" could provide, the more his or her tale was worth. Having been rebuffed by Lambton, and under increasing pressure from the police, Colin Levy resolved to go to *News of the World* with his story and photos. He later claimed he did so because he was afraid the authorities might summarily, and secretly, do away with his wife and him in an effort to protect Lambton and several other titled clients of Norma's, some of them also prominent in the government, from scandal. Most people simply assumed that he sought out *News of the World* for the money he still hoped to earn from his blackmail caper.

Upon making inquiries through a middleman, Levy found himself in touch with Trevor Kempson, one of Murdoch's scandal specialists on the paper's editorial staff. Listening to Levy as he spilled out his tale about Lambton and other well-known figures who were regularly serviced by Norma, Kempson grew suitably excited, though he was careful to conceal it. On hearing that Levy actually possessed pictures of Lambton in bed with Norma, his excitement trebled. He was sure they could do business, he told Levy, but first he would have to consult his *News of the World* superiors.

Soon word traveled back to Trevor Kempson: no decision until we see the pictures and can be sure they're genuine. Kempson, not surprised, met again with Levy and requested the photos. Levy told him they hadn't been developed. Kempson suggested that he bring the film to him so that he could have it processed in the *News of the World* photo lab.

"How much money am I going to get?" Levy wanted to know.

Kempson said that the decision would have to await the authentication of his pictures. Levy agreed to bring in his rolls of film the next day.

Levy duly appeared and handed the film to Kempson. "I'm not letting these out of my sight," Levy said. Kempson nodded.

Together, the two walked to the paper's photo lab. There Kempson gave the film to Brian Thomas, a technician, and asked him to develop it. Thomas went into the lab's darkroom, followed by Levy. Once all the pictures were developed and a print made of each, Levy seized the negatives. Thomas summoned Kempson, who had left to make some phone calls. Kempson arrived back at the lab to find Thomas complaining that Levy had taken the negatives. When Kempson confronted Levy, the failed blackmailer refused to return them. "Not until we have a deal," he said, mistakenly believing that he held the upper hand. He'd forgotten about the prints Thomas made.

But Kempson hadn't. One look at the prints confirmed that the man pictured was Lord Lambton. *News of the World* now had the exclusive story, along with its proof, and there was no need to pay Levy a cent. After consulting with Murdoch, Larry Lamb agreed and ordered *News of the World* to proceed with its publication the following weekend.

The hue and cry that greeted the exposé was furious. Although the disgraced Lambton and a second lord who had also been implicated were forced to resign from the government, much of the public outrage was directed not at the two nobles, but at Murdoch and *News of the World* for having engaged in "such gutter journalism," to cite the quaint words of one critic. Their offense—"dealing with pimps and prostitutes to acquire such sordid little stories"—was denounced as worse than Lambton's. The fact that they had failed to pay Levy seemed to compound the outrage.

Murdoch was astonished. He claimed that he and Lamb had made the decision to break the story solely out of "national security" concerns. After all, he said, who could be sure that Lambton, with access to all sorts of state secrets as a result of his high position in the Ministry of Defense, wasn't involved with spies—a reprise of the Keeler-Profumo scandal? How could anyone in England criticize him or *News of the World* for actions that were in every respect patriotic? Wasn't the primary purpose of the press the exposure of wrongdoing in high places of power and trust? Had the story first been published by one of Fleet Street's more respectable papers, it would have been "praised to the heavens." The outcry was nothing more than an expression of the "raving hypocrisy that infests the establishment in this country."

What Murdoch failed to mention was that Scotland Yard and the British military intelligence agencies, having learned that Levy had been to *News of the World,* had asked the paper's editors not to go public with the story until they had a chance to determine if Lambton's involvement with the Levys indeed had national security implications. Lambton was finished in government anyway, but he was still secretly cooperating with the police and intelligence authorities. To publish the story prematurely would compromise the investigation and allow other possible wrongdoers to cover their tracks.

The consensus of recollection and opinion among those who were on the backstage scene at the time holds that the decision to go ahead with the story was a joint one between Lamb and Murdoch. Lamb was an avid Socialist and Labour Party supporter when he was hired by Murdoch in 1969 to take over the editorship of the *Sun*. In the intervening years, he had been much slower than Murdoch to temper his radical political sympathies. Lord Lambton was not only a pillar of the establishment, but a leading light of the Conservative government of Prime Minister Ted Heath, which had ousted Labour from power in 1970. Lamb's desire to break the story right away, then, was motivated primarily by political considerations. In his view, the immediate exposure of Lambton's sexual hijinks possessed the potential to bring down the incumbent Tory government, as the Profumo affair had helped to do ten years before.

From everything Murdoch has said since then, at least privately, his motives were more a matter of personal revenge. He was "sick of being repeatedly raked over the coals" by the "hypocrites of Fleet Street, Westminster [the government], The City, the clubs, and all the other bastions of British self-righteousness who—half of them, anyway—were just as perverted in their personal practices and tastes as the perversions they attributed to me." He was equally resentful of the countless social insults that various segments of the upper classes had heaped on him and his family, as well as on his cadre of Australian aides in London, since 1969. The emergence of Lord Lambton's sexual plight was a perfect sword with which to launch a counterthrust into the heart of the establishment. What better way to rub its face in its own pompous and hypocritical rectitude than to banner Lambton's escapades on the front page of his most widely read newspaper?

No doubt Murdoch believed he was also doing a public service, in more ways than one, when he put his imprimatur on Lamb's decision to publish despite the police and intelligence authorities' requests. But the personal pleasure he derived from the event is evident to this day whenever he talks about the Lambton affair.

He got no pleasure from the aftermath, though. A subsequent government probe of the scandal resulted in further sharp criticisms of Murdoch and *News of the World*, implying that they had criminally impeded an official national security investigation. Later, Fleet Street's National Press Council chipped in with its own bitter condemnation.

It could be argued that both the government and the press council, being each a component of the British establishment, acted out of their own deviously self-protective motives. It was an argument Murdoch never tired of advancing.

Nevertheless, the post-Lambton attacks convinced him once and for all that he would forever be an outcast in England and reinforced his decision to move himself and his family permanently to the United States. His purchase of the two newspapers in San Antonio ensured that he would have no problems with the American Immigration and Naturalization Service. As the owner and chief executive of a domestic corporation, he and his family could enjoy resident-alien status indefinitely. That was particularly important in view of the Australian law that required him to maintain his Australian citizenship in order to keep his lucrative television holdings there.

The repeated controversies Murdoch triggered in England between 1969 and 1974, although they cast him in a harshly unfavorable personal light, had done nothing to dim the financial prosperity of News International, his main British holding and operating company. *News of the World* and the *Sun* were the principal sources of News International's profits. If anything, each new Murdoch outrage resulted in a further large-increment increase in each paper's circulation. *News of the World*'s weekly circulation was nearing the five million mark, up almost a million since its takeover. At the same time, the daily *Sun*'s had passed three million and appeared definitely poised to overtake that of the *Daily Mirror*, which was battling desperately to reverse its own falling circulation—down nearly two million in four years. Murdoch left it to Larry Lamb and the rest of his *Sun* executives to carry on the profitable battle with the *Mirror*, while he took his taste for journalistic combat to the United States.

Murdoch, his wife, and their three children were about to be comfortably ensconced in a huge, luxurious cooperative apartment on New York's Fifth Avenue. The apartment overlooked lower Central Park and was in a building that housed some of the city's richest and most renowned families, in a neighborhood that the press like to call "the gilded ghetto" and "the clubhouse of the American establishment." Next door was Temple Emanuel, the influential Reform synagogue that symbolized the ascension of New York's Jewish elite into the pantheon of money and power in the city. Within a few blocks stood the great old churches and cathedrals of the equally powerful Protestant and Catholic upper classes. It was a fast-lane neighborhood of the rock-ribbed and the rogue, where television news crews could regularly be seen gathered ouside marbled, brass-inlaid doorways waiting to intercept a Rockefeller or a Kennedy, or, later, a DeLorean or a von Bulow. It was a neighborhood of limousines and leafy streets, a place of great wealth where the ability to master the art of serious social climbing was second only to one's certifiable financial status as the measure of one's acceptance.

Murdoch wasted no time on social climbing. Instead, he threw himself more feverishly than ever into the battle to ensure the success of his newly launched *National Star*, interspersing his labors with trips to England and Australia to expand his operations there further.

As the summer of 1974 progressed, one of his principal outside concerns became what he believed was the "unbelievable crucifixion of Richard Nixon by his own country," as he later put it to me. Sympathizing with a man who was the target of so much public scorn in America, as he himself had been in England during much of the same period, Murdoch defended Nixon with increasing intensity as the embattled President approached his August downfall. He still refused to accept Nixon's offenses as being worthy of the impeachment frenzy that was convulsing America. He remained convinced that if Nixon was hounded out of office, it would be a disaster, not just for the United States, but for the rest of the alliance of democratic nations that relied on America for leadership in the struggle to contain international communism. It would be a disaster, he was sure, because Nixon's ouster would undoubtedly bring about the return of what he saw as the weak-kneed Socialist liberalism that had so pervasively infected the United States in the 1960s and put it on the road to becoming a welfare state. Murdoch had seen at close hand what liberal socialism and welfarism had done to a country like Britain, the cradle of modern capitalism. According to him, they had transformed it over a span of three decades into an economic and political cripple. Moreover, the same impulses were percolating down to the major outposts of the British Commonwealth, most notably to Australia.

Socialism and welfarism in capitalist nations were markedly different from Communist socialism, Murdoch now believed. The more a capitalist nation "gave" to its populace, the more the succeeding generations expected and demanded, until eventually there was nothing left to give without bankrupting the nation's

capital base. It was an insidiously destructive psychology that had
to be stopped before it did to the rest of the English-speaking
world what it was doing to England itself. Richard Nixon and his
Administration represented America's last best hope to reverse
the trend.

Murdoch's political and economic transformation was complete by the time of Nixon's departure in August. There was
nothing he could have done to keep the Nixon Administration in
power, however, for by then events had gotten out of hand—
mostly, Murdoch concedes, as a result of Nixon's and his cohorts'
own panic-induced stupidity. In any event, Murdoch still had no
voice or influence in America.

But that wasn't true for Australia. Almost as if to celebrate
his political conversion publicly, and to compensate for his inability to "save" Nixon in America, he embarked on a concerted
effort there to depose his former friend Gough Whitlam, the
Labor Party leader, as prime minister. His effort not only symbolized his conversion but thrust Murdoch into a Watergate-type
adventure of his own.

Despite Whitlam's failure to heed Murdoch's demands during the 1973 boycott of American shipping by Australia's maritime unions, Murdoch and his newspapers had supported him in
his reelection campaign of 1974. At about the same time, Murdoch put News Limited into partnership with America's Reynolds Aluminum Corporation to develop bauxite mining in Western Australia and applied to the Australian government for the
appropriate licenses. Unable to expand his newspaper and television network in Australia further due to its antimonopoly laws,
Murdoch had been dabbling for several years in Australian oil
and minerals development.

Whitlam was reelected in 1974. However, the Labor Party
failed to recover its majority in the Australian Senate. This soon
produced a government financial crisis, with the Senate, led by
the conservative hierarchy's Malcolm Fraser—a contemporary of
Murdoch's at Oxford—threatening to block passage of Whitlam's
1974–75 budget.

Murdoch would later claim that Whitlam's inept handling of
the budget deadlock was what caused him to turn against the
Labor prime minister. Whitlam would at first attribute it to the
fact that his government had refused, following the 1974 election,
to grant mining licenses to the Murdoch–Reynolds Aluminum

partnership, the expectation of which had been the sole basis of Murdoch's support of him. Other knowledgeable observers would ascribe Murdoch's sudden turnaround to the political transformation he'd undergone between 1973 and 1975, suggesting that he could no longer abide an Australian government based on Socialist principles. Still others would credit it to the fact that after the 1974 election, Whitlam devalued the Australian dollar by 12 percent and thereby adversely affected Murdoch's financial position in the foreign money-exchange markets.

A few years later, another possible explanation surfaced—one that gave Murdoch the appearance of having acted as a secret agent of the American government, and more specifically of the CIA.

In the late 1960s, the United States had entered into a secret "executive agreement" with the conservative government of Australia. The agreement allowed the U.S. to construct a group of high-tech electronics installations near the town of Alice Springs in the Australian Outback. To the sensitive Australian public, the installations were explained away as U.S. Defense Department radio facilities designed to expedite military and diplomatic communications between Washington and the Far East and to assist NASA's space exploration. In reality, they were also ultra–top secret spy-satellite data collection and transmission stations manned and operated by the CIA and other American intelligence organizations.

By 1974, much of what the American intelligence establishment was able to glean about Russia, China, and the rest of the Communist world from its electronic and photographic spy satellites came through the collection of satellite data at the remote Alice Springs stations, which were equipped with huge receiving and transmitting antennas. Indeed, the Alice Springs operation had become a vital link in the American espionage-by-satellite network, and its loss would have been a grave blow to the Cold War intelligence interests of the United States. So vital was it that as an inducement to Australia for permitting its construction, the United States had agreed to share all the satellite data collected at Alice Springs with the main Australian intelligence service.

In 1975, as part of his desperate effort to remain prime minister, Gough Whitlam began to exploit the Australian anti-Americanism that had boiled up over the Vietnam War. One of the tactics he employed was to question publicly the true nature of the American installations at Alice Springs. Eventually, he all but revealed to the Australian public that Alice Springs was a secret CIA operation, the purpose of which was to spy on the Russians and other Communist countries. In so doing, he charged that the previous government—the very same band of conservatives that was trying to force his ouster—had lied to the Australian people, and that in the event of a thermonuclear war between the United States and Russia, Australia would surely be a primary target of Soviet missiles. His intimation was that if he were allowed to stay in power, he would see to it that Alice Springs was closed down and that other suspected clandestine CIA operations in Australia would suffer the same fate.

Whitlam's tactics, cheered and expanded on by other Laborites in Australia, rang alarm bells in the White House and at Langley, Virginia, the headquarters of the CIA. Soon it was decided there that Whitlam and his government definitely must go. There are many in Australia today who believe that Rupert Murdoch became a witting accomplice and surrogate of the CIA in its efforts to achieve that end. Not least among them is Whitlam himself, who still claims that secret CIA funds and political machinations brought about his enforced removal from power.

Whatever his true motives, Murdoch turned against Whitlam with a vengeance early in 1975, using the budgetary crisis as his public rationale and orchestrating a major campaign through his various newspapers—but mostly through the *Australian*—to force Whitlam's ouster. His attack was tantamount to a private impeachment drive.

Late in 1975, the campaign succeeded. Despite months of stiff debate over his constitutional right to do so, Sir John Kerr, the Australian Governor General and a friend of Murdoch's, officially discharged Whitlam as prime minister. At the same time, he put Malcolm Fraser temporarily in charge of the government and decreed that an emergency nationwide election be held a month later, in December, so that the country could choose between Fraser and Whitlam.

Although not demonstrably corrupt, the Whitlam regime was seriously discredited by the attack the Murdoch press and other papers, following suit, mounted against it in 1975. Allegations of a sexual scandal involving a beautiful "mystery woman" from the Philippines, though later disproved, were particularly damaging, as were widely aired charges that Whitlam had sought

$5 billion in secret government loans from the Arab world and that certain Whitlam ministers had engaged in illicit financial dealings with a "mysterious" Pakistani financier. Reacting in the same panicky fashion of the Nixon Administration earlier, the Whitlamites did little to help their cause. When the Governor General dismissed the government in November, Whitlam's unpopularity in Australia rivaled that of Nixon's in America. And although Whitlam waged a strenuous one-month campaign for reelection in December, it was a foregone conclusion that he'd lose.

Murdoch nevertheless refused to let up, thereby precipitating his own crisis. Editors on the *Australian* and Sydney *Mirror* would later say that he'd ordered those papers to embark on their anti-Whitlam smear assault as far back as the time of Nixon's resignation in 1974. And that, beginning in early 1975, he personally took a hand in directing it during his several visits to Australia, driving his chief editors on to greater and more frequent violations of the ethical rules of the Australian Journalists' Association in his zeal to destroy Whitlam's political career. "Given Whitlam's nil chances in the new election," says one today, "it was a pure case of journalistic overkill."

Says another, "It was like Rupert was getting revenge for Nixon, his new hero in America. One could just imagine him declaring: 'If the lefties in America can strike down a conservative like Nixon, I'll show the world what a conservative can do to a lefty leader here.'"

A review of editions of the *Mirror* and the *Australian* of that period thoroughly supports the charges of the near-maniacal anti-Whitlam bias brought against Murdoch and his top editors. It was not just that the papers' editorials and opinion columns incited public passions against Whitlam, however. It was in the two papers' regular news coverage of Whitlam's attempt to win the special election that the bias was most blatant. Photographs of the two candidates were selected to make Whitlam consistently appear harried and feeble, Fraser, firm and resolute. Headlines were invariably worded in a way that promoted a totally negative impression of Whitlam, a totally positive one of Fraser.

For instance, a Sydney *Daily Mirror* headline on November 26, 1975, read: "Gough Panics." And another huge front-page banner on December 3, two days before the election, declared: "Gough Guilty." Nothing in the accompanying news story indicated Whitlam had been on trial, although the story—a rehash of the Arab-loan rumors that had been haunting him for a year—was itself written in a style that left no doubt of the paper's prejudice.

But it was the less garish, once-respectable *Australian*'s approach to the election that raised the sharpest protests. Murdoch had kept the money-losing national paper alive for ten years, it was charged, solely for the surreptitious purpose for which he now appeared to be using it—to make and break governments, to become the unelected premier of Australia. So blatantly slanted was the paper's coverage against Whitlam, and for Fraser, that it triggered an uprising among its staff of reporters and subeditors just before the election.

The rebellion had been brewing ever since the *Australian* embarked on its anti-Whitlam drive late the year before. As early as May 1975, two of the paper's reporters lodged protests with Bruce Rothwell and Leslie Hollings, Murdoch's chief surrogates at the paper. The protests were ignored. August brought another round of objections from a greater number of journalists. These also went unheeded. Finally, early in November, Robert Duffield, an editorial writer who had been with the *Australian* since its beginning, and Barry Porter, a subeditor who was the head of the local branch of the Australian Journalists' Union, wrote a confidential letter to Murdoch. In it they voiced the frustration and anger of the majority of the paper's staff and demanded an immediate meeting. The letter contained the signatures of seventy-five reporters, editors, and other employees. Murdoch, who'd recently arrived in Sydney from New York, refused to acknowledge it.

The Duffield-Porter missive, a lengthy litany of the *Australian*'s journalistic transgressions of the previous nine months, was at once accusatory and imploring. It concluded with a veiled threat: "we can be loyal to the *Australian,* no matter how much its style, thrust and readership changes, as long as it retains the traditions, principles and integrity of a responsible newspaper. We cannot be loyal to a propaganda sheet."

When two weeks passed without a response from Murdoch, Duffield and Porter sent him a brusque follow-up note warning that they were prepared to release the letter to the rest of the media and announce his refusal to acknowledge it. This time Murdoch answered, but it was not the reply the two men had

hoped for. "If you insist on providing ammunition for our competitors and enemies who are intent on destroying all our liveli-
hoods," he wrote, "then go ahead."

Duffield went public with the complaints in the original letter, allowing himself to be interviewed on Sydney television early
in December. Murdoch refused to comment. With the *Australian*
dispute out in the open, journalists on Murdoch's other papers
joined in. In addition, on December 6, the Saturday before the
election, printers preparing to put out his two Sunday papers in
Sydney suddenly went on strike to protest the papers' virulent
anti-Labor editorials. The next day brought a demonstration outside Murdoch's office in which copies of the *Australian* were
burned. This was followed by a noisy rally of more than a hundred journalists from all three of Murdoch's Sydney-based daily
papers—the *Australian,* the *Mirror,* and the *Telegraph.* The rally
resulted in a vote for an immediate strike against the three and a
public statement denouncing Murdoch's "very deliberate and
blatant bias in the presentation of news." The statement went on
to explain that the striking journalists "felt it necessary to dissoci-
ate ourselves entirely from the desecration of the traditional and
historical ethics of journalism" by Murdoch and his editorial
lieutenants.

The strike lasted only a day. Murdoch finally agreed to meet
with Duffield and Porter, representing the dissidents, and work
was resumed. Murdoch listened to the complaints. Then he declared that anyone who didn't like working at his papers was free
to resign and look for employment elsewhere. If there was an en
masse departure—well, he would manage. There were plenty of
people in high-unemployment Sydney looking for jobs.

Duffield and Porter reported Murdoch's response to their
constituents. Only one *Australian* journalist resigned immediately. The rest, although dispirited, went back to work. The election came and went, with Malcolm Fraser and his conservative
plank winning in the widely predicted landslide. The Murdoch-
inspired furor appeared to be over.

But it wasn't. In the aftermath of the election, the "mystery
woman" from the Philippines sued the Murdoch organization for
libel. Actually, she was no mystery woman at all. Named Junie
Morosi, she was an attractive Shanghai-born Eurasian, in her
early forties, who had apparently engaged in some disreputable
business practices with her first husband in the Philippines before

landing in Australia as the wife of an airline executive and becoming private secretary to the Whitlam government's treasurer and deputy prime minister, Jim Cairns. It was the "true" nature of Morosi's relationship with Cairns, as well as with other Whitlam ministers, that the Murdoch papers—especially the Sydney *Mirror*—fastened on in 1975. Their conclusion, garbed in lurid suggestion and innuendo, was that Junie Morosi was busy bedding half the Labor cabinet, if not Gough Whitlam himself. Once the *Mirror* subtly etched the "truth" of that impression, the rest of the Murdoch press made high political capital of it, turning it into a keystone of Murdoch's smear campaign against Whitlam.

One of the *Mirror*'s more prominent "proofs" of the hanky-panky it claimed was going on between Cairns and Morosi was a photo it published of the two eating a cozy breakfast together on a motel balcony. What the paper's readers didn't know was that Mrs. Cairns, present and eating at the same table, had been cropped from the photo. The technique of printing doctored pictures to convey false "facts" was once a time-honored tradition among gutter journalists. Most people, even in journalistically rowdy Australia, believed it a tradition that had died. Murdoch and his subalterns proved it hadn't.

Junie Morosi eventually won most of her libel claim against Murdoch, obtaining a jury award of about $25,000 two years later. In the meantime, Murdoch was desperate to show Australia that he'd been right in his campaign to destroy Whitlam. When he was back in London a few weeks after the election, on his way to New York, the opportunity to do so suddenly, out of the blue, seemed to present itself. His pursuit of it, however, would raise many more questions than it answered. Among them were further questions about Murdoch's use of his newspapers to settle personal scores.

It began on February 17, 1976, with a telephone call to Murdoch at his *News of the World/Sun* office in London's Bouverie Street. The caller was a man named Henri Fischer, a shadowy international businessman from Sydney who boasted of extensive high-level commercial and political contacts in the Arab Middle East. Fischer was aware of Murdoch's recent crusade against the Whitlam government. Following his removal from office, and after his defeat in the previous December's election, Whitlam had been struggling to reassert his leadership of the Australian Labor Party. Fischer, phoning from Paris, cryptically told Murdoch that he possessed information that would finish Whitlam in Australian politics once and for all. Murdoch agreed to meet with him.

Fischer arrived in London three days later. He told Murdoch that he had long been closely connected with the extreme left-wing government of Iraq, which was controlled by strongman Saddam Hussein, the vice-chairman of that country's ruling Ba'ath Party. He professed also to know Gough Whitlam well. The previous December, Fischer went on, three days before the special election, he'd acted as an intermediary between Whitlam and two Iraqi emissaries of Saddam Hussein in a deal whereby Whitlam was to receive a campaign contribution.

The story was essentially true, and much more chillingly convoluted than Fischer's flat recitation made it appear. In November, Fischer had informed the beleaguered Whitlam, whose campaign funds were drying up, that he might be able to engineer a loan or contribution from the Iraqis. Whitlam, despite his awareness that it was illegal to accept campaign money from foreign sources, expressed interest. Fischer then went to the Iraqis and elicited their interest. The two Iraqi emmissaries sent from Baghdad, it turned out, were actually high-level members of Hussein's secret police and, according to the British government, suspected terrorists. When the British embassy in Baghdad turned down their applications for visas to travel to Australia on those grounds, the Australian embassy in Tokyo, acting on instructions from Canberra, issued them papers in false names. The two Iraqis, machine pistols concealed under their clothes, thereupon arrived in Sydney via Tokyo and checked into a cheap motel. The next night, tailed by Australian security officers, they made their way to Fischer's apartment overlooking Sydney's scenic harbor. Awaiting them was Whitlam.

According to Fischer, an agreement was reached—although it was not certain the parties totally understood its terms. With the election only three days away, a series of nationwide polls in Australia had indicated that Whitlam and his Labor plank would be roundly defeated. Only an expensive last-ditch campaign effort on Whitlam's part might reverse the trend. But his campaign coffers were nearly empty. Whitlam apparently was given to understand that if he made the effort, which would cost about $500,-000, the Iraqis would pay for it, win or lose. The two Iraqis, on the other hand, one of them a nephew of Saddam Hussein, evidently interpreted the agreement to mean that they would be required to hand over the money only in the event Whitlam won.

It was this that had prompted him to come forward with his information, Henri Fischer told Murdoch. Now, two months after the election, a furious argument was raging between Whitlam and the Iraqis, with Whitlam demanding the $500,000 and the Iraqis denying any obligation to pay. Both sides were blaming Fischer, especially the Iraqis, and he feared there were plans afoot in Baghdad to do away with him. What he wanted from Murdoch, in exchange for spilling the story, was money and protection.

Fischer's tale was almost too good to be true, Murdoch thought. But then, checking with a friend high up in the Australian security service, he was able to confirm at least one detail— that the two Iraqis Fischer told him about had indeed arrived in Sydney just before the election, that they'd been followed to Fischer's apartment on the night in question, and that Whitlam had also been seen entering the apartment.

With that, Murdoch phoned Bruce Rothwell in Sydney, related the bare outlines of the story, and told him to ready the front page of the *Australian* for a "blockbuster" two days hence. Murdoch had to leave for New York the next day. He said he'd write the story himself on the plane and dispatch it from there. In the meantime, he hired a private security agency to stand guard over Fischer and installed him in an expensive London hotel.

Arriving in New York, Murdoch once again phoned Sydney and dictated the details of Fischer's story to Rothwell and Barrie Watts, an *Australian* assistant editor. They rewrote it in the appropriate *Australian* style and bannered it in the following day's edition, crediting it to a "Special Correspondent." The date was February 25, 1976. Henri Fischer was not mentioned as the story's source.

Predictably, the report stirred a fresh storm of controversy over Whitlam, but it was not enough to lose him his Labor Party leadership or the seat in Parliament he had retained after his prime-ministerial defeat. Although he was forced to submit to an official Labor Party reprimand, he has remained to this day a highly visible presence in Australian political and cultural life and a continuing thorn in Murdoch's side.

An even greater thorn became the bizarre sideshow that developed with Henri Fischer following his meetings with Murdoch in London. In expressing fears for his life, Fischer had told Murdoch that one of those he feared most was a man named Tito Howard, an American businessman and "soldier of fortune" who, he claimed, was known to do "dirty work" for the Arab dictators of Syria and Iraq. Based on Fischer's claims, Murdoch had agreed to provide him with a twenty-four-hour bodyguard.

Murdoch was taken aback, then, shortly after he had Fischer hidden away, when he received a call from a man who identified himself as Tito Howard. According to Murdoch, Howard also asked to meet with him on an important confidential matter. Curious about what Fischer had told him of the American, Murdoch invited Howard to Bouverie Street.

When Howard arrived, Murdoch later recalled, "He said he could produce a certain piece of 35-millimeter film which would prove a major indiscretion by an Australian politician. Would I be interested in buying it? I replied that if it stood up to all the tests for its validity, then I would be interested. Howard then said that he had just such a piece of film . . . and he would get it." But, Murdoch added, "I never saw him again." He became convinced that Howard's visit was nothing more than a clumsy attempt to find Fischer. This, in his mind, increased Fischer's credibility, so he ordered the man's bodyguard doubled while he flew off to New York.

Shortly thereafter, Fischer, hiding out at Murdoch's expense in a suite at London's posh new Inter-Continental Hotel, announced that he had to fly to Australia immediately to get his wife and some incriminating business documents out of the country. Murdoch approved the trip and instructed that one of Fischer's bodyguards, Douglas Sinclair, travel with him.

The journey, by way of Frankfurt and Bangkok, included a stopover in Singapore, where Fischer said he had to tend to some personal business before going on to Sydney. He and Sinclair, his bodyguard, checked into the Singapore Hilton on a Sunday evening. The next morning, according to Sinclair, "I woke up, went to answer a call of nature, and found that Fischer was gone."

Fischer left nothing behind but some empty suitcases and a pile of charred documents in the toilet of the hotel suite. He had been spotted by a Hilton watchman leaving the hotel's back entrance just after dawn of that Monday morning, however. With him was a man who answered the description of Tito Howard.

Had Howard kidnapped Fischer? Not according to Howard. Upon being located in the United States a week later by a British journalist, Howard said that he had merely "rescued" Fischer from the people who were holding him captive.

While in London three weeks before, Howard told Peter Pringle, the journalist, "I went to see Fischer at the Inter-Continental Hotel. There were two men with him . . . both agents of a private detective agency. Fischer appeared really scared."

Howard went on to say that Fischer had slipped him a crumpled piece of paper that read, "I've been kidnapped," and begged for his help. When Howard learned that Fischer would soon be flown to Australia in the company of at least one of his bodyguards, with a stop at Singapore, he said he let Fischer know that he intended to follow them.

Howard arrived in Singapore, he continued, and "discovered" that Fischer was at the Hilton. Checking into the hotel himself, he said that at dawn that Monday morning he went to Fischer's suite with a hired Chinese karate expert, overpowered Sinclair, and enabled Fischer to escape. So far as he knew, Howard concluded, Fischer had gone into hiding with a business friend in Singapore. Howard himself had flown back to the United States a few days later.

When queried about all this, Sinclair vigorously denied having been overcome by Howard and his Chinese karate master; he described Howard's cloak-and-dagger story as "complete fantasy." He hadn't even seen Howard in Singapore, he said, although he acknowledged having met him earlier when the American had visited Fischer at the Inter-Continental in London. Nevertheless, based on the Hilton watchman's description of the man with whom Fischer had been seen leaving the rear of the hotel, Sinclair conceded that the man was most likely Howard.

What was it all about? Had Howard really rescued Fischer, or had he kidnapped him? Had Murdoch really been protecting Fischer, or had he been holding him captive? And what about Fischer himself? Was he pulling some sort of scam on Murdoch, or was he the victim of foul play, as he'd said he feared he would be? If the latter, then why his visits with Howard at the Inter-Continental, which Sinclair later said were friendly? And what about Howard's offer to sell Murdoch incriminating film about an Australian politician? And Murdoch's offer to buy it?*

---

* The mystery would never be solved, at least for public consumption. Except for Murdoch and Whitlam, all the characters disappeared into their prior anonymity.

That last was the most troubling question of the entire affair. It was a question that began to nettle the American journalism community as Murdoch, in the spring of 1976, let it be known that he was intent on acquiring a major metropolitan daily in the United States.

MURDOCH

AMERICA

The Battle of New York

During the same spring, Murdoch and I first met and began to get to know one another. Because I made my living as an independent journalist and author, and more because I generally spent a month or two in England each year, I had heard and read more than a little about him prior to our initial encounter. But I had never laid eyes on him, or even seen a photo. Meeting him, then, was something of a surprise. I'd somewhat expected him to be a figure of commanding, charismatic physical presence and smooth, forceful personality. He wasn't. The man introduced to me as Rupert Murdoch was soft, round, harried-looking, and—well—decidedly unheroic in appearance and manner. However, I was soon to learn the truth of the adage that one cannot always tell a book by its cover.

The giveaway, to begin with, was his face. It was a swarthy assemblage that fronted a large, domed head topped with lank, thinning hair. His brow, broad and high, was terraced by deep lateral creases that provided vivid evidence of his then forty-five, undoubtedly careworn years on earth. A deeper furrow slashed contrapuntally downward between his dark, bushy eyebrows like a nasty dueling scar. His nose, large and broad around the nostrils, had a pronounced ski-jump shape in profile. Below it spread a wide, grimly mobile mouth of the kind Eisenhower was famous for, its generous lips elastically expressive. The entire fleshy construction was framed by pillowy jowls and a chin that lacked definition. Hair grew out of his ears and nostrils, and his jaw was swathed in the hint of a five o'clock shadow.

It could have been the face of a local plumber or house painter—or of a furtive Arab revolutionary. Vaguely Mediterranean in the way Richard Nixon's was, it was certainly not a face one readily associated with a man who devoted all his skills and energies to the world of international big business. Although not altogether unattractive in repose, it was a map of a lifetime of psychic combat; as one mutual friend later described it, it resembled "a sad bruised knuckle." But it could turn outright ugly with gargoylelike distortion when red-zone angry.

In its bulky circularity, Murdoch's head fit well with his thick, knobby body. But at the same time, it seemed oversized and out of proportion, and the hunched, slopelike narrowness of his shoulders made it seem all the more ill-matched.

Nor did his eyes fit, somehow. Large, dark, and liquid, hooded by weighty, slanted prizefighter's lids, they struck me as too gleamingly wizened, too detachedly intelligent, for so blunt and workmanlike a face. They shone with lupine intensity and alertness; though without apparent humor or irony, they smoldered with feral guardedness and snap judgment. They were the eyes of a sardonic brain surgeon set into an Archie Bunker mug. Even when he allowed a smile to flash across his mouth like the swift gleam of sun through a storm cloud, his eyes remained abstract and mirthless, stealthy, and morose.

Murdoch's face and physique were an apt metaphor for his personality and sense of himself. He projected and carried himself in a manner that could only be described as tough. And it was toughness, or at least the illusion of it, that he seemed to value most highly in others, almost to the exclusion of any other trait but business "smarts." He was very much hail-fellow-well-met with those he decided measured up, and with them he would banter and chin in the usual relaxed but studied male-bonding barracks fashion, giving his counterparts the impression that he was meeting them on equal terms. As time went on, it was amusing for me to watch his corporate and journalistic underlings, their own personalities self-consciously molded on the Murdochian model, as they interacted with him. This was especially the case with many among his Australian and British entourage, who generally disported themselves as though they had graduated from the George Raft–Jimmy Cagney school of social behavior. It was like watching a Shavian satire, or an unintended stage parody of toughness, decisiveness, and superiority.

And then there was Murdoch's voice. It was nasal, slightly tinny in timbre, mid-pitched, alternately cautious and abrupt, thickly redolent of Down Under. His manner of speaking, which was mumbly and almost sotto voce in ordinary social situations, gave him an extremely self-effacing, almost apologetic air. But when he ventured onto business subjects, or politics, or social issues, his voice became hard, biting, and judgmental as he weaved his arguments and made his points. Either way, it was a tonically jarring voice that was often accompanied by a nervous cackling laugh. When chewing out a subordinate, it could be downright menacing, and it usually produced the desired response: a sense of abject humiliation on the part of the object of his scorn, who was usually one of his editors.

Soon after we met, Murdoch began telling me about himself—his past, present, and future. Not so much because he wanted to, for by nature he was reticent, even secretive, but because I was nudgingly inquisitive. In 1972, he said, when he'd started to think seriously about moving to the United States, one of the people he relied on to show him around New York was his old friend and quasi-mentor Leonard Goldenson, still the head of ABC. Showing him around meant introducing Murdoch to "the people who counted"—the bankers, lawyers, real estate moguls, politicians, big business executives, media chiefs, and social arbiters who had a major hand in running the city. Since Goldenson's connections were most extensive in the large Jewish sector of that oligarchy, most of the people Murdoch met, or whose acquaintance he renewed after encounters during his earlier visits, were leading members of the city's Jewish establishment.

Among the closer friendships Murdoch formed was one with a lawyer named Howard Squadron, who was five years older than he. A Bronx-born "nobody," to use his own word, Squadron had parlayed a razor-sharp mind, a smoothly assertive personality, and a 1947 Columbia University law degree into a prosperous Manhattan legal practice and, by the early 1970s, a top-rung position in the city's Jewish power hierarchy. As an attorney, he specialized in entertainment, communications, and real estate law. But Squadron was one of those New York lawyers who were much more than lawyers, who achieved recognition and authority more for what they did outside their profession than for what they did within it.

Starting early in his career as general counsel for the American Jewish Congress, one of the country's most prominent Jewish fund-raising and political lobbying organizations, Squadron eventually became its president and, later, the head of the Council of Presidents of Major American Jewish Organizations. A political liberal, he also became a potent behind-the-scenes force in New York's corruption-rife Democratic Party during the 1960s, and in 1970, made an abortive run for Congress. By the time he and Murdoch grew close, shortly thereafter, Squadron liked to boast that he had one of the biggest Rolodexes in New York. Given his vast circle of contacts, it was probably true.

Among those contacts was Dorothy Schiff, the longtime owner of the *New York Post* and a power in her own right in the high-level culture of New York. Murdoch, having become friendly with Squadron and impressed by his easy access to the city's highest corridors of influence, had hired him and his law firm—Squadron, Ellenoff, Plesent and Lehrer—to represent the newly formed News America's legal interests when he expanded his publishing operations into the United States. In many ways, Squadron succeeded Leonard Goldenson as Murdoch's chief guide through the American political, business, and legal maze. It was Squadron who, along with a younger New York investment banker named Stanley Shuman, engineered Murdoch's acquisition of the *Post* and his invasion of New York in general.

Shuman was the third of New York's Jewish-establishment figures upon whom Murdoch came to rely. A Bostonian by birth, he was four years younger than Murdoch. After obtaining a law degree from Harvard in 1959 and an MBA in 1961, he had joined the mysterious and controversial Wall Street investment bank of Allen and Company. By 1970, he'd elevated himself to the position of executive vice president and managing director of the firm. Specializing in media mergers and acquisitions, he'd earned himself a tidy fortune in the process.

Allen and Company was a prosperous, secretive, family-owned firm. Its dominant figure was Charles Allen. The firm had played key financial roles in the development of the Bahamian gaming industry in the early 1960s and in the financing of postwar Hollywood movie productions. In 1973, the company gained control of Columbia Pictures, one of Hollywood's major studios, and then became centrally embroiled in the David Begelman embezzlement scandal that shook Columbia and the rest of the movie industry in the late 1970s. By 1976, the firm was still dominated by the *éminence grise* presence of the aging Charles Allen, but its primary operational control had passed to Herbert Allen, Jr., Charles's thirty-five-year-old nephew. While "Herbie" Allen supervised the firm's private investments and holdings, Stanley Shuman became one of its principal deal makers for outside clients seeking corporate mergers, acquisitions, and takeovers.

Shuman was stockily handsome, athletic, and "smart as a whip," to use Howard Squadron's phrase. As an aggressive and still relatively young partner in Allen and Company, because of that connection he was as much a controversial "outsider" in his own trade as Murdoch was in his.

"Forget all the garbage stories you hear about Allen and Company," Squadron told me. "It wasn't the firm that interested Rupert, anyway, it was Stan himself. It was natural that they should gravitate toward each other. They were two sides of the same coin—Rupert the rough side, Stan the smooth."

Gravitate toward one another the two did. By 1976, Shuman had joined Squadron at the center of Murdoch's tight circle of New York friends and advisers. And each was an intensely interested onlooker when Murdoch met with the elderly Dorothy Schiff for lunch at her office in the decrepit *New York Post* plant in lower Manhattan, hard by the East River and Brooklyn Bridge, in September of that year.

Another close observer was a third American enlistee in Murdoch's enlarging New York circle. Clay Felker was the imperious, mercurial founder-editor of the trendy, popular *New York* magazine and the putative inventor of the "new journalism" that had become the newspaper and magazine rage in the United States during the late sixties and early seventies. The success of both had turned Felker into a powerful media force and a leading social lion in status-conscious Manhattan. After Murdoch settled there in 1974, the two became fast friends. To be sure, the journalist in Felker was appalled by the *National Star* when it first appeared. But he respected Murdoch's money and his apparent desire to invest it further in American publishing ventures.

Although he had accumulated plenty of prestige, the high-living Felker had never been able to make enough money of his own to expand his publishing operation in the fashion he'd hoped to. That was because the operation wasn't really his. The ownership of the New York Magazine Company was split up among a variety of stockholders, some of them jealous of Felker's celebrity, others resentful of his abrasive personality. A minority owner, he was in many respects little more than a high-salaried employee of the company, and he saw in Murdoch, among other things, a potential route to gaining personal autonomy over it. In the meantime, he busied himself as an almost daily adviser to Murdoch on the personalities and complexities of New York journalism. He, in fact, had been the first to suggest that Murdoch look into acquiring the *New York Post.*

In the winter of 1962–63, a long and bitter labor stoppage had forever changed the face of the newspaper industry in New York. In its wake, four major dailies were eventually forced to close. Among them was the high-quality *Herald-Tribune, The New York Times'*s principal competitor and the paper from which Clay Felker's *New York* magazine later evolved. By all rights, the *Post* should have succumbed, too; it had been struggling financially for a long time and was being held together solely by annual infusions of money from Dorothy Schiff's personal fortune. She had saved it early in the strike by breaking ranks with her fellow publishers, making a separate settlement with the unions, and getting the *Post* back on the streets well ahead of the city's other dailies. The paper was given a further breath of life when its two afternoon-evening rivals, the chain-owned *World-Telegram and Sun* and *Journal-American,* went out of business not long after the strike.

Despite having the market almost exclusively to itself, however, the *Post* still failed to thrive as it entered the 1970s. This was due in part to its outdated editorial style, and in part to its antiquated plant and machinery and to the steep increase in its labor, manufacturing, and distribution costs—the chief legacy of the 1963 strike settlement. The international oil-and-monetary crisis of 1973–74 compounded the paper's problems, the resultant inflation further driving up the costs of newsprint and other production essentials.

Now, in 1976, another round of labor negotiations anticipated the expiration of the latest print union contracts. From her conversations with the city's other remaining publishers—the owners of the *Times* and *Daily News*—Dorothy Schiff knew that they were intent on digging in hard against what they were sure would be the unions' exorbitant demands. Moreover, they were set on making their own stiff counterdemands in the hope of reducing their union work forces and increasing automated production.

Schiff envisioned a repeat of 1962–63, and she wasn't sure she wanted to go through it again at her age. What's more, in the previous year the *Post* had lost nearly a million dollars, and the prospects for 1977 were even grimmer. Those realities, along with the likelihood of future inheritance tax problems should she die while still in possession of the paper, had finally persuaded her that she should sell it. Her lunch with Murdoch reinforced her resolve. He seemed eager to buy, promising that he would invest millions to modernize the paper but would retain its liberal, "progressive" character and maintain its top editorial staff. Yet for all that, Dorothy Schiff was not yet ready emotionally to part with it.

Murdoch grew impatient. Despite the warnings of several of his American friends to the contrary, he was convinced that he could turn the *Post* around by doing to it what he had done to the comatose left-wing *Sun* in London eight years before. If he had any doubts, they were dispelled by the fact that just a few months before, the *Sun* had finally surpassed the London *Daily Mirror* in circulation. He couldn't wait to get his hands on the *Post*. But the hesitant Dorothy Schiff wasn't cooperating.

Murdoch therefore embarked on a ploy. In London, the money-losing *Observer,* a quality Sunday paper that competed with the *Sunday Telegraph* and *Sunday Times,* had been put up for sale by its owners, members of England's wealthy Astor family dynasty. On the board of the *Observer* was Arnold Goodman, an illustrious academic, lawyer, and government adviser who had also been on the board of *News of the World* when Murdoch bought it. After becoming Lord Goodman in 1970, he and Murdoch had remained distantly friendly. When it was decided to sell the *Observer* in the fall of 1976, Goodman asked Murdoch if he would be interested.

Murdoch was, but more for the indirect pressure he hoped such interest would put on Dorothy Schiff than for any other reason. If word reached her that her dilatory response to his expression of interest in buying the *Post* had "forced" him to enter negotiations to buy another British paper instead, she might then decide to sell, especially since there was no one else around who wanted the *Post*. Furthermore, the fact that Murdoch was negotiating for a quality paper, for a change, might ease any doubts

Schiff was reported to have about his promise to maintain what she believed to be the *Post*'s "high quality."

The tactic worked. In October, Murdoch's involvement in negotiations for the *Observer* were widely publicized. Schiff called Howard Squadron and said: "What's this?" Squadron offered the appropriate disclaimers, which amounted to his telling her that "Rupert couldn't wait forever for her to make up her mind." Schiff made her decision and within hours asked for a money offer.

By then, however, Murdoch's interest in the *Observer* had become genuine. When his name was first mentioned in the British press as a potential buyer, there had been a chorus of protest. "Giving the *Observer* to Rupert Murdoch is like giving your beautiful daughter to a gorilla," one veteran newspaper editor was quoted as saying in London's *Sunday Times*. And the well-known Australian television reviewer, Clive James, exclaimed: "Rupert Murdoch was one of the main reasons that people like me have come 12,000 miles to work in Britain." The "rain of insults" prodded Murdoch into going after the *Observer* for real. But now it was a case of his having been dilatory. While he was using the *Observer* solely to pressure Dorothy Schiff, another buyer had appeared on the British scene—Atlantic Richfield, or ARCO, the American oil company.

Why an American oil company would want to buy a tired British Sunday newspaper raised a number of unanswered questions in England. But when the dust cleared a few weeks later, ARCO was the new proprietor of the *Observer*. And Murdoch, through his American corporation, was the new owner of the *New York Post*, for which he paid $30 million.

Among the first to rush into print in praise of Dorothy Schiff's good judgment, and Rupert Murdoch's "splendid potential" for reinvigorating daily journalism in New York, was the trend-setting Clay Felker. As one of the authoritative cultural voices of the city, when Felker "spoke," his pronouncements were taken seriously in many quarters. If he approved of Murdoch, then Murdoch must be worthy of the city's hope and respect—or at least that portion of the city that mattered, which consisted essentially of the lower half of Manhattan and a few isolated cultural outposts in Brooklyn and Queens. What most readers didn't know was that Felker, in addition to being Murdoch's pal, had another reason for stamping him with his imprimatur. In November, at the very time Murdoch was sewing up his deal with

Dorothy Schiff, Felker was immersed in an increasingly bitter battle to maintain his tenuous grip on the New York Magazine Company he had founded, with the help of a few rich and friendly backers, ten years earlier.

New York's rapid success had enabled Felker to take the company public in 1969. The move had increased his net worth considerably, but it also diluted his control and inflicted on him an independent board of directors that was not always unanimous in its support of his expansion aspirations. In 1974, however, he had persuaded the board to let him buy *The Village Voice,* the city's free-wheeling, left-wing "counterculture" weekly whose readership was a bohemian downtown counterpart of *New York*'s high-toned uptown audience.

The purchase, though, was not made with cash; it was accomplished instead through a swap of stock. The majority owners of *The Village Voice* were the wealthy socialite-politician Carter Burden and his close friend, lawyer Bartle Bull. In exchange for placing the *Voice* in Felker's domain, they were given 34 percent of the stock in the New York Magazine Company and two major seats on its board. This had the effect of diluting Felker's share of the ownership and further weakening his influence over the board.

Early in 1976, under the company banner, Felker launched a California version of *New York.* Called *New West,* the magazine's start-up costs and postdebut losses, a significant part of which were attributable to Felker's unbridled spending, aroused the ire of several of the major stockholders of the parent company in New York. Not the least of those was Carter Burden. Since the time of his transfer of *The Village Voice* two years earlier, Burden and Felker had become harsh enemies. Now, in November, Burden was using Felker's soaring *New West* losses as a reason to mount a putsch among the board to remove Felker totally from the company.

Felker had only two hopes of survival. One was to reconcile with Burden, clearly an impossibility given the acrimony between them. The other was to bring in an ouside party, friendly to him, who would help him buy out the majority Burden-Bull holding in *New York* and restore his executive and editorial authority. Rupert Murdoch was to be Felker's savior—at least in Felker's mind.

Thus, only a few days after his purchase of the *New York Post,* Murdoch found himself being "romanced" by Felker.

Felker's proposal was for a joint takeover between them of the New York Magazine Company and its three publications, with Murdoch putting up the money. Murdoch was sympathetic to the notion of acquiring *New York* magazine. Since it was profitable, he wouldn't have to think about changing it appreciably, and its slick, sophisticated style would serve as a congenial counterpart to what he had in mind for the *Post*. Indeed, it might even blunt the criticism he was sure to receive when he began to revamp the *Post*.

Murdoch did not commit himself to Felker's proposal, however. Instead, he sent him away with an "I'll have to think about it." Then, privately, he asked Stanley Shuman to investigate the company's finances and learn if its principal stockholders would be receptive to a buyout.

It took Shuman little more than a week to return an affirmative and enthusiastic answer, along with an estimate that a buyout would cost well under $10 million. For less than $40 million, Murdoch in one fell swoop could become a major publishing presence in New York with the *Post, New York,* and *The Village Voice.* What made it especially attractive was the fact that he could use the *Post*'s large cash reserves—funds he had just "inherited"—to cover most of the purchase of the New York Magazine Company. Those funds amounted to more than $6 million, which meant that he'd be getting *New York* for practically nothing.

But what to do about Felker? Murdoch knew that *New York*'s staff was intensely loyal to him. But he had begun to sour on Felker, both personally and as a publishing executive. After watching him in action the year before in the Hamptons and on New Year's Upper East Side, Murdoch found his social pretensions irksome. What's more, he had reason to suspect Felker of abusing their friendship by denigrating him behind his back—a pastime in which Murdoch himself was well practiced. Murdoch's suspicion was sharpened by the fact that Felker was friendly with David Frost.

Murdoch told Shuman and Howard Squadron that he didn't want Felker as a partner if he took over *New York*. He'd be willing to keep him on as the magazine's editor for a reasonable time, under a tight financial rein, but he was sure Felker would reject such a reduced role.

There was only one solution, the three concluded. Since

Felker at that time was almost totally involved in trying to keep *New West* afloat, Murdoch should offer to spin off the California magazine as a separate company, sell Felker a piece of it, and let him run it. In that way, Murdoch would discharge whatever moral duty he owed Felker. And if Felker eventually succeeded in making *New West* profitable, he would share in the rewards. It was, as Squadron put it, "a perfect incentive plan." To Murdoch, it was a convenient way to get Felker "out of my hair."

By the time this was all worked out, in early December 1976, Felker was in Los Angeles on *New West* business. Murdoch phoned him, informed him that he had decided to proceed with the takeover bid they'd discussed, and asked him to return to New York for a meeting. Felker, much relieved, flew out of Los Angeles the next morning. He spent most of the flight plotting what he intended to urge as his and Murdoch's joint strategy for the company once the takeover was completed and he was back in full charge.

Felker could barely hide his shock when, the next day, Murdoch revealed what he really had in mind. And with the realization that the Australian intended to dispose of him, his shock quickly turned to rage. Murdoch apologized, but said he "just didn't think" they could work together. Felker accused him of betrayal. Murdoch shrugged, then repeated his offer to sell Felker a third of *New West*—for a million dollars.

A sop! Felker cried. Anyway, he had no way of raising such an amount, and Murdoch knew it.

Murdoch used Felker's anguish to give him a lecture on thrift. Had Felker had the wisdom to save some of his money instead of spending it the way he did, he might be in a position to take up the offer. It was precisely that big-spender aspect of Felker's nature that had made Murdoch realize that he could not have him running the *New York* organization when he took it over. "It's a lifelong habit with you, Clay," Murdoch said. "You're too old to change your spots."

Felker barely heard the sermon. By then he was formulating a counterattack. Murdoch said that Stanley Shuman's preliminary inquiries indicated that he would easily and quickly be able to acquire 51 percent of the stock in the New York Magazine Company through a generous tender offer. Once that was accomplished, the rest of the shareholders would sell out, too, giving Murdoch the company in its entirety.

"You're forgetting one thing," Felker said. He reminded Murdoch that under his contract with *New York*, Carter Burden and Bartle Bull could not sell their 34 percent holding to anyone else without giving him—Felker—an opportunity to buy it first.

Murdoch replied with a smile tinged with pity. He hadn't forgotten at all, he said. In fact, he had made the clarification of that first-refusal clause his first order of business.

"It's you who're being the forgetful one," Murdoch told Felker. He pointed out that under the language of the clause, Felker's right to buy the Burden-Bull percentage existed only if the company was operating at a profit. As it happened, it had been operating at a loss for the past year. It was ironic, Murdoch added, but the only reason for that was Felker's extravagantly expensive launch of *New West*. What it meant was that Felker himself had rendered the first-refusal clause null and void.

Felker, stunned again, fought back. He insisted that the loss the company had reported on its books was there solely for tax reasons, and "that doesn't count."

"Sorry," said Murdoch. "The figures are down in black and white. You can't change the figures."

"We'll see about that," Felker snapped as, near tears, he got up to leave the meeting. He promised to fight Murdoch "tooth-and-nail" for *New York*.

"Teeth and nails are fine," Murdoch rejoined sarcastically. "But it's money that wins this kind of scrap."

The battle lines were drawn. And although the battle itself lasted several weeks, becoming a hotly covered city media event as the New Year ushered in 1977, its outcome was never in doubt. Lawsuits were filed, ugly charges were hurled in the press, and the writing and editorial staff of *New York* magazine threatened to walk out en masse if Murdoch succeeded in his bid to take over the company.

In the end, though, the whole affair climaxed more in a whisper than a bang. The court actions over the question of Felker's contractual right to purchase the Burden-Bull shares were quickly resolved in Murdoch's favor. A brief flurry of interest in bidding against Murdoch by the Washington Post Company, an interest solicited by Felker, died aborning. A number of *New York* staffers made good on their promise to quit, but for all practical purposes the magazine remained intact. When it was all over, on January 7, 1977, Murdoch was the new owner of the

New York Magazine Company and Felker, as one of Murdoch's allies gleefully put it, was "history."*

Aside from shifting one of his own people into the editor's chair at *New York* and installing a News America financial team to reduce the magazine's expenses, Murdoch did little at first to interfere with its editorial direction. The new editor was James Brady, a brash ex-Marine who had made his mark in New York as editor of *Women's Wear Daily,* the trend-setting "Bible" of the fashion industry, and then joined the Murdoch organization to become the first American editor of the *National Star.* Brady's appointment was only an interim one, however. Not long after, Murdoch would hire a young Texan, Joe Gravitt Armstrong, to run *New York.* Armstrong, a breezily personable but high-strung "boy wonder" of the magazine industry, was given almost complete autonomy over *New York* until, a few years later, he also came to grief with Murdoch.

The iconoclastic *Village Voice* was much more of a hallowed institution to its readership than *New York* was to its. And the paper's longtime staff of highly opinionated, mostly left-wing writers—writers who seemed to champion everything the establishment abhorred—had an even more proprietary attitude. Because the *Voice* made money, mostly through its huge volume of counterculture advertising, and because Murdoch realized that its market was beyond his ken, he was content to leave it alone. A single brief attempt to change the paper's editorship produced a raucous house revolt, and he beat a hasty retreat. Thereafter, he would let the *Voice* march to the beat of its own drum, erupting only occasionally to complain about its journalistic "foolishness" and excesses and especially about its writers' regular attacks on him for what he was doing with the *New York Post.* The *Voice,* he often claimed, a paper that itself fed readers a steady diet of "sexual prurience and partisan political prattle," had no business criticizing Murdochian journalism—particularly when it, too, was often guilty of distortion and error.

Indeed, Murdoch had little time to spend on either *New York* or *The Village Voice.* His most pressing concern was the

---

* Not exactly. Felker walked away with a nearly million-dollar settlement, and he would remain a significant publishing presence in New York, often using his positions to continue his war against Murdoch. Most recently, he has served as editor of *Adweek,* an advertising industry journal.

Post, and once the Felker fight was behind him, he devoted practically all of his time and energy to it.

Murdoch's formal takeover of the *Post* had created considerable anxiety among its top editorial and writing staff. At that time, he had been reassuring, announcing that he intended few personnel changes and hoped only to tighten the paper's belt to stem its losses. But soon he changed his tune. In an interview he gave to *The Village Voice*'s Alexander Cockburn, he trotted out his usual criticisms of American journalism and aimed them directly at the *Post.* American reporters "can't even bloody write," he said. "Importing English sub-editors is dangerous, but I wish to God the Americans would learn the techniques of English subbing." The *Post* itself was "not very well written and they go on too long. There's no subbing. There's no one writing headlines down there."

The first thing Murdoch did was to start "importing English sub-editors," by which he meant editors expert in Murdochian-formula journalism. Among the first to arrive was Peter Michelmore, actually an Australian who most recently had worked on the two-year-old *Star.* Murdoch instructed Michelmore to "make suggestions" to the *Post*'s longtime executive editor, Paul Sann, on how to enliven the paper's front page.

Sann, along with James Wechsler, had dominated the *Post*'s editorial staff for years. Both were serious newsmen and zealous protectors of the paper's liberal tradition and tabloid dignity, a combination most New Yorkers were bored with by then. Both were also keenly aware of Murdoch's reputation and, nearing retirement age, had steeled themselves to being pushed aside once "Murdoch got up to speed at the paper," as Wechsler said. They thought that might take a few months, possibly even a year. But they didn't know their new boss. Murdoch operated in time frames of days and weeks, not months and years.

The initial indication of this came from Peter Michelmore. One of the major national news stories during the weeks following Murdoch's takeover was the execution of mass murderer Gary Gilmore in a Utah prison. There were two news angles to the story. One was the fact that Gilmore was the first convict to be put to death in almost a decade, thereby inflaming the long-standing controversy over capital punishment in America. The other derived from the fact that Gilmore had for some time been demanding his own death, a peculiarity that endowed him with an extra dollop of fascination, at least in the view of the news media.

The night before Gilmore's January execution, a band of opponents of capital punishment mounted a vigil outside the prison. The event—singing, chanting, a few shouts—was covered by national television and proved altogether peaceful. The next morning's reports from the army of print reporters on the scene confirmed that fact, including the wire service dispatch that arrived at the *Post*. But Michelmore was not content with the facts. Under orders from Murdoch to start "punching up" the paper's front page, he wrote a headline for that afternoon's first edition that portrayed the Utah protesters as having "stormed" the prison in their anguish and having been brutally repelled by the authorities.

When Paul Sann saw the headline he ordered it changed and then angrily confronted Michelmore. The Australian defended it by saying that he was simply trying, per Murdoch's instructions, to "juice up" the front-page treatment of an important story, a story that had considerably more importance than the mere event of Gilmore's death. Sann knew better, though, and the realization confirmed that his days at the *Post* were numbered.

Read All About It!

"For many years," Rupert Murdoch said to a New York advertising group soon after taking over the *Post,* "the story of newspapering in New York was one of constant erosion, failure, defeat. To be successful today, newspapers must grab the reader with the right headlines, with the very first paragraph, or not grab him at all. . . . What major city newspapers are coping with these days is a generation weaned on television. We have got to win back readers who do not have the daily newspaper habit. Our entire editorial thrust at the *Post* will be to provide New Yorkers with brighter, shorter, more clearly understood stories and to marry the words with better and sharper pictures, better quality printing, and more appealing design."

Such was Murdoch's declared prescription for the ailing *Post.* Despite its implied insult to the intelligence of many New Yorkers, it seemed a valid attempt at a cure. What Murdoch really appeared to be saying was that he was going to reform the *Post*'s character and personality to turn the paper into an afternoon version of the best-selling morning *Daily News*—"saucy, irreverent, graphic and fun," as one *News* editor described his own paper at the time, yet journalistically reliable. The *News* had a daily paid circulation of nearly two million, while the *Post*'s had dropped below the 500,000 mark by the start of 1977. The *News* had attained its decades-long popularity through the very newspapering methods Murdoch seemed to be espousing, and clearly he wanted to gain a large part of that market for the *Post.* Thus, most New Yorkers were prepared for a "new" *Post* early in 1977, one that would be an afternoon manifestation of the brassy but respected *Daily News.*

Most New Yorkers were unaware of Murdoch's history, however. To remake the *Post* into an afternoon-evening version of the *News* was not enough, he knew. Market studies showed that the majority of people in the city preferred to get their morning news from the papers, their news at night from television. If Murdoch's ambitions were to bear fruit, he would have to go into direct competition with the *News* by printing the *Post*'s first edition early in the morning instead of in the afternoon. This became his opening gambit, and although it would require some time to implement because of its labor and distribution complications, he would eventually manage to put it into operation.

The second component of Murdoch's plan was to redesign the physical appearance of the paper within its tabloid format. Here he followed his usual practice, resorting to what has come to be known as the Murdochian "circus layout" and adding a strip of red color to the otherwise black-and-white front page to give the paper a new visual trademark. In conjunction with that, he mandated a much larger sports section than the old *Post* contained, with a heavy emphasis on horse racing, and a lot more news pages given over to *National Star*–style celebrity gossip and advice columns, many of them tinged with the occult.

The third and most vital component of Murdoch's strategy was simply to out-sensationalize the moderately sensationalist *Daily News*. Of late, the mildly right-wing *News* had been on a campaign to upgrade its journalistic image. While retaining its trenchant blue-collar personality, it had spent the recent years trying to improve its "character," devoting more space to national and international concerns—much as London's *Daily Mirror* did in 1968 when Murdoch took over the *Sun*—and examining the volatile issues of the day with more depth and seriousness than it had ever done before. The effort, however, had to some degree been responsible for a gradual erosion in the paper's circulation during the period. And it was further proof to Murdoch that the *News* was vulnerable to a circulation war based on a revival of the very sex-crime-and-scandal journalism and simplistic editorializing that the *News* had begun to soft-pedal.

In this last regard, a few years after Murdoch took over the *Post,* the well known "diet-doctor" Herman Tarnower was murdered by his mistress, the upper-crust prep-school headmistress Jean Harris. Tarnower's fame derived from his authorship of a best-selling diet book, and the *Post* covered the event with what by then had become its usual feverish and exaggerated exploitation of death and scandal. So bizarre had some of the paper's advice and "how-to" feature pages become by then that one enterprising Australian member of the editorial staff sent an earnest memo to Murdoch's office that read in part:

> Suggest we immediately capitalize on the Tarnower murder by paraphrasing a series of excerpts from his *Scarsdale Diet* book and working them into a series of columns which we could call "Dr. Tarnower's Diet Tips From The Grave."

Although the idea was not pursued, it was symptomatic of the journalistic wackiness that had infested the paper.

Time was of the essence, though, and Murdoch felt he had no time to "reorient" the large staff of local editors and reporters he'd inherited from Dorothy Schiff. Moreover, Paul Sann's stubbornly principled reaction to Peter Michelmore's Gilmore-execution headline left no doubt in Murdoch's mind of what he already suspected—that the incumbent editorial staff would resist his every move.

To replace Sann as top editor, Murdoch recruited Edwin Bolwell, a chunky, boyish-faced, forty-four-year-old Australian who'd had extensive experience on tabloids in Australia and Canada before ending up in New York as a journalist, first at *The New York Times* and then at *Time* magazine. Murdoch figured that Bolwell's recent "legitimate" background would stand him in good stead at the *Post,* while his eagerness to run a major American paper would compel him to follow unquestioningly Murdoch's directives for the revamping of the *Post.*

The pugnacious Bolwell was a disaster from the start, however, from everyone's point of view. According to several *Post* veterans, he took over the *Post* newsroom in the manner of a military commander occupying the homeland of a defeated enemy, issuing an endless stream of "do-it-my-way-or-else" orders and acting, says one, "like some tin-horn banana-republic dictator on speed." At the same time, Bolwell proceeded with increasing frequency to ignore Murdoch's suggestions, on the ground that once having appointed him, Murdoch was obliged to leave him alone and not interfere.

That was not quite what Murdoch had in mind when he chose Bolwell for the job in January. As the spring of 1977 progressed, he began to have second thoughts about the wisdom of his choice. By June, Bolwell was gone.

At the time, Murdoch bitterly described Bolwell's departure to me as "a noble experiment that failed." What he meant was that he had endeavored to show New York, and particularly the staff of the *Post*, that he'd been willing to entrust the paper to an independent editor with good journalistic credentials (*The New York Times, Time* magazine) so that he could not be accused of setting out from the start to turn it into another typical Murdoch tabloid. But with the departure of Bolwell, he no longer had to be so cautious. He could take credit for having endeavored to apply reasonable journalistic standards to the new *Post*. He could blame the *Post*'s veteran staff for refusing to accept Bolwell. And he could then proceed with the task of putting his own indelible stamp on the paper without further ado.

The time could not have been more favorable for the likelihood of success, for the summer and fall of 1977 were about to become one of the most newsworthy periods in recent New York history. It started with the "Son of Sam" multiple-murder case, a story that the *Daily News* had been the first to develop. It continued with a series of Puerto Rican nationalist bombings, then a July heat wave, then a power blackout followed by an outbreak of looting in several black slums, then a crowded, bitterly contested mayoral election—all occurring in a New York that had stumbled to the edge of bankruptcy two years before and was being governed by a board of financial controllers created by the state.

Having named himself the *Post*'s editor-in-chief as well as its publisher, Murdoch proceeded to act the former role fully. There would be no further trusting of outsiders to put out the paper, he declared. The first thing he did was to gather round him a group of his own fiercely loyal, tabloid-experienced editors and writer-reporters, many of them straight from the *National Star,* to help him run the *Post* in the manner he dictated. He appointed Bruce Rothwell as his overall deputy and would soon put him in charge of the *Post*'s editorial pages. He brought in Roger Wood, an English newspaperman who had recently been editing the *National Star,* as the *Post*'s new executive editor. Peter Michelmore became metropolitan editor. Another ambitious young Australian named Steve Dunleavy, a favorite of Murdoch's at the *Star,* led the influx of foreign writer-reporters with whom Murdoch fleshed out his new staff. Suddenly the *Post* masthead had almost nothing but British and Australian names on it.

Murdoch's second order of business was to decree that the *Post* would go immediately into head-to-head competition with the *Daily News*. The *News* had been making much of the case of the ".44 Caliber Killer," a description that derived from the gun used in a series of unsolved ambush-murders by an apparently deranged gunman during the previous months. The *Post* had given the case only cursory coverage prior to July. By then, the unknown killer was being called "Son of Sam," based on a letter he had written to the *News*. Murdoch decided that the exploitation of such a crime story was just what the *Post* needed to challenge the *News*. "It was all we had at the time," he told me.

And so the exploitation began. Soon the *Post* was outdoing its new rival with increasingly bizarre "Son of Sam" headlines and stories, many of the headlines written by Murdoch himself, many of the stories totally fabricated. Soon *Post* circulation began to rise, proving to Murdoch that New York was more than ready for his type of daily journalism. Late in July, after the final murder, the *Post*'s front page screamed: "No One Is Safe from the Son of Sam!" Early in August, on a day when "Sam news" was particularly thin, the *Post* published a garishly bannered story, written in what had become its trademark London *Sun–National Star* style and attributed to Mafia sources, that claimed that New York's major crime families were out hunting for the still-at-large killer. The story was pure fantasy, as Murdoch told me with a laugh a few days later.

The *Daily News* struggled to keep up, matching the *Post* headline for headline and abandoning all its previous efforts at dignity. By the time the killer was arrested in the second week of August, the hysteria created by the two papers was at a fever pitch. The *Post* announced the arrest with a simple, huge "Caught!" emblazoned across its front page. The fact that the man arrested—a twenty-four-year-old post office worker named David Berkowitz—was for legal purposes nothing more than the "accused" at the time was ignored. As far as the *Post* was concerned, Berkowitz *was* the killer.

Berkowitz's capture provided the excuse for a further round of fake sensationalism by the *Post*. Soon after, the paper appeared with the front-page headline: "How I Became a Mass Killer." The headline attributed the statement to Berkowitz, gave the impression that he had made it directly to the *Post,* and suggested that the story beneath it would be some sort of confession of guilt.

It was a favorite Murdoch technique. What the headline referred to was nothing more than a collection of old letters Berkowitz had written to a girlfriend when he was in the Marine Corps, a collection the ex-girlfriend had sold to the *Post* when she learned of Berkowitz's arrest.

Ultimately more costly for the *Post* was the payment of a bribe, through a freelance photographer, to a jail guard for access to Berkowitz's cell. At a later criminal trial on the matter, the photographer testified that he had been given a "spy" camera and a large sum of money by one of Murdoch's top aides. Part of the money, the photographer claimed, was intended for the guard. When Murdoch himself testified, he disclaimed any personal knowledge of the transaction. The *Post* and its hierarchy eventually escaped prosecution. A curious sidebar to the whole affair, however, was a report of an allegation made by an investigator employed by the New York State Special Prosecutor's Office that he had been ordered by a superior "not to actively seek" evidence linking Murdoch and the *Post* to the bribery scheme. The claim was never pursued in court.

The *Post*'s performance in the "Son of Sam" case was New York's full-scale introduction to Murdochian journalism, and it was followed in short order by equally misleading and distorted coverage of that summer's heat-wave blackout and looting. "24 Hours of Terror," blared the paper's front page after electricity was restored and the *Post* was able to print.

Two months earlier, Murdoch had given a speech to a group of Rotary Club members in which he voiced anxiety over "a divided New York" and added: "The racial discord in the city is aggravated by demagogues playing cynical and political games. . . ." There was no doubt that the looting and vandalism that occurred during and after the blackout were eminently newsworthy events. But they were confined mostly to a few poor, largely black neighborhoods and bore little resemblance to the citywide "24 Hours of Terror" portrayed in the *Post.* The paper's reaction seemed motivated mostly by the fact that the violence in Harlem had spilled southward into Manhattan's Upper East Side, where Murdoch and many of his top deputies were living. The *Post*'s coverage made it appear that a horde of rampaging blacks had descended on that traditional enclave of white wealth and power and that the deep-seated racial fears of countless white New Yorkers were about to be realized.

Who was kidding whom? Out of one side of his mouth Murdoch decried the city's long-standing racial discord and the cynical demagogues who regularly aggravated it. But at the same time he made it clear that he depended on such discord to trigger the kind of events he could then exploit—again—to "enliven" his front pages and sell newspapers. Not only that, but by sensationalizing such events, Murdoch exacerbated the city's racial tension. Who was the cynic? many asked; who was the real demagogue?

As with the "Son of Sam" case, Murdoch was fully in charge of the *Post*'s hysteria-laden coverage of the blackout and its aftermath. City officials spoke out angrily at the falsities, distortions, and racial stereotypes printed by the paper during the brief paroxysm, and many accused the *Post* of fostering it. Mayor Abraham Beame, who was in the midst of a reelection campaign, called Murdoch an "Australian carpetbagger" and accused him of slanting the *Post*'s coverage of the blackout to embarrass him in the forthcoming primary. Osborn Elliott, formerly the editor of *Newsweek* and a deputy mayor, and then the dean of the Columbia University journalism school, added to the critical din with a public letter that began: "Dear Rupert: So your *New York Post* has now covered New York City's first big crisis since you took over. Are you proud of what your headlines produced?"

Murdoch lashed back with his own heated replies. With respect to "Son of Sam," he told *More* magazine, a journalism review, that the *Post*'s treatment had "encouraged the police to get off their tails and go catch him," a claim the police department immediately refuted. He took the blame for the "How I Became a Mass Murderer" headline, admitted it was inaccurate and wrong, but sloughed it off by saying, "When you get in there at 3 o'clock or 5 o'clock in the morning, you've got five minutes to make an edition, and you're trying to choose between two headlines, it's easy to make a mistake."

What he didn't say was that the early morning newsroom frenzy he alluded to was entirely of his own making, brought about by the pressures he had exerted on his new editorial staff to produce more saleable stories than the *Daily News* was coming up with. And implicit in his excuse was the inference that it was permissible to publish deliberate falsehoods so long as it was done under the pressure of deadlines. Murdoch didn't realize it, but he was actually giving himself and his newspaper methods away.

He did so in other ways, too. August 29, 1977, was a slow news day in New York. The *Post*'s lead front-page story, suitably headlined, was about an apparent attempt in Memphis, Tennessee, by a bunch of crackpots to rob Elvis Presley's grave. When asked by *More* why that particular story dominated the *Post*'s news reportage for the day, Murdoch replied, "You've got to put something on page one. . . . That week we had Presley on the cover of the *Star*. The sales went up one million copies. Call it what you like—call it rubbish, I don't care. . . ." In other words, on a day when there's no earth-shaking news, pluck some obscure note off the wires from Memphis, blow it up all out of proportion with a sensational headline and mawkish *Star*-style rewrite, and splash it all over the front page—solely because "Elvis sells papers."

Murdoch's cynicism, and his belief that he had the right to use his news pages to manipulate public opinion, knew no bounds. A few days before the *Post*'s Presley edition appeared, on another slow news day, the paper's front page headline read: "Alice Crimmins: 5–20 Years."

The story of the beautiful, adulterous Alice Crimmins was well known in New York. In 1971, after a series of highly publicized trials, she was convicted for the 1965 murder of one of her children. She was assumed to have been responsible for the slaying of her second child as well. Following her conviction, she was sentenced to serve five to twenty years in prison. Now, in the summer of 1977, she was in a prison work-release program and was due to be paroled on September 1. That her forthcoming parole was a legitimate news story—even a front-page story—could not be argued. But the way it appeared in the *Post* had little to do with journalistic legitimacy.

First of all, Murdoch himself wrote the headline. It was an eye-catcher, to be sure. But it was entirely misleading, since it gave the distinct impression that Crimmins had just been sentenced, or re-sentenced, to serve another long stretch in prison.

The accompanying story was blatantly slanted to paint Crimmins in a bad light and rearouse a negative public reaction to her. Such would have been perfectly acceptable in an editorial, or in one or more of the paper's opinion columns. But this was a front-page news story. No doubt many New Yorkers continued to harbor hostile feelings toward Crimmins—I know I did. Murdoch's treatment, however, had the curious effect of evoking a certain amount of sympathy for her. After all, she had paid the legal debt that society—the people—had mandated, and she wasn't breaking any law by her conduct in the work-release program. The news of her forthcoming parole was certainly sufficient reason for her reexposure to the public limelight. But did she deserve to be pilloried on the front page in the fashion Murdoch had decreed?

When queried about it, Murdoch made it clear that his purpose in printing his headline and story was indeed to pillory her. He did it, he said, "Because I think any woman who murders her kids is a poor woman." So, although Crimmins had served her time, and the law had said, in effect, "Debt Paid," Murdoch was not going to let her escape so easily. He contended to me that the law had been too soft on Crimmins, that "she should have been locked up for life." He indicated that since the law had failed in the Crimmins case, it was up to him to use the *Post* to inflict the appropriate additional punishment on Alice Crimmins through a "different kind of law"—the "law" as it was codified in a newspaper publisher's mind.*

Murdoch was not just intent on using the *Post*'s news pages to punish those he held in disfavor, however. He also made it abundantly clear that he intended to employ them to give aid and succor to those he favored. Evidence of that surfaced most compellingly with the start of the 1977 New York mayoral race.

The political infrastructure of New York City had long been dominated by a labyrinthine web of informal alliances among various interest groups in the city's business, legal, property, and labor sectors, most of it strung together under the mantle of the Democratic Party. Like any big-city system of governance, the mechanism was controlled by personalities and power blocs, pro-

---

* Although Murdoch often claims to be against the death penalty, he is an avid proponent of stiff criminal punishment and is very much in favor of mandatory life sentences for all convicted murderers and other perpetrators of extreme violence. As for his stand against capital punishment, one can never be sure if it is motivated by the usual religious or humanitarian concerns, although he insists that it is. He once told me in deadly earnest, after a few drinks, that "electrocution is a waste of good electricity. The real answer is to kill them all before they have a chance to kill others."

pelled by the fuel of political ambition and favor. It was as crooked as it was honest, as devious as it was straightforward, as wasteful as it was efficient. To a foreigner, even one experienced in the urban politics of his own democratic country, its operation was a mystery.

Soon after his arrival in New York, Rupert Murdoch set out to penetrate the mystery. By 1976, he had mastered, if not the mechanism itself, at least a knowledge of the individuals and groups, public and private, that constituted its vital parts and the many ways in which they interacted in their ongoing dominion over the city. And by the time he acquired the *Post,* he could count himself as being among them.

Murdoch's acquisition of the *Post* turned him automatically into a major player at the volatile checkerboard of New York politics. It also came at a time when his personal sea change to political conservatism had hardened into dogma, and the fiscal framework of the city was for all practical purposes bankrupt. It did not take him long to put two and two together and conclude, as many others already had, that the labor unions that had long exercised a kind of despotic control over the city's vast municipal work-support system were primarily responsible for its financial woes.

But, he also realized, the unions would not have been able to wreck the city had it not been for the complicity of a series of weak-willed mayors—including the 1976 incumbent, Abe Beame. Those mayors had allowed themselves to be coerced into bowing to the unions' wildly escalating demands during the previous two decades. Thus, as far as Murdoch was concerned, whoever was to be the next mayor had to be willing, and tough enough, to resist any further giveaways to the city's unionized work force. Abe Beame had already proved himself to be totally ineffective in that regard, and Murdoch had written him off at the start of 1977.

For Beame to be reelected, he would first have to win the September Democratic Party primary election against several other well-known candidates. Among them were Bella Abzug, the ultra-liberal feminist congresswoman from Manhattan; Herman Badillo, a Puerto Rico–born congressman from the Bronx; Percy Sutton, the black Manhattan Borough President; Mario Cuomo, a Queens lawyer who had run unsuccessfully for the state's lieutenant governorship three years before; and Edward Koch, another Democratic congressman from Manhattan. A woman, a Puerto Rican, a black, an Italian, three Jews, two Catholics—the primary arena was a typical cross section of ethnic aspiration in 1970s New York; it lacked only an Irish name to make it complete.

Murdoch could not abide the stentorian Abzug. Nor could he tolerate the idea of a black mayor. So Abzug and Sutton were quickly dismissed from his endorsement consideration. Beame, of course, had been dispelled earlier. That left Badillo, Cuomo, and Koch.

Murdoch met with each. Early in the campaign, he seemed to lean toward Cuomo, a man who bore a physical resemblance to him. As the primary race intensified during the summer of 1977, however, he changed his mind. Murdoch later explained it publicly by saying that "Cuomo was coming across as a man who couldn't make up his mind on things." But the explanation hid the fact that he had begun to dislike Cuomo, as much for what he saw as his sanctimonious personality as for his refusal to take political advice from Murdoch. (Five years later, when Cuomo ran for governor, Murdoch would grow almost apoplectic in private at the mere mention of the prospect of his winning.)

It therefore came down to Badillo and Koch in Murdoch's mind. For a time he flirted with the idea of Badillo. But then his expanding circle of Jewish friends and advisers persuaded him to back Koch, even though Badillo was married to a Jewish woman and Koch was rumored to be a homosexual. Koch, with a relatively undistinguished record in Congress and not a great deal of mainstream Democratic Party support, had entered the race as a distinct underdog. Moreover, along with his petty-minded ego, he was possessed of a generally unattractive public personality. Yet to New York's "white shoe" Jewish establishment he was far preferable to Cuomo or Badillo. Furthermore, he yearned so passionately for the job that, if backed and elected, he could be trusted to follow the more conservative dogma that was then emerging within the city's Democratic Party and among its Jewish rank and file.

With his decision in August to back Koch, several weeks before the Democratic primary, Murdoch ran a front-page editorial in the *Post* enthusiastically endorsing him over the other candidates. That was a journalistically acceptable procedure, certainly, although most such endorsements are usually not made so far in advance of an election. It was what ensued that once again revealed Murdoch's manipulative streak. During the following weeks, the paper's news pages became increasingly—through headline, story lineage, story placement, and story tone—a forum in which Koch was subtly and subliminally championed and his opponents disparaged.

The practice continued well into the fall, while Koch, having won the September primary, campaigned toward the general November election that would determine the city's next mayor.

Soon, in a repeat of the *Australian* uprising of two years before, more than fifty of the *Post*'s reportorial staff, most of them leftovers from the Schiff-Sann-Wechsler regime, solemnly dispatched a group letter to Murdoch protesting the one-sided coverage. His answer was the same as earlier: he invited anyone at the paper who questioned his integrity to leave. Few took him up on the invitation. Once and for all, Murdoch's authority was solidly established.

And it was established not just at the *Post*. Koch won the November election and was inaugurated as the new Mayor of New York at the start of 1978. Murdoch boasted of having elected him, and Koch was quick to agree. Although the crusty Koch liked to crow about his independence, much of his mayoralty since then has been conducted in accordance with the Murdoch worldview. If Koch has been the official Mayor of New York since 1978, it can fairly be said that Murdoch (then still an Australian citizen) has been one of its chief unofficial mayors. According to what Murdoch has told me on more than one occasion, since becoming mayor, Koch has seldom made a move of any consequence in New York without consulting him. The way Murdoch says it, "consulting" means "requesting permission."

"Just for a Handful of Silver . . ."

Protest against Murdoch's transformation of the *Post* during the summer and fall of 1977 was widespread in New York. But in the end it was feeble and ineffective, as he predicted it would be. The paper's rising circulation demonstrated that there were plenty of New Yorkers who enjoyed his brand of "shock-and-schlock" journalism, and he was sure that many of "those elitists who seem to be making a career of blasting me" were buying the paper, if only to give themselves "a chance to further cluck their tongues."

At the start of 1978, with the new *Post* established and daily circulation revenues on the rise, the time had come for Murdoch to begin applying the flip side of his newspaper formula, which addressed itself to a sharp reduction in the costs of producing the paper. In addition to his constant criticisms about the "pitiable" quality of American journalism, Murdoch had often sounded off about the unproductive bloatedness of the country's major news-paper organizations. From the moment he took over the *Post*, he regularly cursed what he saw as its own bloated journalistic staff, claiming that it was loaded with "dead wood" and insisting that he could "put out the paper with half the number of people." The only problem was that the majority of reporters and editors he wanted to get rid of were there under contracts protected by the Newspaper Guild, the journalists' union. To reduce the staff by the desired half would have required a vast mount of money in severance payments. Murdoch had already committed more than a million dollars to refurbishing the *Post*'s run-down plant and distribution facilities, so he decided to defer action on the matter of staff reductions until that chore was completed.

In February 1978, he made his move, announcing to the entire staff that financial requirements mandated a wholesale shrinkage of the paper's journalistic work force—reporters, editors, and clerical workers. He presented a list of 148 people who had to go, many of whom had signed the previous fall's protest letter objecting to the paper's 1977 election coverage. Although Murdoch realized he could not fire them outright due to their membership in the Newspaper Guild, he said that he was prepared to offer each a generous severance package. Of the 148 people listed, more than a hundred took up the offer and left by summer. Most of the rest were consigned to journalistic limbo at the paper, told that they had no chance to advance, until their contracts ran out. In the meantime, Murdoch imported a further handful of British and Australian reporters and editors to fill out his freshly streamlined staff.

Another component of the cost-cutting drive was a corresponding reduction in the *Post*'s blue-collar labor force—the typographers, printers, and others who worked in the physical production of the paper. Here, however, Murdoch had none of the autonomy he possessed when disposing of the journalists. As in England, he was at the mercy of a confederation of unions much more powerful and intimidating than the Newspaper Guild alone. What's more, the contract between the pressmen's union—representing the operators of the printing presses at all three New York newspapers—and each of the papers' managements was up for renewal. In preliminary negotiations, on the grounds that under the expiring contract they had been forced to employ many more press operators than they needed, the *Times* and *Daily News* had informed the union that they intended to hold out for a radical reduction in pressroom manpower requirements under any new contract. The pressmen's union, just as resolutely, had indicated that it would strike, taking the papers' other unions with it, if such was to be the case. If it made good on the threat, it would produce a replay of the 1962–63 strike that had nearly destroyed daily journalism in New York.

The *Post,* too, was overburdened with excess printing press operators and wasteful union make-work rules. Murdoch's hope of even beginning to reduce the paper's production force, then, was tied directly to hammering out a new contract with the pressmen's union. He could not do it unilaterally, however, since he had returned the *Post* to membership in the New York City Publishers Association the previous fall. (After the *Post*'s separate settlement with the unions during the 1962–63 strike, Dorothy Schiff had kept the paper out of the association.) Thus he was committed to joining the *Times* and the *Daily News* in pressing for the reduced-manpower contract they had pledged to hold out for.

The *Times* and *Daily News* had each appointed its own high-level corporate labor-relations specialist to represent it in joint negotiations with the pressmen's union. The *Times* representative was Walter Mattson, a tall, burly, taciturn man who had much expertise in the latest computerized printing technologies and was a veteran of the New York labor scene. Standing in for the *Daily News* was Joseph Barletta, a polite, soft-spoken lawyer who had been director of operations for the Chicago Tribune Company, the longtime corporate owner of the *News,* for many years and who had recently moved to New York to become the *News's* general manager. They, along with Murdoch, constituted the combined negotiating front of the publishers association, which—it was agreed among the three—would function as a union in its own right, a management union.

Their opposite number in the negotiations was William Kennedy, the gruff, stocky, fifty-six-year-old president of the pressmen's union, the formal name of which was New York Newspaper Printing Pressmen's Local Union No. 2. Kennedy had been a working printing press operator at various New York newspapers for twenty-five years and had been the union's president since 1966. In 1974, the New York typographers' union had entered into a new contract with the publishers association that many in local labor circles believed to have been a cowardly capitulation to management. Kennedy had been one of the severest critics of the pact, contending that it set a precedent that would be ruinous to hard-line labor solidarity in New York. Consequently, in 1978, he was determined in his refusal to repeat the mistake of the typesetters.

Preliminary talks between Kennedy, Mattson, and Barletta had been conducted throughout the spring of 1978 while Murdoch was diverted by his separate effort to reduce the *Post's* white-collar staff. By July, it was clear that there would be no agreement between the pressmen and the newspapers. On July 18, Murdoch met with Barletta and Mattson over dinner at a popular New York restaurant, Christ Cella. There, according to Murdoch, they reached an agreement to maintain their initial hard-line demands for sharply reduced manning-and-work rules under the proposed new contract, even if it meant enduring a strike. There could be no individual wavering in their common front, Murdoch insisted, no matter how long a strike might last. He says that Mattson and Barletta concurred fully, and that the three of them decided to give Kennedy a deadline of three weeks to conclude a new contract with the newspapers. If the union didn't meet the deadline, and with the old contract having expired, the papers would immediately begin on their own to make the desired personnel reductions in their printing plants, in effect daring the union to call a strike and thus close down the three papers.

Barletta and Mattson each disagree with Murdoch's version of their dinner accord, Barletta calling it a "fiction." He adds, "We agreed it was not wise to freeze ourselves in concrete." This was significant because later, once a strike was underway, Murdoch would suddenly abandon the management troika and make a separate settlement with the union, thereby getting the *Post* back in print well before the *Times* and *Daily News*. His rationale would be that he was double-crossed by Barletta and Mattson.

But before that happened, the strike began—on August 9, 1978. With their papers shut down, Murdoch, Barletta, and Mattson remained publicly unified. And Murdoch, on the theory that he was the most experienced of the three in dealing with television cameras, became the spokesman for the publishers during the intensive video coverage of the strike negotiations.

Privately, though, they grew less unified, primarily because Murdoch suspected that Mattson, whose enigmatic, closemouthed personality he didn't like, was operating under a secret agenda dictated by his bosses at the *Times*. Murdoch knew that he was held in contempt by the *Times* senior executives, mainly for the kind of journalism he'd brought to the *Post,* and he began to believe that Mattson had agreed to his ultra–hard-line strategy only in the expectation that a prolonged strike would force him to shut down the *Post* for good. Once that happened, Murdoch imagined, the *Times* would proceed immediately to settle with the union on much less stringent terms than it appeared to be demanding and would be in a position to boast of having driven the alleged evil of Murdochian journalism out of the city. He imagined further that Barletta and the *Daily News* were covert participants in the scheme, if for no other reason than the *News*'s desire to see the *Post* wiped out as a competitor.

Murdoch's suspicions were fueled by none other than William Kennedy. At a private meeting with Kennedy at Murdoch's office on New York's midtown Third Avenue, Kennedy warned the *Post* owner that "the other publishers are going to do a number on you." According to Kennedy's later account, Murdoch seemed already alert to that possibility.

His suspicions were heightened on August 18, when he had a second meeting with Barletta and Mattson over another meal at Christ Cella. The strike was entering its second week. According to Murdoch, Mattson was beginning to waffle about the agreement Murdoch believed the three had reached at their July dinner. A week later, on August 24, he became convinced the *Times* was playing a double game when Mattson proposed a new offer to the pressmen that constituted a radical softening of their original demands on manning-and-work rules.

At the time, in addition to my relationship with Murdoch, I had a social acquaintance with Arthur "Punch" Sulzberger, the owner and publisher of *The New York Times,* and others at the paper. As well, although I knew no one in the top management of the *Daily News,* I was well acquainted with a pair of partners in the *News*'s principal New York law firm. As a result of that connective circuit, I became a kind of independent junction box for the often conflicting currents of opinion and strategy advanced by the three principals on the newspaper side of the strike. Had I been required to paint a picture of the underlying motives of each, as I gleaned them through various casual conversations, I would have been forced to resort to the surrealist's brush.

Each publisher seemed to be following his own secret agenda, much of it molded from motives that had little to do with the urgent labor issues at hand. As the business chief of the *Times,* the innately cautious Sulzberger for many years had suffered under the stigma of being the "boss's son" and had not been looked upon kindly by most of the paper's professional journalistic hierarchy. Murdoch saw the *Times*'s original hard-line position vis-à-vis the union, therefore, as "Punch Sulzberger trying to prove his manhood." High-placed executives of the *Daily News,* however, viewed him differently. To them, the weak, indecisive Sulzberger—"a man who's never had an original thought in his life," in the words of one—was simply "going along with his top management, as he's always done."

For his part, Sulzberger found Murdoch "charmingly repul-

sive," whereas most of his top aides at the *Times* perceived him—
as one put it a year later—as "a force for evil." The *Daily News*
view of Murdoch, as filtered through the voice of Barletta, was
more simplistic. To him, Murdoch was a "dirty street-fighter,"
and a "totally amoral man."

Given all the interpersonal contempt, it is no wonder that
the avowed unity of the three newspapers quickly unraveled.
Whether Mattson, representing the *Times* and in secret conjunction with the *News,* was really carrying out some devious plot
against Murdoch and the *Post* is debatable. In any case, both
Mattson and Barletta adamantly deny such a suggestion to this
day, as do Mattson's colleagues at the *Times.* What is not as debatable is the fact that Murdoch became increasingly convinced
of it, almost to the point of paranoia. Already a man with a powerful persecution complex stemming from the twenty-five years of
criticism that had been leveled at him and his work, and still
gripped by his outsider's insecurities, Murdoch's near-paranoia
repeatedly evinced itself in his descriptions to me of his strike
woes. "The *Times* and the *News* are out to get me," and "I not
only have to worry about the unions, but the *Times* and *News,* as
well," were just two of his frequent plaints.

Suspicion became certainty when the strike was a month old.
Although Kennedy and his pressmen had been the focus of the
dispute, all the other major newspaper unions had joined the
strike. Now, a month later, and despite the efforts of a federal
mediator, negotiations between the pressmen and the Murdoch-
Barletta-Mattson team were at a standstill. The Chicago Tribune
Company had hinted that it would consider a permanent shutdown of the *Daily News* if the strike was excessively prolonged.
Murdoch had dropped similar hints about the *Post.* The other
unions began to worry about the loss of thousands of jobs.
Through the New York City Allied Printing Trades Council, an
umbrella organization of union leaders, they called for a special
labor mediator in an attempt to speed up its resolution. The man
they recommended was Theodore Kheel.

Kheel was another of those New York attorneys who were
more than just lawyers. At sixty-four a senior partner in the law
firm of Battle Fowler Jaffin Pierce and Kheel, he was well known
around the city as a behind-the-scenes political power broker and
high-level problem-solver with an aggressive taste for the limelight and an often overweening pride in his own growing renown.

He had made his career in labor law as a specialist in collective bargaining, had been instrumental in the settlement of several major strikes in the past, was a longtime adviser to the Allied Printing Trades Council, and was on a friendly first-name basis with all of the city's print-union leaders. Kheel was intimately acquainted with most of the members of the Publishers Association as well, having been involved as a mediator or adviser in several prior disputes between the unions and the newspapers, including the 1962–63 strike.

Kheel and Murdoch had a curious, if brief, history. Kheel had been the main lawyer for Clay Felker and *New York* magazine, and a member of the magazine company's board, when Murdoch accomplished his unfriendly takeover at the start of 1977. In that context they had been adversaries, especially since, as Kheel says, "Murdoch had me immediately fired from the board and dismissed as the company's lawyer." Their unfriendliness had sharpened a short while later when Kheel presented Murdoch with a bill for his legal services to *New York* during the takeover—a bill Murdoch found "outrageously excessive" and refused to pay. Thereafter, though, the two settled their quarrel, and Murdoch even hired Kheel to work on a minor labor problem at the *Post*. At the time, Kheel employed as his special assistant a thrustingly ambitious young protégé named Martin Fischbein, a colleague he characterizes as "a fellow I was extremely fond of." Murdoch became fond of the disingenuously manipulative Fischbein, too, "and before I knew it," says Kheel, "Marty was leaving me to go to work for Rupert." Thus, when he was asked by the unions to become involved in the 1978 strike, Kheel had keenly ambivalent feelings about Murdoch.

There was no ambivalence on Murdoch's part about Kheel, however. After his few prior contacts with the labor lawyer, and having heard a series of damaging stories about him from the indiscreet Fischbein, Murdoch now saw Kheel as a clear-cut enemy. No matter how much objectivity Kheel claimed to exercise, by virtue of his long association with the Allied Printing Trades Council he was a union man. To Murdoch, the proof was in the pudding. He pointed to Kheel's mediatory involvement in previous strikes and threatened strikes in which settlements engineered by Kheel had resulted in great gains for the unions and costly setbacks for the publishers. When George McDonald, the head of the Allied Printing Trades Council, proposed Kheel's intervention in the stalled strike negotiations on September 8, 1978,

Murdoch protested to Barletta and Mattson on those grounds. Also, from what he'd heard from Fischbein, Kheel himself had engineered the unions' invitation because he couldn't stand being out of the spotlight. When Barletta and Mattson outvoted him in favor of Kheel's entry into the deadlock, it confirmed in Murdoch's mind that there was an evil conspiracy afoot to do him in.

On September 11, Kheel agreed to enter the dispute as "fact-finding adviser" to the Allied Printing Trades Council. "My job was to clarify the issues and make recommendations that would speed up a settlement," Kheel says. "I was not acting as a mediator, since there was already a federal mediator involved."

Murdoch thought otherwise. As the publishers' spokesman during the first four weeks of the strike, he had spent much time before the television cameras discrediting the unions and promoting the newspapers' hard-line position, which was mainly his position. Now the public spotlight had turned to Kheel, who was highly adept at conducting televised news conferences and one-on-one print interviews. In his usual smooth style, he managed to project himself as a clear-thinking savior. No one was listening to Murdoch anymore; they were all listening to Kheel. And even though he denied being a mediator, that was the public's perception of him, abetted by the television cameras, by the city's weekly magazines, by the temporary daily "strike newspapers" that were being published by independent entrepreneurs, and by the pontifical statements of Kheel himself. Murdoch now feared that Kheel would go beyond mediation to become a full-scale arbitrator of the dispute.

All of Murdoch's suspicions about a plot to wreck the *Post* came to a boil during the late afternoon of September 11, the day of Kheel's entry into the strike. Part of the earlier unification pact between Murdoch, Barletta, and Mattson had been their agreement not to talk individually to anyone outside their circle about matters relating to the strike. In other words, there were to be no unilateral discussions with the opposition or with the mediators. At about five in the afternoon of September 11, Murdoch tried to reach Mattson by phone in his office at the *Times* to talk about Kheel. He was told that Mattson had left for the day. When he asked where he could be reached, Murdoch was innocently told by a secretary that Mattson had mentioned something about stopping to visit with Theodore Kheel before catching a train for his suburban home.

Murdoch, infuriated, had Martin Fischbein call Kheel's Park

Avenue office to learn if it was true that Mattson was "secretly meeting with Kheel." Fischbein was told by the office's receptionist that Kheel had just gone up to the building's top-floor private dining club, called The Boardroom, to have a drink "with another gentleman."

Did she know who the other gentleman was? Fischbein asked the operator. The operator, who knew Fischbein from the days when he'd worked for Kheel, did not think twice about answering. "I believe it's Mr. Mattson from *The New York Times.*"

Mattson would later say—and Kheel would agree—that the purpose of the meeting was to talk only about labor matters relating specifically to the *Times,* and that the position of the Publishers Association in the strike was not discussed. But to Murdoch it was an act of treachery and betrayal on Mattson's part, a secret meeting doubtlessly convened to further the *Times-News* plot against him and the *Post.*

Thereafter, the relationship between Murdoch on the one hand, and Mattson and Barletta on the other, rapidly deteriorated, as did Murdoch's already antagonistic links with Kheel. As Kheel became more and more of a presence in the renewed but still-deadlocked strike negotiations, Murdoch stepped up his public objections to Kheel's role and drew into a thickening cocoon of incommunicativeness when dealing with Mattson and Barletta.

On September 27, an afternoon meeting was scheduled between the three newspaper representatives and Kennedy of the pressmen's union, along with Kheel and other members of the Allied Printing Trades Council, at the offices of the federal mediator in downtown Manhattan. The purpose of the get-together was for all sides to hear Kheel's proposals. Murdoch, however— counseled by Howard Squadron, who also disliked Kheel—had already concluded that Kheel and Mattson were conniving to impose a settlement formula on the three papers that would be far more lenient on the pressmen than the hard-line demands they had originally agreed on. "No more meetings," he said to Squadron. "It's time we went our own way."

What Murdoch was saying was that he had secretly decided to do the same thing Dorothy Schiff had done fifteen years earlier—bolt the Publishers Association and work out an immediate deal of his own with the pressmen's union. At a lunch with Barletta just prior to the September 27 meeting, he tried to persuade the *Daily News* representative that Mattson and the *Times* were playing a double game. Barletta, who was by then exasperated by Murdoch's "panicky paranoia that everyone was out to screw him," denied the *Post* owner's claim and defended Mattson and Kheel. That confirmed to Murdoch that Barletta was either blindly naive or in cahoots with Mattson against him.

It was the last straw, and as they left the restaurant to go to the meeting, the agitated Murdoch muttered something about having "reached the end of the line." Barletta wasn't sure what Murdoch meant, although he wondered if he was talking about shutting down the *Post* for good—something he'd been threatening to do with increasing frequency. When they arrived outside the federal mediator's office, Barletta was surprised to discover that Murdoch did not intend to go in. Howard Squadron was with them, and Barletta heard Murdoch say to Squadron, "You go in and toss the bomb, toss the bomb." Now Barletta was sure Murdoch intended to terminate the *Post,* and his heart "did a little dance." With the *Post* gone, the *Daily News* would have the New York tabloid field all to itself.

But Barletta, to his great disappointment and anger, would soon learn that Murdoch's intentions were just the opposite. Squadron took the floor at the Kheel conclave and informed everyone that Murdoch and the *Post* were that day withdrawing from the Publishers Association and would seek to negotiate separately with the pressmen. They hoped to make an immediate deal with the union so that the strike against the *Post* would end and the paper could start publishing again. Murdoch no longer cared what the other two papers did. Squadron invited Kennedy to meet with Murdoch that night.

The meeting took place. As a result, a little over a week later the *Post* was back in business, while the *Daily News* and the *Times* remained shut down. Not only that, but Murdoch announced that he would immediately launch a Sunday edition of the *Post* to fill the vacuum left by the absent Sunday *News* and Sunday *Times.* Murdoch's separate deal with the pressmen and the other unions was simply the promise that he would go along with whatever contracts the unions eventually worked out with the *Times* and the *News.* In the meantime, as the only major daily—and Sunday—paper available in New York, the *Post* would enjoy a windfall in advertising revenues.

"Monopoly is a terrible thing, till you have it," Murdoch

said. He added that he was planning to start a new morning paper, to be called the *Sun,* to fill the vacuum left by the *Daily News.*

Kheel's reaction was to circulate Xeroxed copies of the Robert Browning poem, "The Lost Leader," among the remaining *Times* and *Daily News* negotiators. The poem began: "Just for a handful of silver he left us."

During October, with the other papers still struck and the *Post* continuing to collect massive advertising revenues, it occurred to Murdoch—or so Kheel would later allege—that a prolongation of the strike against the *Times* and *Daily News* would be eminently desirable. "Murdoch saw that I was making headway toward a settlement," Kheel says. "He thought if he could discredit me with the unions, he might be able to bring about a breakdown in the negotiations and keep the strike going, all for the purpose of continuing the *Post*'s advertising bonanza."

How did Murdoch attempt this? A few months earlier, a New York freelance magazine writer named Richard Karp had written an article about Kheel on commission from Murdoch's *New York* magazine. The article, which would eventually be entitled "The Many Worlds of Ted Kheel," was a litany of sinister suggestion and innuendo about Kheel's private business dealings over the years. In addition, it accused Kheel of being a longtime "fixer" of the newspaper unions on behalf of the *Times* and *Daily News.* Karp wrote that Kheel had frequently used his position as a trusted labor mediator to favor the city's publishers at the expense of the unions, for which he was consistently paid off by the publishers with heaps of favorable publicity, plus protection against any journalistic investigations into his allegedly sordid, scandal-ridden personal business enterprises.

Kheel says that when he learned of the nature of Karp's article in August, about a month before he stepped into the newspaper strike, he called Martin Fischbein, who by then was working for Murdoch, to complain. As a consequence, publication of Karp's article was "killed" by Murdoch, evidently as a favor to Fischbein—although Joe Armstrong, *New York*'s Murdoch-appointed editor-in-chief and publisher, said at the time it was canceled for other reasons.

Whatever the case, early in October, according to Kheel, just after the *Post* was back in print, Murdoch ordered Armstrong to revive the article and publish it in *New York* as soon as possible.

The surprised Karp was summoned back from San Francisco, where he had gone to pursue other work, and was asked by Richard Berendt, the magazine's editor, to polish up the "killed" draft he'd handed in two months earlier.

With Kheel playing a pivotal role, the strike against the *Times* and *Daily News* finally came to an end on November 6, 1978. "By then," Kheel said to me, "it was too late for Murdoch to use Karp's story to attack me for the purpose of delaying the strike's settlement. So he took a different tack. With the *Times* and *News* back on the streets, his bonanza was over, and in fact he was forced to terminate the Sunday *Post* he'd started to capitalize on in the absence of the other two Sunday papers. I knew from Marty Fischbein* that Murdoch was feeling very vengeful toward me. So he ordered Armstrong to run Karp's story anyway."

The long article appeared in the January 8, 1979, issue of *New York,* with Kheel's picture on the magazine's cover under the headline, "The Survivor." The subhead read: "Theodore Kheel, labor mediator, seen as hero in local press. Good-guy role in newspaper, railroad, transit, and longshoremen strikes, played up. Links to $50-million bank swindle, $100-million stock fraud, etc., played down."

Kheel denied all the charges and later that year, after failing to produce a retraction, sued Murdoch, Karp, Armstrong, and *New York* for libel, claiming $8 million in damages. Under the current libel law, Kheel was a "public figure" and as such had almost no chance to succeed in his suit. Nevertheless, three years later, Murdoch, on behalf of himself, Armstrong, and *New York,* settled the case before it could reach trial. To Kheel, "The settlement was very satisfactory to me, although I am forbidden by its terms from revealing its details." Karp refused to join in the settlement, even though it would have cost him no money, on the grounds that to do so would have been an admission on his part that his article contained the many falsehoods alleged by Kheel.

Murdoch, too, refuses to reveal the details of the settlement. But since then, he has never been hesitant about betraying to me and others his continuing dislike for Kheel.

* Fischbein subsequently died in an automobile accident. After a dinner date with television journalist Jessica Savitch in 1983, he drove his rented car into a rural Pennsylvania canal, killing himself and her. According to Joe Armstrong, Fischbein was a principal source for Karp's article.

The article on Kheel was not the only time that a Murdoch publication published this type of story. Another example was the case of Pete Hamill, a well-known New York columnist who criticized the *Post*'s treatment of the Alice Crimmins parole story during the summer of 1977. When Murdoch complained about Hamill to Rinker Buck, a journalist interviewing him for an article in *More* magazine, Buck asked him if he'd called Hamill to protest.

"No," Murdoch said, "I retaliated. I ran little excerpts of a column he wrote about Jackie Kennedy years ago." The column Murdoch referred to was one in which Hamill had discussed Jacqueline Kennedy Onassis in harsh and unflattering terms. But in 1977, Hamill was engaged in a romance with the former First Lady. Following Hamill's attack on the *Post*'s Crimmins coverage, Murdoch ordered his old column dug up and excerpted in the *Post* to embarrass Hamill and perhaps ruin his relationship with Onassis.

"That was self-indulgent on my part," Murdoch told Buck, "but I don't apologize for it. People have got to learn."

Actually, the incident was an amusing bit of mischievous byplay on Murdoch's part and of no great consequence in itself. But the dark impulses that lurked behind it—"People have got to learn"—were disturbing.

Sprouting Wings

Much was made in the 1970s about Murdoch's talent for rescuing and reviving sickly newspapers. One must wonder about that. The month's monopoly he enjoyed in the New York daily market during the 1978 strike afforded him a splendid opportunity to re-revamp the *Post* in a way that might have enabled it to depose the *Daily News* as the city's best-selling paper. In that month, the *Post*, the only metropolitan paper available, saw its daily circulation rise to almost double that of the prestrike period. Over the nearly two years of Murdoch's stewardship, his cheapening of the paper had failed to increase circulation appreciably following its initial rise and had actually caused it to lose a significant amount of mainstream advertising revenue. From his point of view, by deserting his fellow publishers and settling early with the unions, he did everything right, since circulation and advertising income soared once the *Post* was back in print. But for all that, during its month-long monopoly, it remained its dreary downscale self, its appeal still deliberately pitched to the least-common-denominator segment of New York's collective intelligence.

Had Murdoch used the opportunity to upscale the paper during that period, even to elevate it no more than slightly above the level to which the *Daily News* had sunk prior to the strike in its endeavor to match the *Post*, it is quite possible that he would have kept much of the captive readership he gained, and over the next few years might have overtaken the *News* in circulation and ad revenues. That he didn't reflected negatively on his alleged genius. Once the *Daily News* resumed printing in November 1978, the *Post* quickly settled back into its prestrike financial doldrums.

Thereafter, Murdoch was forced to resort to increasingly

drastic and expensive measures to boost circulation. The one seemingly surefire way of doing it would have been to introduce a New York version of his London *Sun*'s Page Three—a daily full-page nude feature. The reason he didn't was due partly to the fact that his three children by Anna Murdoch were growing older and more impressionable. He was afraid they might suffer by association from the angry mass outburst such a departure from journalistic propriety would likely have produced. But it was due also to Anna Murdoch's own growing independence as a woman and her increasing objection—very much in tune with the times—to the commercial exploitation of women as sex objects. As she said to me and my wife at the time, "How can I teach the boys [her two sons, James and Lachlan, then in their early years at a leading New York private school] respect for women if every time they pass a newsstand they see some naked girl sprawled in their father's paper?"

With all her children in school and under the daily protection of an ex-London police sergeant recently hired as a live-in bodyguard, Anna Murdoch, by then in her mid-thirties and unhappily overweight, had returned to school herself on a part-time basis, taking courses—first at Fordham and then at New York University—toward a college degree in history and literature. As she increased her complaints to friends about her husband's frequent absences from New York, she also made it clear that she was no longer content to play the role of complaisant housewife but intended to forge a separate and serious career of her own in writing. The lack of confidence she suffered with respect to her literary ambitions in the late 1960s, fostered by Murdoch's curt dismissals of her efforts, was ameliorated somewhat by the more positive reactions of others who got to see recent samples of her work. As a result, she began to sketch the plot of a novel she had been germinating, a semiautobiographical family saga set in Australia. The international success of *The Thorn Birds*, the colorful Australian best-seller by Colleen McCullough, reinforced her resolve to produce a book of her own.

Anna was also growing exasperated by the stories that inevitably came back to her about the dozens of women who claimed to have known her husband well. Given Murdoch's wealth and his expanding notoriety in New York, there was no dearth of such tales. One such woman went so far as to install herself as a neighbor of the Murdochs near their upstate New York country estate in the late 1970s. She was a regular visitor to the Murdoch house while boasting to others of "my importance to Rupert." Anna Murdoch eventually put her foot down, her anger over the woman's almost daily presence in their lives exploding directly in front of me. The woman soon vanished from the scene.

But then, a year or two later, another woman appeared with a similar repertoire of claims. She was a fortyish divorcée whom I knew to be an aggressive celebrity groupie—a woman who spent much of her time and energy in pursuit of famous, powerful, and (usually) rich men. She made no secret of her purported closeness to Murdoch.

Whatever the case, beginning in 1978, Anna Murdoch's attitude toward her husband, even in public, underwent a marked change. Where before she had been a devoted and seemingly doting wife, she now became caustically critical of many aspects of Murdoch's character, often whispering clenched-teeth reprovals at him in the company of others, frequently patronizing him aloud with an "Oh, Rupert, don't be daft" when she took annoyed exception to something he said. The edges of her personality, theretofore blunted by her Grace Kelly serenity, suddenly grew sharp and serrated, and her eyes became regularly cold with contempt.

The tension between the Murdochs lasted for several years. Then it relaxed. By then I knew them well. Without saying it in so many words, Anna Murdoch indicated to me that she and Rupert had reached an accommodation, one of those *ententes cordiales* carved out by sophisticated people who have been married to one another long enough for their familiarity to spill into boredom, if not dislike. What could have become ugly and permanent marital discord between the Murdochs was nipped in the bud and transformed instead into a kind of polite deference to one another, although Rupert remained by far the more deferential.

It was largely because of Murdoch's need to get back in his wife's good graces, then, that the *New York Post* remained free of naked starlets and models. Instead, as circulation remained sluggish following the 1978 strike, and it appeared that no amount of further journalistic sleaziness would improve it, Murdoch, in 1981, introduced an entirely different strategy, a money lottery called "Wingo."

Along with its diet of daily nudes, the London *Sun*'s circulation triumph during the early 1970s had been based largely on its frequent promotional giveaways and contests. Graham King, the Murdoch organization's longtime promotional specialist, takes credit for most of them. "The idea was to always have something to advertise," King told me. "And to get women to buy the *Sun* as well as men. Research showed us that men would buy it for the daily Page Three nude and the sports. Women, on the other hand, responded more to the advertising carried in newspapers than to the editorial stuff. It didn't matter what kind of advertising, so long as it was aimed at the particular acquisitive interests of particular economic classes of women.

"Our market was the lower classes. And lower-class women like nothing better than the idea of being able to acquire something for nothing. So we invented giveaways and contests and advertised them heavily in the paper. One was where we gave away a bra-and-panties set packaged in a match box. Of course, to get their gift, women had to buy the paper. So they really weren't getting it for nothing—they were paying a few pence. But still, to them it was a bargain, and that's what counted.

"We ran those things constantly. Often we'd tie them into feature articles appearing in the paper. For instance, one week the paper ran a feature on the history of the bathroom. In conjunction with that we did a contest in which a set of bath towels was the prize.

"We went after the men with similar promotions. We had the usual stuff, like Page Three nude calendars, *Sun* T-shirts, that sort of thing. One male-oriented campaign that turned out to be a great circulation booster was when we ran a contest in which the prizes were ponies. We were going after the younger generation of working-class fathers there. We figured, what young father wouldn't be eager to win a pony for his kid?"

Murdoch and King had tried similar promotions in the *New York Post,* but their success in raising circulation during the first few years was only marginal. "There was a different psychology in New York about material things," King says. "With much more so readily available, even to the lower classes, the average New Yorker was pretty blasé about the possibility of winning a toaster or a weekend in the Poconos. So we had to up the ante."

The upped ante was Wingo, a daily newspaper numbers game that was a variation of the hoary game of bingo and one that Murdoch had already used successfully in London and Sydney. Printed cards containing a series of random numbers were mailed to millions of households in New York and its suburbs. The idea was for each recipient to buy five consecutive copies of the *Post* during each of the weeks that followed. If the numbers printed in the paper matched those on one's card, the cardholder could win a large cash prize.

Wingo seemed to be the answer. The *Post*'s daily circulation climbed rapidly toward the million mark, a fact the paper daily gloated over in print. Yet the increase did little to improve its profit-and-loss statement. In the first place, the expenses of launching and running Wingo—including its payoffs, which proved more sparse than the paper's promotions promised—were punishing. And the sharp increase in circulation still failed to lure major new advertisers. They feared that the greater number of people who were buying the *Post* were doing so only to check their Wingo results. As one prominent advertising man quipped, "Wingo has simply turned the *Post* into another OTB parlor." OTB stands for Off-Track Betting, a form of legalized gambling started in New York a few years earlier. The city's OTB parlors were notorious for their scruffy environments and clientele.

Wingo, then, rather than solving the *Post*'s financial problems, compounded them. By late 1981, four years after Murdoch acquired the paper, it was clear that that no matter what he did, it would continue to lose large amounts of money annually. But that was by then a secondary consideration. The *Post*'s losses remained useful in reducing taxes on the profits of his other American ventures—*New York, The Village Voice,* the *Star,* and his San Antonio papers—and were still easily coverable out of the huge profits of his British and Australian press operations. Because the *Post* served as the primary seat of his burgeoning influence in the United States, Murdoch resolved to keep it going.

The extent of that influence was demonstrated early in 1980. The year before, Murdoch had turned his attention back to Australia, where much corporate turmoil had erupted in that country's media establishment. Still a relatively small television proprietor with his Adelaide and Wollongong stations, Murdoch suddenly had an opportunity to take over Sydney's third major television outlet, Channel 10. It was an expensive opportunity but he seized it, compulsively attracted by the high advertising revenues Channel 10 enjoyed. Within weeks, with the help of a massive line of bank credit, and despite a fierce campaign of resistance mounted through the Australian Broadcasting Tribunal by the still vengeful Labor Party, Murdoch won control of the Sydney station. As a result, because of the Australian law limiting individual ownership of television stations to two, he was forced to sell Wollongong.

Murdoch then went after Melbourne's Channel 10, which was wholly owned by a company that also owned and operated one of Australia's two domestic airlines. The company was known formally as Ansett Transport Industries and was still presided over by its founder, the elderly Sir Reginald Ansett. It became clear early on that to get the station, Murdoch would have to gain control of Ansett in its entirety—the airline itself and its other subsidiaries. Since Ansett, a public company, was experiencing financial difficulties, several other wealthy Australian takeover entrepreneurs were already pursuing it.

Murdoch, who had recently added more than $50 million in surplus cash to News Limited's treasury through the sale of its Australian bauxite holdings, proposed a joint takeover plan to one of his main rivals, saying that he was interested only in having the Melbourne television station. When that failed to materialize, he sought out another prosperous partner, Thomas Nationwide Transport, which already owned 15 percent of Ansett. Thomas, built up and headed by Sir Peter Abeles, a postwar Hungarian immigrant to Australia, was more amenable to a joint takeover, and soon it was accomplished. By late 1979, Murdoch not only controlled two major Australian television stations, but was 50 percent owner of the country's second largest airline.

In addition, through a separate stock raid on the Melbourne *Herald* organization, he almost came away with his father's old company. Just prior to making the Ansett deal in the fall of 1979, Murdoch—some say out of his residual vindictiveness toward the *Herald* for the way it had treated him and his mother after Sir Keith's death twenty-five years before—decided to use some of his $50 million in bauxite earnings to put a scare into the still-powerful *Herald* organization. He started to accumulate *Herald* shares on the open market and then announced a tender offer for enough remaining publicly held stock to give him 51 percent ownership.

The entire takeover attempt lasted a mere two days. The *Herald* organization's management reacted in panic. Enlisting the aid of Murdoch's old Sydney enemy, the Fairfax newspaper company, it immediately began to buy its own shares, at a price in excess of that offered by Murdoch, in the hope of preventing him from getting the 51 percent majority he'd said he was after. By the end of the second day, the *Herald*-Fairfax alliance had spent more than $53 million—most of it borrowed—in public stock purchases to ward off Murdoch's attack. What it didn't know, however, was that at the start of the day, rather than going after additional stock of his own, Murdoch secretly started to sell the shares he'd accumulated, at the price being paid by the *Herald*-Fairfax group. Most of the stock bought by *Herald*-Fairfax, then, was Murdoch's, and the price he got was nearly $1.50 per share more than he'd paid for it. By the time the day was over, Murdoch, having unloaded his shares at a profit of more than three million dollars, proudly revealed his coup and announced that he was no longer interested in the *Herald* organization.

The *Herald*-Fairfax group tried to put the best public face on its humiliation. But a furious outcry came from other quarters—especially within the government—over the ethics and legal propriety of Murdoch's financial machinations. Since the time of his role in the ouster of Gough Whitlam as prime minister, Murdoch had seldom been in Australia. Although not forgotten, he had drifted into the nether regions of the Australian public's consciousness. Now here he was, back again four years later, roiling up greater turbulence than ever. Even the four-year-old conservative government of Malcolm Fraser—a government that in large measure owed its position to Murdoch and his newspapers—was hard put to excuse his actions.

Once his Melbourne *Herald* adventure was over and he'd gone on to acquire his half-ownership of Ansett, Murdoch was forced to undergo another round of hearings before the Australian Broadcasting Tribunal to obtain approval to operate Ansett's Melbourne television station. This time the opposition Labor Party, well-represented in the Tribunal, declared outright war on him and managed to block his clearance—partly on the grounds of his heavily partisan political history as a publisher, partly over questions about his business ethics, and partly because he was no longer a resident of Australia.

Murdoch fought back stormily, not least because he had put News Corporation, his brand-new public holding company, deeply in debt to acquire Sydney's Channel 10 and the half-share in Ansett. He had reorganized News Limited, his original Australian holding company, into a larger entity called News Corporation Ltd. to accommodate those major purchases. But in so doing, he had been forced to dilute marginally Cruden Investment's majority percentage in News Corporation—or "Newscorp," as the new holding company soon came to be called. Although he still had full control of the Newscorp board, which was made up mostly of his business cronies and personal friends in Australia, England, and America, because of his recent heavy borrowing he knew he would be increasingly subjected to the watchful eyes of his bankers.* To allow the Broadcasting Tribunal's decision to stand would be a signal to the banking community of a weakening of Murdoch's executive and entrepreneurial resolve and a dreadful public relations start for Newscorp.

Once again, Murdoch took on an incumbent Australian government and won. This time, rather than threatening to expose political wrongdoing through his papers, he simply reminded key members of the conservative cabinet and Parliament of their collective debt to him. A bill was passed quickly in Parliament amending the legislation that governed the criteria of the Broadcasting Tribunal in approving television licenses. The new, less restrictive standards enabled Murdoch to appeal the Tribunal's original decision denying him Melbourne's Channel 10, and his earlier rejection was overturned. With Melbourne and Sydney in his stable, Murdoch now possessed a much more profitable and powerful television network than he'd had with Wollongong and Adelaide. Together, the country's two largest metropolitan regions contained more than 70 percent of Australia's televiewing public and produced about 60 percent of its TV advertising reve-

---

* News Limited became a subsidiary Australian operating company of News Corporation, as did News International in England and News America in the United States, Murdoch's principal operating companies in those countries. Richard Searby, Murdoch's old schoolmate and his chief Australian lawyer, became chairman of the twelve-member board of Newscorp, as he had been of News Limited. Other directors included Lord Catto, Stanley Shuman, Donald Kummersfeld (a former deputy mayor of New York whom Murdoch had hired in 1977 to run News America), and several of Murdoch's top editors and financial aides. Cruden Investment's ownership of Newscorp shrunk from about 47 to 43 percent. One reason Murdoch borrowed so heavily from bank sources, rather than raise money through a public stock flotation, was because he didn't want to reduce Cruden's percentage any further. Newscorp, the parent Australian company, should not be confused with Newscorp Investments Ltd., a subsidiary Murdoch later formed in England.

nue. What's more, he was half-owner of a profitable major airline.

Ownership of Ansett provided the fodder for Murdoch's first direct exercise of political influence on a national scale in the United States. Ansett had an Australian government–owned counterpart in Trans Australian Airlines (TAA). The two were the country's principal domestic carriers, while Qantas, also government-owned, served the international market. Although they were competitors, Ansett and TAA usually made their new aircraft purchases under a joint arrangement to get reduced prices and favorable financing. When Murdoch took on Ansett late in 1979, he learned that it and TAA were each tentatively committed by option to purchasing new fleets of European-made wide-bodied passenger jets—the Airbus Industries' A-300. As a result of the combined Ansett-TAA commitment, Boeing, the American manufacturer of a soon-to-be-introduced competitor of the A-300, the twin-engined 767, would lose a major sale. Given his own commitment to expanding his operations in the United States, Murdoch decided that it would be politic to have Ansett reconsider the 767. If the airline could get a better price and financing deal from Boeing than it had been offered by the European consortium that made the A-300, he might abandon the Airbus and go with Boeing.

On his way back to New York from Sydney in January 1980, Murdoch traveled by way of Seattle, where Boeing was headquartered, to look into the prospect. The aircraft manufacturer's top management had been alerted to his visit by Boeing agents in Australia. When he arrived, they offered to supply Ansett with twelve 767s and thirteen smaller jets at a total price of $657 million. The figure was competitive with that of the Airbus consortium, and even though Boeing couldn't deliver as fast as Airbus, Murdoch conditionally agreed to forgo the A-300s in favor of the 767s. All that remained to be determined was whether the financing he could get for the Boeing planes would also be competitive. The proposed Airbus financing deal, a complex one involving several different national currencies, had been structured to require repayments over a ten-year period at an interest rate of just under 8 percent. Could the Americans match that? Better yet, could they improve on it, in view of the fact that Ansett would have to wait longer than its rival, Trans Australia, to get its planes?

The Boeing executives grimaced at the condition. Their main source of financing aircraft sales to foreign airlines was the Export-Import Bank, an agency of the U.S. government whose mission was to foster American exports by providing low-interest loans to overseas buyers of American products. Since Boeing sold many of its various passenger jets abroad, it had a long and close relationship with the Eximbank, as the agency was commonly called.

Boeing's treasurer, John Pierce, told Murdoch that the Eximbank was likely to oppose an interest rate of less than 8½ percent. On a loan of $657 million, Murdoch quickly calculated, the difference between 8½ and 8 percent would mean an additional three million dollars in annual interest payments. Over ten years, that thirty million dollars would almost equal the cost of another Boeing 767.

Surely the bank would go lower than 8½ to guarantee the sale of twelve American planes, Murdoch said to Pierce. Well, answered Pierce, they'd never know unless they tried. He reminded Murdoch that the Eximbank made its financing approvals more on the basis of the foreign buyer's persuasion than on that of the domestic seller's, for the buyer was the direct recipient of the government's credit. "If you're willing to argue for eight percent, we'll do everything in our power to help you," he promised.

"I'll not only get eight percent," Murdoch said. "I'll do better than that."

At the time of the Murdoch-Boeing meeting in Seattle, the national political campaigns leading to the November 1980 presidential election were just getting underway. There was no doubt in Murdoch's mind about what had to happen in the United States. The imperative was a sharp swing to the right, such as had occurred the year before in England with the election of Margaret Thatcher on a platform of economic reform designed to stem the tide of welfarism, reduce the costs of government, and stimulate free enterprise and employment. Murdoch had climbed on the Thatcher bandwagon early. He had used the *Sun* and *News of the World* to support her rise to power and by early 1980 could rightfully take some of the credit for it.

Economic and political impulses similar to those that propelled Thatcher into office had also been gathering force for several years in the United States. They were especially palpable within the right wing of the Republican Party and in the increasingly persuasive speeches of former California governor Ronald Reagan, its most visible spokesman. Reagan had entered the 1980 Republican presidential primary race. Murdoch quickly became convinced that Reagan could not only win the Republican nomination, but the Presidency itself, particularly in view of incumbent President Jimmy Carter's timid, weak-willed performance up to that point. From the very outset of Reagan's drive for the White House, then, Murdoch was firmly in his camp and had begun to gear the *New York Post* in his favor.

But there was also the question of who the Democratic candidate would be. A number of hopefuls had announced their intention to wrest the nomination from Carter, among them Jerry Brown of California, John Connolly of Texas, and Teddy Kennedy. A key event in the selection process would be the 1980 New York primary. Like every other newspaper in New York, the *Post* would be expected to endorse both a Republican and a Democrat as the specific candidate it preferred in the state's respective primaries.

Jimmy Carter's Administraton was in deep political trouble—trouble that would intensify as a result of the seizure of the American embassy in Iran and the President's failure to react in any dramatic, strong-armed way to the long hostage crisis that followed. The possibility that Carter would lose several key primaries, and thus fail to win renomination at that summer's Democratic convention, had become very real early in 1980. As the date of the New York primary approached, he badly needed press support, particularly in the Democratic stronghold of New York City. His New York campaign managers had been trying for months to gauge the intentions of the *Post,* traditionally a knee-jerk Democratic paper but, under Murdoch's three-year reign, clearly no longer so. Fresh from his initial Boeing agreement and faced with the task of trying to negotiate a favorable financing deal through the Eximbank, Murdoch put out word that he would have to meet with all the Democratic candidates—including the President—before deciding which one the *Post* would endorse.

At the time Murdoch posed his condition, he had been made aware that the president of the Eximbank, John Moore, was a longtime Georgia crony of Jimmy Carter's and had been appointed by Carter in 1977 to run the bank. Word came back from Washington early in February that Carter would be willing to meet with Murdoch over lunch at the White House on February 19, 1980, to discuss the New York primary election. That was only nine days before the date Murdoch, under Ansett's provisional contract with Airbus Industries, had to decide whether or not to proceed with the A-300. Since his decision hinged on the reaction of the Eximbank to his demand for a better financing deal than Airbus had offered, Boeing had already started to put pressure on John Moore to act fast and favorably on Murdoch's loan application. When John Pierce, Boeing's treasurer, learned that Murdoch would be in Washington on February 19 to lunch with President Carter, he called Moore and persuaded him to meet with Murdoch and himself that morning for a preliminary discussion of the Australian's financing needs.

The meeting took place at the Eximbank offices at 11:15 in the morning of the nineteenth. Murdoch quickly put his demands to Moore and informed him that he had only nine days to wrap up a deal. The centerpiece of their discussion became Murdoch's insistence on an interest rate lower than the one offered by Airbus. Moore seemed doubtful that the bank, whose loan decisions had to be approved by both the Treasury Department and Federal Reserve, could do better than 8½ percent.

Murdoch shrugged and left for his lunch at the White House. Pierce, who remained behind, continued to work on Moore over their own lunch. Although Murdoch had insisted on 7.9 percent, Pierce said, he would accept a flat 8 percent—but not a percentage point higher. If the bank refused to grant a loan at that rate, Boeing would lose a major sale and the American commercial aircraft industry would suffer immeasurably. Moore began to squirm.

Except for his complaint that "he served me a bloody hamburger," Murdoch's White House lunch with Jimmy Carter seemed unremarkable. It appeared to be a routine meeting between an incumbent President seeking renomination and a prominent big-city newspaper publisher deciding on whether to support him. Three days later, on February 22, the *New York Post* endorsed Carter in the New York primary race. And thereafter, it intensified its often negatively slanted reporting on Teddy Kennedy, Carter's most threatening rival.

Within days after the *Post*'s Carter endorsement and just two days short of Murdoch's deadline, Ansett was given an unprecedented 8 percent financing deal by the Eximbank on the first four

767s it ordered from Boeing, with an identical rate all but promised on the purchase of additional planes. It did not take long for the press to begin questioning the propriety of the arrangement, given its timing. Murdoch's lunch with Carter on the same day he met with Carter's man at the bank, John Moore, was revealed. The fact that the *Post* had endorsed Carter almost immediately afterward, and that Moore had rushed through the Eximbank's loan approval soon after that, together became a fox's scent to a pack of aroused media hounds.

The first questions were raised publicly in March by *The New York Times* following Murdoch's announcement in Australia that Ansett had agreed to buy the Boeing 767s instead of the Airbus A-300s. Three days later, Senator William Proxmire, chairman of the Senate Committee on Banking, Housing and Urban Affairs—the committee overseeing the Eximbank—wrote to John Moore questioning the bank's seemingly overgenerous loan to Ansett and suggesting that Moore had allowed the bank "to be used to further the President's reelection." Dissatisfied with Moore's reply, and discovering that the Treasury Department had unsuccessfully attempted to block the loan on the ground that it "fritters away bank resources," Proxmire called for a full-scale committee investigation.

As Senate investigations go, the Proxmire Committee's probe might itself have been described as one that frittered away federal resources. Further interesting—even startling—facts developed. Among them was the revelation that the Carter-appointed American ambassador to Australia, another of his Georgia associates and an ex–law partner of John Moore, had played an active role in pressuring the Eximbank into approving the Ansett loan. Another was that there had been considerable resistance among the Eximbank's four-person board of directors—not counting Moore—to granting the loan on Murdoch's terms. Still another was the testimony of several Treasury Department officials that they felt Moore had exercised inappropriate haste in promoting the loan, as well as undue pressure on the Treasury to get it approved.

Murdoch himself testified. After categorically denying any "deal" between Carter and himself, he conceded that the timing of the events surrounding the loan was "unfortunate" and blamed most of the brouhaha on *The New York Times.* The *Times,* he later told me, had been out "to get" him ever since the denoue-

ment of the 1978 newspaper strike and had used the Eximbank-
Ansett loan to carry out its "evil scheme." "I'll have my day with
the *Times,*" Murdoch promised just after he testified in the Proxmire investigation. In his lingo, that meant that he would have his
day of revenge. When the day came, as it did in 1985, it would not
even come close to fulfilling his expectations.

The Proxmire probe was totally unproductive, at least in the
view of those who had hoped to discover a major scandal. Although the American government was perceived by many as
having been duped by Murdoch into subsidizing his privately
owned Australian airline, he was absolved of wrongdoing, as was
President Carter. John Moore and the Eximbank came away with
nothing more than a verbal slap on the wrist from Proxmire for
wasting public money. With Ronald Reagan's defeat of Carter in
the November 1980 election, the incident became little more than
a footnote to the history of the period.

The Times *Are A'Changing*

The question of whether Murdoch dissembled when he told the Proxmire Committee there was no connection between the *Post*'s endorsement of Carter and the Eximbank's loan grant to Ansett remained a problematic one in the minds of many in Washington. Not long before, Murdoch had bought two of Australia's largest sheep-breeding farms for four million dollars. Upon learning of that after Murdoch completed his testimony, a member of the panel quipped to an aide, "He not only pulled the wool over Treasury's eyes, now he's pulled it over ours."

There was considerable precedent to support this educated conclusion. In the first place, through more than twenty-five years of newspaper publishing—an implied form of promise to be truthful—he had practically institutionalized the practice of exaggeration for the sake of improving his commercial fortunes. Moreover, his promise the year before to the Australian Broadcasting Tribunal, when asked if he intended to make any changes in the top management of Sydney's Channel 10 should his license be approved, was not kept. "I wish to give an assurance to the Tribunal that no change is contemplated," Murdoch had testified. "Channel 10 will continue exactly as it is today."

Two weeks after the Tribunal granted the license, however, Channel 10's experienced general manager, Ian Kennon, was unceremoniously fired and replaced by one of Murdoch's News Limited functionaries, a man who had no experience in television. Two months later, Sir Kenneth Humphreys, the television company's longtime chairman, followed Kennon.

I asked Murdoch about his testimony before the Proxmire

Committee a few months later. My question was posed while he was in the midst of his latest—and in a sense most momentous—acquisition struggle: his pursuit of the *Times* newspapers of London. In order to buy the daily *Times* and *Sunday Times,* separate papers owned and published by the same corporation, Murdoch had to make several solemn legal vows to the British government that as their new proprietor he would allow the two papers to continue to operate editorially without any interference. I coupled my query regarding his testimony to the Proxmire Committee with one about his intention of living up to the promises he'd just made in England.

"One thing you must understand, Tom," he replied. "You tell these bloody politicians whatever they want to hear, and once the deal is done you don't worry about it. They're not going to chase after you later if they suddenly decide what you said wasn't what they wanted to hear. Otherwise they're made to look bad, and they can't abide that. So they just stick their heads up their asses and wait for the blow to pass." It was a prophetic boast.

Although suffering from a long history of unprofitability and racked by recent labor disputes that had shut it down for more than a year, the ultra-sober *Times* of London remained Britain's most prestigious newspaper, a virtual national monument. When it, along with the more lively and profitable *Sunday Times,* was put up for sale in the fall of 1980, Murdoch quickly entered the bidding. Ownership of two such well-thought-of papers, notwithstanding their financial problems, would be an expeditious way for him to rehabilitate his miserable journalistic reputation throughout the world and gain him acceptance at last into the higher echelons of the British establishment. It was just that reputation, though, when Murdoch loomed as the *Times*'s most financially qualified buyer early in 1981, that caused the government to insist on guarantees of noninterference. The fear was that he would attempt to do with the *Times* and *Sunday Times* what he'd done with the *Sun* and *News of the World*—not only cheapen and sensationalize them, but turn them into another collective organ of his increasingly vocal right-wing political ideology.

The conditions were originally set forth in the purchase negotiations between Murdoch and the board of the paper's parent corporation, Times Newspapers, which was owned by the rich Canadian publisher-industrialist Kenneth Thomson. Thomson's late father, Lord Thomson of Fleet, had acquired the *Sunday*

Times in 1950. In 1966, when he bought the separate daily *Times*, he had been required to guarantee the editorial autonomy of both papers by the appointment of four independent "national" directors to the board of Times Newspapers. Theoretically the national directors, representing British society as a whole, had the power to prevent the Thomsons from meddling in the papers' editorial direction. As it happened, since the Thomsons proved to be hands-off owners, their authority was never tested. But in any event, it was mostly window dressing. It carried no veto power, and the four national directors were outnumbered by other directors serving the Thomson interests.

In deciding to sell Times Newspapers to Murdoch in 1981, the Thomson organization knew that in light of his record, the British government would insist on more stringent editorial guarantees. So, too, would the journalists who staffed and ran the *Times* and *Sunday Times,* without whose approval the sale could not expeditiously go forward. While Murdoch negotiated with the Thomson ownership over the price, a committee of journalists, led by the editors of the *Times* and *Sunday Times,* haggled with the board of Times Newspapers over the demands that would be put to Murdoch concerning beefed up guarantees of continuing editorial independence.

Murdoch quickly reached an accord with the Thomson group on a price—a very favorable one of just under $30 million. Next he had to discuss with the Times Newspapers board and the journalists the question of guarantees. When the strengthened guarantees were put to him, including an increase in national directors from four to six and the stipulation that editors could be appointed and dismissed only with the national directors' concurrence, Murdoch readily agreed. "Almost too readily," said a member of the journalists' committee later. "One got the feeling that even if we'd asked for a different set of assurances, he'd have given them equally easily."

What it all came down to was that Murdoch would run the business side of the *Times* and *Sunday Times* and would leave the news function to the journalists, with no attempt to meddle in either paper's "editor's business." That included each editor's autonomous right to hire and fire journalistic staff, shape his paper's journalistic content, maintain authority over its opinion pages, and refuse to publish advertisements. The *Times* would remain England's staid "paper of record," and the *Sunday Times* would be allowed to retain its own character as a weekly that combined serious, probing journalism with more lighthearted fare.

The guarantees were designed to avoid having Murdoch's purchase of the two papers submitted to England's Monopolies Commission for official approval. With his latest acquisition, Murdoch would be the proprietor of four major national newspapers. Ordinarily such a concentration of press power would demand official review under Britain's antimonopoly laws. And the possibility was strong that such a review would result in a prohibition against Murdoch's takeover, particularly in view of the number of enemies he had made in Parliament.

One politician who was not an enemy, though, was Prime Minister Margaret Thatcher. She "owed" Murdoch and was happy to do her part to help him avoid a full-scale probe by the Monopolies Commission. The man charged with the decision on whether or not to refer the case to the commission was a member of her cabinet, John Biffen, the Secretary of State for Trade. Biffen conducted a cursory review of the matter, in the course of which Murdoch assured him and Parliament that he fully intended to abide by the conditions and guarantees he'd agreed to with the Times Newspapers board. The guarantees also included Murdoch's promise to keep the legal titles of the *Times* and *Sunday Times* in the name of Times Newspapers, rather than put them under News International. The purpose of that condition was to ensure that if Murdoch ever decided to close down the two papers and liquidate the Times Newspapers company, the titles would remain assets of the company and would be available for sale.

In the year following Parliament's approval of Murdoch's purchase, the usual disorder attendant to newspaper publishing in London turned into chaos at the *Times* and *Sunday Times.* The abrasive fifty-two-year-old Harold Evans, formerly the editor of the *Sunday Times* and a man with a sterling newspaper reputation, took over as editor of the *Times.* He was succeeded at the *Sunday Times* by Frank Giles, his sixty-one-year-old longtime deputy and also a man of high journalistic repute, if not of Evans's aggressive temperament.

Soon Murdoch's promises about editorial independence began to unravel. Although Evans brightened the appearance and tone of the *Times,* and circulation began to inch upward, Murdoch grew increasingly unhappy with Evans's refusal to follow his policy wishes, not the least of which was his demand that the *Times* become an indiscriminate advocate of the Thatcher government in England and Ronald Reagan's in America. Murdoch's usual insistence on severe reductions in the *Times*'s unionized labor force was for the most part justified. Nevertheless, it caused regular disruptions in production and further serious morale problems among the paper's staff, all of which impeded Evans in his efforts to improve the paper. Personal antagonisms between Evans and Murdoch's chief News International deputies did nothing to ease the rising tension.

By early fall of 1981, Murdoch and Evans were clearly on their way to becoming bitter adversaries, Evans intent on enforcing the guarantees he'd had a hand in formulating when Murdoch bought the *Times,* Murdoch equally determined to rid himself of them. As the *Times*—the *Sunday Times,* too—became increasingly critical in print of Thatcher's economic policies, Murdoch grew increasingly outspoken in his dissatisfaction with Evans and Frank Giles. To guests at a dinner party in New York, he characterized Giles and his wife as Communists. Evans, he called worse. Then he went on to blast the two papers as being "lily-livered" and "straining my patience." No one at the dinner who heard Murdoch's diatribe had any doubt of what was about to happen. Few were aware of the real reasons for it, however.

I had learned, during our five-year relationship, that Murdoch was very much a creature of his financial fortunes. His daily mood and outlook were almost childishly affected by every minuscule shift in one or more of his corporations' latest fiscal reports. This psychic condition was not so much a matter of greed, or a sense of fiscal responsibility, as it was of—well, vindication. Murdoch was too intelligent not to be aware of, and highly sensitive to, his terrible journalistic reputation. Counterbalancing that was his reputation for making money and keeping people employed and the high satisfaction he got from it. So long as his weekly corporate balance sheets reflected vigorous overall profitability, he was able to suppress the underlying guilt and chagrin he felt about his newspaper practices and convince himself that what he was doing was worthwhile. That made him feel good about himself. But when a glitch appeared in his profit-and-loss statements, it served as a harsh reminder of his suppressed shame. His mood darkened. His behavior became erratic. His usually calm demeanor grew agitated, and he lashed out compulsively at those he thought were to blame. His whole purpose in life seemed suddenly and obsessively to erase the glitch through radical, almost panicky counteractions of one kind or another. When those failed, he simply became more morose and abusive.

During 1981, the glitches began to turn up with increasing frequency, particularly in the financial statements of News International, Murdoch's British operating company. His major television and airline expansion in Australia in 1979 and 1980 had brought about a corresponding increase in the gross income of Newscorp to about $800 million. However, because of Murdoch's refusal to finance any of that expansion through public stock offerings, thereby avoiding a further dilution of his own equity in Newscorp, the Australian parent company was now highly leveraged by bank borrowings. With interest rates rising rapidly worldwide, Newscorp's debt service had started to take greater and greater chunks out of the company's revenues. Financial tolerances were narrowing, and Murdoch's willingness to carry money-losing papers began to be questioned.

As early as the late 1960s, Murdoch had recognized that his empire, then still limited to Australia, could not rest on printing and newspapers alone. His initial forays into Australian television reflected his determination to diversify, and his later ventures in Australian mineral and mining projects underlined it. Now, in 1981, Newscorp was well-diversified, yet the bulk of its revenue still came from its newspaper-based subsidiaries—News Limited, News International, and News America. But each was growing less profitable, its revenues being drained by rising labor, plant, and promotional costs and by the single major money-losing paper each operated.

The 1981 woes of News International in England were particularly unsettling. Although the *Sun* and *News of the World* were still the country's circulation leaders, the costs of keeping them in the forefront had magnified considerably. Rival papers were constantly mounting circulation wars. Murdoch, hating to lose the preeminence he'd established in the 1970s, had been forced to pour extra millions into the battles merely to maintain the status quo of the two papers. Of his two more recent purchases, the *Sunday Times* continued to operate near the profitability line, but the *Times* was losing even more money than it had before he took it over, notwithstanding the trend toward modernization Harold Evans had started. In addition, all four papers were being squeezed by spiraling labor and production costs, most of which were caused by the print unions' intransigence in refusing to reduce rampant job duplication and featherbedding at Murdoch's two London plants. As he said to me at the time, "If it's the last thing I do, I'll make the goddamn unions pay dearly for their idiocy." He was gearing up to launch a full-scale war against the Fleet Street unions, and his threat would prove prophetic.

For the fiscal year 1980–81, News International had made a pretax profit of $62.4 million. But only $15 million of that had come between January and June of 1981, the second half of the fiscal year and the period during which Times Newspapers had entered the Murdoch fold. Murdoch's accountants were projecting that in the fiscal year 1981–82, the two *Times* papers together would lose upward of $30 million. With the profits of the *Sun News of the World* group expected to drop off by about $20 million due to bloated labor expenses and the special costs of launching a new Sunday magazine supplement to *News of the World,* it was likely that News International's overall profit for the coming year would be in the neighborhood of only $12 million, a huge drop from the previous year and a serious dent in the income the parent Newscorp needed to service its rising debt. Should such sharply reduced profit become a pattern over the next several years, and should it be repeated in the United States with News America, which had recently recorded a nearly $2.5 million loss, the likelihood was that Newscorp would have to begin raising money in the Australian stock market through new stock offerings. What that would produce would be a substantial weakening of Murdoch's proprietary hold on the entire organization.

That sort of financial anxiety brought out the worst in Murdoch. Rather than admit that his acquisition of the two *Times* newspapers—especially the daily *Times*—had been a profound mistake in business judgment, he began to blame those who were running them. Fiercely convinced that he knew how to popularize the still-bland *Times* into profitability, he was just as fiercely resentful of the constraints that prevented him from doing so. His resentment and name-calling intensified during the fall of 1981, as Harold Evans continued to resist his editorial "suggestions." According to Evans, those suggestions had to do not only with turning the paper into a right-wing propaganda sheet, but with transforming its journalistic style and format into tha. of an "up-scale *Sun.*"

The clash between the two came to a head at the start u 1982 when Murdoch, in the midst of his latest labor dispute with the *Times* and *Sunday Times* print unions, threatened to shut down the papers for good unless he obtained a sharp reduction in jobs. According to Evans, Murdoch's warning seemed serious, although he had made it many times before in similar situations. The first question asked was: If Murdoch followed through and liquidated Times Newspapers, what would become of the two titles? Evans still believed that Murdoch's guarantee to keep the titles in the name of the Times Newspapers corporation ensured that each would be available to be sold and the papers restarted by another buyer or buyers. It was then that he learned that Murdoch, two months before, had hatched a plan to transfer the titles into the name of News International.

To Evans, this was an outright breach of the promises Murdoch had made to the government. The particular guarantee in question had been inscribed into law by Trade Minister John Biffen's formal parliamentary decree consenting to Murdoch's acquisition.

> News International shall not without the consent of a major-ity of the independent national directors procure or permit any-thing to be done which shall result in Times Newspapers selling or otherwise disposing of any interest in the *Times* or *Sunday Times.*

Evans's brief investigation showed that News International had "disposed of" the *Times* and *Sunday Times* titles by secretly transferring them from Times Newspapers to itself and had done so not only without the consent of the national directors, but without even consulting them.

When confronted, Murdoch claimed that he'd done nothing illegal, since the titles in the two papers did not amount to the interest referred to in the parliamentary decree. Evans found that to be casuistic and proceeded, over Murdoch's objections, to publish a story in the *Times* about the transfer. The inferences to be drawn from it were clear. Murdoch, the paper's owner, had violated the law, and the *Times* was now hostage to his whim. Moreover, by virtue of the subterfuge by which the titles had been switched, he may well have violated other laws pertaining to "fraudulent conveyance."

The entire matter caused an uproar in Parliament. Murdoch summoned lawyer Richard Searby from Australia to try to patch things up. Searby concocted a plan designed to rescind the transfer and then reimplement it through a proper submission to the national directors of Times Newspapers. Evans announced his intention to fight the new transfer. Before he could, though, in a hail of publicity in mid-March 1982, Murdoch succeeded in ousting him as editor of the *Times*—again without approval of the independent directors and thus contrary to the promises he'd made the year before.*

By April, when the furor subsided, Murdoch was in full editorial control of the *Times* and *Sunday Times* and had achieved some of the labor-reduction concessions he'd demanded from the unions. Since then, despite regular threats to close them, he has managed to keep the papers afloat by means of promotions, contests, and other forms of popularizaton. There is no question that the *Times* is a more lively and readable paper today. But its reputation for accuracy and precision in news reportage has suffered seriously as a result.

But it was the *Sunday Times*'s credibility that was most damaged by Murdoch once he rid the organization of Harold Evans. The crucial event occurred in the spring of 1983, when he personally plunged both the *Times* and the *Sunday Times* full-tilt into the "Hitler Diaries" hoax. No other episode more strikingly revealed Murdoch's career-long habit of ignoring minimal journalistic standards for the sake of selling newspapers than this.

The truth about the so-called Hitler Diaries is now familiar enough to require only a brief retelling. Konrad Kujau was a German handwriting expert and collector of Nazi memorabilia who had forged a few handwritten notebooks in the late 1970s and attempted to peddle them to Franz Tiefel, a dealer in Nazi artifacts, as Adolf Hitler's secret diaries. Tiefel knew Gerd Heidemann, yet another collector of Nazi mementoes and a writer for the flashy German weekly picture magazine *Stern*. He showed

---

* Evans, however, declined to invoke the authority of the national directors in his fight with Murdoch to retain the job. He was persuaded by some of them that his departure might be best for the strife-ridden *Times*. The financial settlement he received evidently helped to seal the persuasion.

Heidemann one of Kujau's "diaries." Heidemann, who was deeply in debt, approached Kujau with a scheme designed to earn them both a fortune. Kujau would produce further fake diaries, sixty in all. Heidemann would then foist them off on *Stern* as the actual journals of Hitler, personally written by the German führer and hidden away for safekeeping by Nazi loyalists in East Germany at the end of the war. Kujau agreed and began to churn out additional forgeries, all neatly chronologized and each in a script almost identical to that of Hitler's.

Late in 1980, Heidemann succeeded in convincing *Stern* that the first few samples of Kujau's forgeries were really Hitler's diaries and that through his "secret contacts" in East Germany he would produce the entire collection. Thereafter, between January 1981 and early 1983, with Kujau continuing his work, *Stern* paid Heidemann $3.1 million for the collection. Of that, Heidemann gave Kujau $100,000 and kept the rest for himself. In the meantime, with the fiftieth anniversary of Hitler's rise to power at hand, *Stern* began secretly planning the diaries' publication. The magazine fully expected to stun the world with its coup, particularly because the documents "revealed" an Adolf Hitler markedly more human and humane than the monster depicted by postwar history. But before it started publishing in April, *Stern* would have to sell the diaries' foreign-language rights to recover its outlay to Heidemann and reap the full commercial dividends of its investment.

Based on the evidence later developed at the trial of Heidemann and Kujau, *Stern* was unaware of the diaries' phony provenance. However, the magazine's publishers were roundly criticized by the German trial judge for having made no efforts to authenticate them.

On March 9, 1983, Peter Wickham, *Stern*'s agent in London, contacted the Murdoch organization with the first hint of the magazine's plans. He asked if Murdoch would be interested in bidding on the exclusive English-language newspaper rights to a super-secret publishing project, one that would easily treble the circulation of Murdoch papers around the world. Wickham received an affirmative reply, but was reminded that Murdoch could not bid on something he knew nothing about. Wickham said he understood and promised that once he had a written pledge of secrecy from Murdoch, he would divulge the nature of the project in its entirety.

Shortly thereafter, with a secrecy guarantee in hand, Wickham spelled out the details to Murdoch's top men at the *Times* and *Sunday Times*. He told them that *Stern* had no doubts about the diaries' authenticity and that it intended to start publishing the first installments in late April. Any deal would have to be concluded before then, he insisted. He invited Murdoch to *Stern*'s headquarters in Hamburg to inspect samples of the diaries. London's *Daily Mail* had already expressed an interest in bidding, he added.

Murdoch traveled from New York to Hamburg with Bruce Rothwell. There he learned that *Newsweek* was already well along toward sewing up the American magazine rights. Murdoch papers had been victimized on several prior occasions by journalistic hoaxers. But any misgivings he might have had about the diaries' authenticity were dispelled by the fact that *Newsweek*, one of the world's most prestigious publishing organizations, was about to acquire them for the United States. His only concern, then, was to get the English-language newspaper rights as cheaply as he could while at the same time outbidding the *Daily Mail*.

As it happened, the *Daily Mail*'s interest was short-lived, and in mid-April Murdoch came away with the rights for $400,000. Immediately he, Rothwell, and his top *Times* editors in London, all still pledged to secrecy, began to plot their strategy on how best to use the acquisition. They decided to start by publishing the first English-language installment in the *Sunday Times* of April 24, 1983, four days before it was scheduled to make its debut in *Stern*. They would break the news of the existence of the diaries the day before in the *Times*.

Since they had less than ten days to accomplish their plan, they were forced to bring an increasing number of lower-echelon editors on both papers in on the secret. On April 15, Frank Giles, the *Sunday Times* editor, told Eric Jacobs, the editor in charge of the paper's features section, to begin preparing space in the April 24 edition for the first diary installment. Jacobs was instantly suspicious—he recalled that the *Sunday Times* had been badly burned in the 1960s after purchasing and publishing excerpts from diaries of Benito Mussolini that had later proved to be fake. When he reminded Giles of the Mussolini episode, the chief editor assured him that the Hitler diaries had been thoroughly checked and that there was no doubt about their authenticity. "In the event," Giles added, referring to Murdoch, "the proprietor has no doubts."

That hardly soothed Jacobs's qualms. He mentioned the

matter to Phillip Knightly, a veteran investigative reporter for the *Sunday Times.* Knightly came back five days later with a detailed memorandum questioning the wisdom of publishing the Hitler material on what appeared to be nothing more than blind faith in its authenticity. When the memorandum reached Giles, he dismissed Knightly's warnings with the assurance that the *Times* organization had by then independently verified the diaries.

Enter Hugh Trevor-Roper. One of Times Newspapers' six national directors and a leading British expert on the Hitler era, Trevor-Roper had just returned from the bank in Switzerland where the diaries were stored and pronounced them authentic. Bruce Rothwell, who had accompanied him, seconded his declaration by remarking that the diaries "gave off good vibes." And Charles Douglas-Home, Harold Evans's successor as editor of the daily *Times* and another visitor to the bank vault, clinched matters by describing the documents as smelling properly "old and musty." On the basis of all that, Murdoch ordered the April 24 publication to proceed. Later, when the diaries were shown to be fake, he would say to me, "It's all that fucking Trevor-Roper's fault."

Save for Knightly and one or two others who had learned about the project, apparently everyone in the Times Newspapers hierarchy was smugly confident of the diaries' authenticity on Friday, April 22. The forthcoming weekend's *Sunday Times* was being prepared to receive the first excerpts, along with a number of sidebar stories about the diaries' "history." As well, the next day's Saturday edition of the *Times* was about to be printed, and it would lead with an exclusive headlined preview of the story, in effect announcing to the world the discovery of the trove. The *Times* blurb would describe the diaries as "astonishing" and "of momentous historic significance," and it would herald the fact that its sister paper, the following morning's *Sunday Times,* would have the first exclusive extracts.

On Friday afternoon, Knightly phoned Trevor-Roper to learn more about his authentication methods. Oddly, while Knightly came away from their conversation reassured, Trevor-Roper, who had written several noted books on Hitler, grew unsettled by some of Knightly's queries. By the next morning, he says, he had begun to have second thoughts. They intensified when he picked up the Saturday *Times* and read its announcement under the headline: "Hitler Secret Diaries to Be Published." The story contained several statements from him attesting to the diaries' authenticity. As soon as he read the quotes, his second thoughts turned into overwhelming doubts about what he had seen, smelled, and handled in Switzerland. He immediately phoned Charles Douglas-Home to tell him he had changed his mind. He was not saying the diaries were fake, though, only that he was no longer sure they were real.

Douglas-Home was the editor of the *Times*, not the *Sunday Times*. Although Trevor-Roper's Saturday morning call reached him eleven hours before the *Sunday Times* was scheduled to go to press, he failed to pass the news on to Frank Giles or anyone else at the *Sunday Times*. That evening, as the *Sunday Times* began to rumble off the presses at the Times Newspapers plant in Grey's Inn Road, north of Fleet Street, Frank Giles called his editorial staff into his office for a drink to celebrate the paper's publishing coup. The edition contained four full pages devoted to the "Hitler Diaries," all of them brimming with self-congratulation and the promise of future weeks' installments.

While the journalists chatted smugly over their drinks, Giles sat at his desk and started phoning higher-ups in the Times Newspapers and News International organizations to tell them that the paper was on its way. Among those on his list of people to call was Trevor-Roper. According to Magnus Linklater, one of the editors in Giles's office, when Giles reached Trevor-Roper, "We were all talking. But gradually each one of us shut up as we caught words from Frank's conversation. The room was completely silent by the time Frank said, 'Come on, Hugh, don't tell me you're having doubts *now*. I trust you're not making a 180-degree turn. Oh, you are . . .' "

Within days, the forgery was exposed. In Germany, a scientific analysis of some of the original documents proved that their glue, bindings, and thread were all of postwar material and manufacture. Other tests showed that the paper on which the diaries were written contained a chemical that was not manufactured until after the war. A further examination of the text found that it was based on a clever compilation of Hitler's speeches and official Third Reich edicts. Soon thereafter, the true story of how Heidemann and Kujau perpetrated the fraud began to emerge.

The *Sunday Times* put the best face on its role in the scandal by printing a feebly reasoned apologia in which it neglected to report the details of its participation and declined to take any responsibility for it.

Once again, a major newspaper owned and actively managed by Rupert Murdoch had been revealed as a publisher of sensationalist bogus "news." That the paper was London's *Sunday Times,* and by extension the daily *Times,* compounded the offense. Although it was true that Murdoch had "saved" the two papers, he proved once again that his much heralded entrepreneurial and business acumen often relied on exaggeration to achieve its ends.

"Voodoo Killer"

In the United States, much of that technique continued in the pages of the *New York Post*. During the summer of 1980, the *Daily News* had attempted to stem the erosion of its own circulation by starting a separate edition designed to break the *Post*'s monopoly over the city's late afternoon and evening market. Hired to organize and edit the new paper, called *Tonight* and launched at a cost of $20 million, was none other than Clay Felker. Murdoch quite accurately interpreted the *News*'s move as an outright declaration of war motivated by the *News*'s hostility toward him because of the 1978 strike and meant to eradicate the *Post* for good. He fought back in kind, moving the *Post*'s first edition up to 7:00 A.M., dropping the paper's price from thirty to twenty-five cents—the price of the *News*—and increasing the octane of the paper's sensationalism-cum-invention formula.

The *News*'s strategy failed, not so much because of the *Post*'s counterattack as because *Tonight* was ill-conceived and poorly executed. As put together by Felker, *Tonight* was more sophisticated and restrained in tone than the morning *Daily News* and thus hardly competitive with the increasingly shrill, cheap-thrill *Post*. Moreover, the inside of the new paper was little more than an amalgam of that morning's *News* and the next morning's. People who bought the *News* in the morning would find many of its features—columns, puzzles, sports coverage, and other items—repeated in *Tonight*. Similarly, features that were new in *Tonight* were repeated in the next morning's *News*. The *Daily News* organization was in effect asking its readers to buy three papers every twenty-four hours but giving them only two.

In the end, *Tonight*'s circulation settled at about 80,000 while the *Post*'s rose by about the same amount, thanks to its earlier first-edition time, its reduced price, and its higher level of sleaze. But both organizations suffered financially. In August 1981, the *Daily News* terminated *Tonight,* admitting that it had suffered an overall loss well in excess of its start-up costs. And despite the rise in the *Post*'s circulation, the expenses of its earlier edition far outstripped the additional $10,000 it grossed each day from increased sales. What's more, despite its circulation boost, advertising revenues remained as stale as ever.

Murdoch's difficulties were underlined by a yarn that made the rounds of New York newspapermen's hangouts at the time. The tale had Murdoch himself on the phone to a top executive of one of the city's leading department stores and a lavish advertiser in the *Times* and *Daily News.* The purpose of his call was to plead for more advertising in the *Post.* Murdoch purportedly argued that the great increase in the paper's circulation justified an increase in the store's advertising. "The only trouble with that," the executive was said to have replied in declining Murdoch's pitch, "is that *your* readers are *our* shoplifters."

Although Murdoch denies this occurred, the story accurately reflects the cause of his continuing problems in New York. Yet with characteristic stubbornness, once his skirmish with the *Daily News* over *Tonight* ended, and despite the renewed barrage of criticism he received for his further downscaling of the *Post,* he refused to modulate the paper's progressively more bizarre and frenetic style. By then he was ready to concede that he would never be able to make the paper profitable through advertising revenue. Since additional increases in circulation would not do the trick either, mainly because of the additional costs they entailed, Murdoch's only purpose in keeping the paper alive and pressing for wider circulation was to expand his political influence. So long as his other properties made money, he could continue to maintain the money-losing *Post* for his personal ambitions.

By 1981, the violently alarming and grossly misleading headline had become staple fare of *Post* style, whether related to a genuine news event or to some minor "human interest" concoction of the editorial staff. With it went the terse, rat-a-tat story that as a rule was less concerned with the facts of the event than with what could be made of it in the service of sensationalism and fear- or thrill-mongering. The paper's vocabulary relied on a daily cascade of buzzwords, most of them nouns magically transformed into adjectives and all of them worn thin and trite from obsessive overuse—"hero," "miracle," "slaughter," "outrage," "vermin," "terror," "sex," for instance. Other features of the basic formula were the graphic and, whenever possible, gory or macabre photo and the preening self-promotion that seemed to blare out from every news and opinion page. Accompanying it all was a busy and often confusing salad of typography and layout that symbolically screamed "Urgent!" but delivered much less than it promised.

The *Post* as a news organ was mostly tantalizing facade and little substance. It was frequently offensive to all but the densest readers because of the presumption of public gullibility it operated from. Even its gossip pages were, though suitably catty in tone, pallid in their effect. Editorials, most of them written by Bruce Rothwell but faithfully voicing Murdoch's now-didactic right-wing stridency, usually contained conspicuous boldface and underlined passages in the World War II Nazi propagandist style, as though readers could not be trusted to absorb the salient points without such guidance. Having reconciled with the bombastic, self-important Maxwell Newton, Murdoch brought him up from Australia to cover national business and economic affairs. As a result, *Post* buyers were treated to yet another editor who seemed to reside on the far side of coherence. Only the paper's expanded sports section, which remained in the hands of a native-born editor, continued to be a genuine reflection of New York. However, it, too, suffered from the typographical murkiness and schizophrenic layout imposed on it by the original redesign of the *Post*. It suffered also from its reporters' tiresomely cute dependence on mock-words like "bleep," "bleeper," and "bleeping" when reproducing profanity-ridden postgame quotes of the athletes they wrote about.

Murdoch continued to defend his transformation of the *Post* at every turn, regularly denying that its journalism was often based on distortion and untruth. "It's a much more lively paper now," he kept insisting. That depended on what one understood as lively. From an Anglo-Australian point of view, perhaps it was. From an American viewpoint, and more particularly from a New York one, Murdoch's "lively" was analogous to lower Times Square at night. The district was certainly lively and had a certain visceral fascination for tourists. But except for the nightly assemblage of local dopers, muggers, sex hustlers, and other metropolitan lowlifes, few New Yorkers cared to frequent it with any regularity.

"Aha!" Murdoch exclaimed when I made that analogy to him in 1981, "then how do you explain that we sell nearly a million more copies of the *Post* today than were sold when we started out with it? We're only giving the public what it wants to read."

The claim was a typical Murdoch exaggeration—the increase in circulation had been less than half a million. But beyond that, it revealed the blind spot he constantly suffered from. How could a New York paper increase its paid circulation by nearly half a million in five years, yet during the same period lose increasing amounts of money annually?

He blamed it solely on labor, distribution, and promotional costs. But *The New York Times,* with an infinitely greater overhead, yet a smaller circulation, had reported handsome profits during the same span. The difference, of course, consisted of advertising revenues. The *Times,* with its high-quality, upper-income circulation, was an advertising gold mine, whereas the *Post,* even though it once again had a virtual lock on the afternoon-evening New York newspaper market, was a slag heap. Wouldn't the potential for eventual profitability rise if the *Post* was transformed into an afternoon tabloid version of the *Times,* I asked Murdoch—a paper that appealed to those who bought the *Times* in the morning, often along with *The Wall Street Journal?*

His answer revealed his sore spot. He despised the *Times* and every other paper in America that strived for journalistic quality as "snobby enterprises." What he really meant, if my personal knowledge of him was accurate, was that he knew that the sophisticated audience of the *Times* and *Wall Street Journal* would never swallow his blunt, simplistic, reactionary, political conservatism, and that if he tried to turn the *Post* into a tabloid *Times* he would be forced to give up its right-wing proselytizing through news-slanting and editorial-page sermonizing. The *Post*'s audience, Murdoch felt, was basically a poorly educated, narrowly experienced mass of New Yorkers unaccustomed to contemplating the complexities and nuances of history and contemporary life. It was a mass mind that could easily be exploited, manipulated, and propagandized, one that in Murdoch's view craved guidance, flourished on simple black-and-white answers, and cared little about the journalistic deceptions by which its emotions and re-

sponses were manipulated. Or so he told me—although not in
those precise words—after he single-handedly polished off two
bottles of wine with dinner one night in 1982.

Our dinner took place not long after Murdoch had failed in
what many insiders took to be his own grandiose attempt to put
the *Daily News* out of business and thereby gain much of its advertising for the *Post*. Soon after the *News* terminated its *Tonight*
edition in 1981, Murdoch introduced Wingo to the *Post*. Almost
immediately, the *Post*'s circulation started to rise again, while the
News's stalled. The *News* tried to counter the inroads the *Post* was
making by hurriedly creating and promoting its own lottery,
called Zingo. The prospect of such an expensive new circulation
fight quickly paled, however. To the Chicago Tribune Company,
the *Daily News*'s corporate parent, Murdoch seemed intent on
committing financial suicide with the *Post* and taking the *News*
with him. Despite the fact that the *News* remained well ahead of
the *Post* in circulation, its steep overheads had produced a loss of
$11 million in 1981. Forecasts for the next four years predicted a
series of even greater deficits, which would only be inflated if the
News was forced to continue Zingo in order to keep up with
Murdoch. Thus, in December, its Chicago parent decided to put
the paper up for sale.

Three months later, in the early spring of 1982, the Tribune
Company announced that it had found a buyer in Texas millionaire Joseph Albritton. In 1974, Albritton had purchased the ailing
Washington Star but had been unable to save it. He had more recently acquired a Trenton, New Jersey, daily. Acknowledging on
April 5 that he was prepared to take over the *Daily News*, he dis-
closed a plan by which he intended to reduce the paper's unionized work force of 3,800 by 1,600, thereby trimming $85 million
from its $200 million yearly wage costs. Stanton Cook, president
of the Chicago Tribune Company, warned the New York newspaper unions that if they put up a fight, thereby scaring Albritton
away, the *News* would simply be shut down for good. Albritton,
in effect, was the "buyer of last resort," and the unions stood to
lose 3,800 jobs if they didn't go along with his cost-cutting conditions.

The Allied Printing Trades Council, still headed by George
McDonald and advised by Theodore Kheel, didn't take kindly to
Cook's threat. According to Kheel, he initially suggested that the
unions make an alternative bid for the *News* based on an Em-

ployee Stock Ownership Plan, or ESOP, which would give the Tribune Company several tax advantages. The union leadership rejected the idea on the ground that there was no one in its ranks with any experience in running a major paper.

"It was then," says Kheel, "that I thought of Murdoch." Kheel approached Murdoch with a proposal that the *Post* owner purchase the *News,* possibly in partnership with the ESOP Kheel had devised. Murdoch wasn't interested in a partnership, but he immediately warmed to the idea of obtaining the *News*—provided he could get union concessions on major work-force reductions for both the *News* and the *Post.* With such a monopoly over New York's tabloid market, he could finally build up a profitable newspaper organization and at the same time expand his political power. Kheel persuaded the union leaders to commit themselves to working with Murdoch on the theory that he would be a better choice than Albritton for the ownership of the *News.* "At least Murdoch was a known quantity," Kheel said.

The only fly in the ointment was Stanton Cook of the Tribune Company, who abhorred Murdoch. When Murdoch announced on April 12 that he intended to make a bid for the *News,* Cook accused him of being interested only in upsetting the Tribune Company's negotiations with Albritton, of making "a transparent attempt to destroy and shut down" the *Daily News* at the last minute. Cook was referring, of course, to his earlier announcement that Albritton was the Tribune Company's only choice to buy the *News* and that if the negotiations with him failed, the company would have no other alternative but to put an end to the paper.

Mainly because of Murdoch's intrusion, Albritton quickly withdrew, leaving Cook with no choice but to make good on his promise to close the *News.* He never did, though. Heatedly rejecting a vague follow-up bid from Murdoch, Cook announced that the *News* would stay in business under the Tribune Company's sponsorship and would do so on the basis of its own cost-cutting deal with the unions. The *Daily News* published Cook's rejection under the headline: "Trib to Rupert: Drop Dead," with Cook quoted as claiming that the only reason for Murdoch's intercession had been to bring about the shutdown of the *News.*

The headline was guaranteed to inflame Murdoch—not because of its public-slap-in-the-face character, but because it reminded him he would have to continue the *Post*'s money-losing struggle against the *News* for at least another few years and he would not gain the political dominance in New York he had begun to count on. Murdoch reacted in two ways. One was to further intensify his circulation attacks on the *News* by adding yet another layer of sensationalism, distortion, and slantedness to the *Post*'s news pages and by stepping up the *Post*'s efforts to embarrass the *News* in print. The other was to begin looking beyond the New York newspaper world for opportunities to spread his political creed and influence.

By 1982, the nature and purpose of the marriage between Murdoch's journalistic sensationalism and his politics had become clear. Quite simply, beyond its money-making blueprint, Murdochian journalism was designed to manipulate readers' emotions to buttress the ideological debating points made by its right-wing editorializing. Although examples of this were many and varied, a typical one pertained to the issue of welfarism as a prime symptom of the disease of liberalism in America. Murdoch's *Post* editorial writers, along with most of his columnists, were tireless in their attacks on the liberal and Socialist strains that had long dominated the American political process, especially in the major urban regions of the country. With the advent of Reaganism in 1980, their attacks grew more frequent and pointed. At the same time, the *Post*'s news pages increasingly sensationalized incidents of crime involving members of the metropolitan area's large welfare class, often distorting facts and always employing the purplest of prose to paint those involved in the worst possible light.

There was no question that the American welfare system, and the political philosophy behind it, were riddled with imperfections and ripe for reform. There was no question either that the emergence of Reaganism, whose principal domestic ideological imperatives were based on severely reducing the citizenry's dependence on government for its daily welfare, had touched a responsive nerve in America. Its main difficulty was that it increasingly appeared to be inequitably selective, favoring certain small classes of people and enterprise while depriving larger groups, mainly those in the country's lower, mostly nonwhite, economic strata. It could fairly be said that although Reaganism made no overt appeals to the inherent racism and ethnocentrism of America's economically dominant classes, those impulses were very much a part of the nation's favorable response to it, especially in racially and ethnically mixed urban areas.

Unlike Reaganism, however, Murdochism thrived on overt

appeals to ethnic biases in the journalistic prosecution of its right-wing ideology. An example of this bias, when it came to violence in New York, was in the way the *New York Post* handled the case of the "Voodoo Killer" as compared to that of the "Subway Vigilante."

"Voodoo Killer: Crazed Mom Slays Two Tots" was the headline on the *Post*'s November 30, 1984, front page. The gruesome incident was real enough. The day before, a husbandless black woman living on welfare in a South Bronx slum tenement had stabbed to death her own three-year-old child and the infant son of her sister. As it turned out, the woman had a history of mental derangement, most of it rooted in religious delusion, and had been in and out of city psychiatric welfare wards as recently as a few weeks before. The twin slaying had apparently been triggered by some sort of argument between the woman and her sister (who was also stabbed, but escaped death) over food. Other members of the family told reporters about the woman's past spiritual hallucinations, and police confirmed that upon her arrest she was spouting inanities about the Bible and the devil.

Murdoch's *Post* immediately transformed the woman into the "Voodoo Killer."

What was the factual justification for the headline? None, unless one credited a single cryptic quote from a purported aunt of the murderer, buried at the tail end of the *Post* story, that described the woman as having "known" a "voodoo priestess" three years before. The so-called aunt later denied having said anything of the sort or having talked to any *Post* or other reporter. In their coverage of the story, the *Daily News* and the *Times,* though they pointed out the woman's history of apparent religious psychosis, made no connection between her deranged acts and voodooism. Nor, in its three separate follow-up stories the next day, did the *Post.*

The only justifications for the *Post* headline were economic, ethnic, and political. Murders are everyday occurrences in New York. They are particularly routine in the many black and Spanish ghettos of the city, and reading about such rampant homicide becomes a ho-hum proposition. It was made even more of a yawn by the *Post*'s past saturation of its readers' sensibilities with sensationalized, but not very startling, stories of urban brutality.

So "Voodoo Killer" was concocted by Murdoch's editors to

pierce that ennui, "juice up" a commonplace event, and produce a big sale of *Posts* on November 30. (By comparison, the *Daily News* front-page headline was: "Crazed Mom Stabs Two Kids to Death"—a little less compelling in its inflammatory news appeal, yet truthful.) But behind the obvious economic motive lay a more sophisticated one that dovetailed neatly with the racial and ethnic mind-set of Murdoch and most of his Australian and British deputies on the *Post.* The posture was antiblack, anti-Hispanic (which in New York is to say, for the most part, anti–Puerto Rican), and "anti" every other component of the city's economic under-class. What it sought to accomplish was to reinforce the standard *Post* editorial line that welfare-subsidized minorities were prone not only to violent crime but to heinously bizarre violent crime. By playing the story the way it did, the *Post* could then come back with yet another editorial about the folly of welfarism in America and how it encourages crime and violence.

The case of the "Subway Vigilante," a month later, had a similar use. Bernhard Goetz, a white man, shot down four black teenaged hoodlums in a New York subway car after one or more apparently tried to gouge money from him. He then fled, becoming the object of a massive manhunt. Even before he was apprehended and identified a few days later, Goetz became the darling of the *Post,* a symbol of Murdochian frustration over "the way the energy and prosperity of industrious white America was being drained by the tremendous black problem," as Murdoch had earlier expressed it to me. In this case, a white man had spoken with a gun. Whether he had acted in self-defense or not remained unclear, but the question was almost beside the point so far as the *Post* was concerned. And it became of no greater significance once Goetz gave himself up and it was learned that he was a man with an emotionally checkered history. The *Post* continued to play him up as a gallant white-versus-black hero, and the four teenagers as irredeemable thugs who thoroughly deserved their fate.

No doubt the paper's treatment of the case rang a responsive bell in the passions of many readers, for New York was indeed a fertile garden of race-oriented fear and outrage, much of it caused by just the sort of people gunned down by Goetz. But much, too, had been cultivated by the *Post* itself, so that an incident such as the Goetz carnage provided it with still another chance to practice the journalism of self-fulfilled prophecy. One could only wonder about the paper's coverage had Goetz been a black man and the four youths he shot white.

"Voodoo," a term loaded with negative emotive content, was applied to a violent black. "Vigilante," a word that resonated with rectitude and glory, was applied to a violent white. Such was the *Post*'s clever subtextual methodology under Murdoch. It was exploited not just on those two isolated occasions, however. Practically every day, in almost every conceivable way, the paper continues to betray sharp ethnic prejudices, whether in its headlines or in the language of its stories or in the pictures it runs and captions. The function of Murdoch-*Post* journalism is not to report, but to suggest, to sway, to manipulate its readers' passions and responses.

And then there is the reverse-prejudice, reverse-manipulation regularly practiced by the paper. Between the end of the 1978 newspaper strike and the election of Ronald Reagan in 1980, the *Post* had completed its political metamorphosis. Now, without apology, the paper proceeded to function as an organ of the strident right-wing politics and socioeconomics symbolized by Reaganism and the neo-conservative movement. Although Murdoch had endorsed Jimmy Carter during the 1980 New York Democratic primary, he made no secret of the fact that the endorsement was pro forma and that come the November election the paper would firmly support almost any Republican pitted against Carter. He made no secret either of his hope that the Republican candidate would be Reagan, for the tough, pragmatic conservatism preached by Reagan and his circle was the closest in America to the type of bellicose conservatism increasingly espoused by Murdoch. Thus, when Reagan was nominated to run against Carter, the *Post* went all out for the former movie actor and California governor, using its news pages in much the same blatantly slanted way it had done three years earlier when it promoted the election of Ed Koch as Mayor of New York.

Murdoch did not exactly brag of having single-handedly brought about Reagan's election. But he took as much credit for it as he reasonably could, claiming that the *Post* had "delivered New York State to Reagan." He saw his boast acknowledged when, shortly after the new President's inauguration in January 1981, Reagan thanked Murdoch personally and sent him a presidential plaque honoring his singular contribution.

Thereafter, just about the only way the *Post* failed to follow the new right-wing party line was in its continued strident advocacy of Israel in its opinion and news pages. Arch-conservative politics in America—including the so-called neo-conservative doctrines that had propelled Reagan into office—are centered in that simultaneously real and symbolic region of the nation known as Middle America, a region where American Jews have long been, at best, tolerated outsiders, at worst, obsessively hated aliens. The traditions and culture of mainstream American Jewry are largely urban-oriented and politically progressive, which is to say Democratic and Liberal Party–associated. Even in its most socially benign Republican Party manifestations, the militant conservative movement in the United States has never been much interested in Jewish concerns and is often rabidly opposed to them, usually for reasons rooted in the virulent anti-Semitism that continues to this day to be part and parcel of right-wing American orthodoxy. To be sure, the Reagan Administration did not get elected on an anti-Jewish or anti-Israel platform. But Reagan's 1980 campaign was little more than lukewarm in its embrace of traditional Jewish parochial interests, the foremost of which was the United States' continuing unconditional support of Israel.

Murdoch, on the other hand, as publisher and editor-in-chief of the *New York Post,* had a large Jewish constituency, as he did to a lesser degree with *New York* magazine and *The Village Voice.* Not only had the pre-Murdoch *Post* readership been heavily Jewish, so, too, were the present *Post* advertisers. Moreover, most of Murdoch's closest friends and business advisers were wealthy, influential New York Jews intensely active in pro-Israel causes. And he himself still retained a strong independent sympathy for Israel, a personal identification with the Jewish state that went back to his Oxford days.

There was no way, then, that Murdoch could allow the *Post* to relax its traditional advocacy of Israel as he turned it into New York's main organ of Reaganite orthodoxy. His first solution to the problem was to expand and banner the paper's stable of politically conservative columnists who also happened to be Jewish. Norman Podhoretz and Dorothy Rabinowitz were just two of the *Post*'s new right-wing voices. Interestingly, their often convoluted and long-winded "egghead" writing style was at extreme odds with Murdoch's prescriptions for snappy, entertaining journalism.

His second solution, which was to use the paper's news pages to glorify Israel more intensively than ever while regularly deriding the actions of its Arab enemies, was not so subtle. Knowledgeable Jews even complained of the campaign, theorizing that Murdoch was interested in nothing more than exploiting and sensationalizing Middle East violence to sell newspapers. Much of the *Post*'s reportage of events in the region was shamelessly slanted, distorted, and on more than one occasion, fabricated from the bare, dry, factual bones of wire service copy.

I was witness to some of the *Post*'s coverage of the Israeli invasion of Lebanon in the summer of 1982 and of the subsequent siege of Beirut. Throughout that period, the paper was without a single reporter on the scene, yet its stories were laced with unattributed "eye-witness" descriptions of Arab atrocities and Israeli heroics, many of them invented in its New York City newsroom. In the meantime, the paper's conservative Jewish columnists regularly attacked what they took to be the anti-Israeli coverage of the war by the American television networks and other New York papers that had reporters at the battlefront and in Beirut.

Soon, Murdoch himself was on his way to Israel for a helicopter tour of the combat areas in Lebanon and to meet with Ariel Sharon, the right-wing Israeli general who had mounted and still commanded the invasion. The tour was arranged by Howard Squadron, Murdoch's New York lawyer and, as head of the American Jewish Congress, one of Israel's most influential lobbyists in the United States. From the very start of his ownership of the *Post*, Murdoch had opened the paper's opinion pages to columns written by Squadron and his counterparts in other major Jewish organizations. In April 1982, Squadron's Jewish Congress had obligingly named Murdoch "Communications Man of the Year" and thrown a lavish banquet in his honor, a signal to New York's liberal Jewish community that despite his suddenly hard-nosed journalistic devotion to Reaganism, Murdoch was still a dedicated friend and supporter of Israel.

Murdoch returned from his trip singing the praises of Sharon in particular and Israel in general. Predictably, the *Post*'s pro-Israel slant grew even sharper, notwithstanding the serious questions by then being raised, especially in Israel, about Sharon's and the government's conduct of the war. If there was any real benefit of the trip, it was that Murdoch eventually established a resident *Post* reporter in Israel. Thereafter, stories emanating from Israel would at least have the appearance of first-person authenticity.

Perhaps the ultimate in *Post* distortion and hysteria-mongering occurred in the days immediately following the Soviet nuclear power-plant accident near Chernobyl in the western Ukraine at the end of April 1986. Throughout that week, Murdoch's New York minions published all sorts of "factual" scare stories based—to put it charitably—on pure rumor and speculation.

For example, on May 2 the paper appeared with this almost full-length front-page headline: "Mass Graves For 15,000 N-Victims." A second banner across pages two and three repeated the astounding news: "15,000 Already Dead In Russia." The story relating to the two headlines gave as its "source" for this "horror" an obscure Ukrainian-language newspaper published in New Jersey. Here's how *Post* reporter Leo Standora wrote it:

> Information gathered by Ukrainian Weekly, a newspaper in New Jersey, from relatives of people living near what may be the world's worst nuclear disaster indicate as many as 15,000 are already dead.
>
> It said they were being buried in a mass grave 150 miles from the Chernobyl reactor complex. . . .

Since no other paper contained such an alarming announcement—indeed, since the other New York papers and TV news broadcasters had begun cautiously to credit Soviet assertions that the immediate death toll was practically nil (a fact subsequently substantiated)—the *Post* headlines and story seemed designed expressly for the purpose of selling extra copies of the paper that day.

Nor did Standora bother to inform readers that his only source, the *Ukrainian Weekly,* was a virulently anti-Soviet "exile" publication that seldom let an opportunity pass to propagandize against Communist Russia. It could be said, of course, that the use of facts by the news media in the West to embarrass the Soviet Union and to demonstrate its many faults is a legitimate journalistic pursuit. But to tee off on the Russians solely on the basis of rumors gathered by a barely read foreign-language weekly with a perpetual ax to grind is another matter altogether. But then, like its source in New Jersey, the *Post* under Murdoch never made any secret of its own feverish anti-Soviet bias.

Naturally, the next day's editions of the *Post*, those of May 3, 1986, made absolutely no reference to the previous day's sensational report of 15,000 deaths in the Chernobyl area.

Pie in the Sky

One of Murdoch's first priorities on his return to New York from Israel in the late summer of 1982 was to implement his decision of a few months before, following his failure to bring about the shutdown of the *Daily News,* to begin "nationalizing" the American branch of his newspaper empire. His ambition was no less than to establish a Murdoch-owned paper in every major city of the United States. Oddly, the first paper he considered buying was the money-losing *Courier-Express* of Buffalo, New York, not exactly a major metropolis despite its rank as the state's second largest city. I asked him, "Why Buffalo?" Murdoch replied that the *Courier-Express* was the first paper to become available. Soon, though, he revealed another reason.

The previous winter, Hugh Carey, New York's contentious, controversial, two-term Democratic governor, had indicated that he wouldn't run for reelection in November 1982. The news produced the usual jockeying for political position among a flock of Democratic politicians across the state who hoped to succeed him. Conspicuously absent from the group was New York City's Mayor Ed Koch, who had just been reelected in part on his promise that he entertained no higher political ambitions and would serve a full four-year second term at City Hall. For that reason, Koch could not toss his hat into the gubernatorial race on his own initiative, although he ached to run. The New York governorship was a traditional stepping-stone to the White House. Koch, whom many jokingly described as the only mayor in the United States with his own foreign policy, often fantasized to friends about one day being the first Jewish president. As governor of New York, his fantasy would no longer be farfetched.

Murdoch had solved Koch's problem in January by launching a much publicized write-in ballot campaign in the *Post* to persuade New Yorkers to "draft" the mayor as a Democratic candidate and thereby release him from his promise to serve out his recently begun second term. The promotion was Murdoch's most shamelessly partisan abuse of his journalistic power in New York since he'd taken over the *Post.* Few were seriously disturbed by it, however, finding it more humorous than harmful. Nevertheless, the fact that Koch coyly participated in it made it clear that for all his self-alleged feisty independence, he was little more than Murdoch's lackey.

Predictably, Koch was duly "drafted" by *Post* readers and in February "accepted" the so-called mandate that he run for the Democratic nomination, which would be determined in the September 1982 primary. What he failed to take into account was the possibility that Murdoch might be setting him up as a fall guy. All appearances pointed to the likelihood that Lewis Lehrman, a wealthy businessman who if anything was a more militant and energetic conservative than Ronald Reagan, would be the Republican candidate in November. Mario Cuomo represented the only other realistic prospect for the Democratic candidacy—the same Mario Cuomo whom Murdoch had grown to dislike, not only for his "stale liberal politics" but for his "weak, holier-than-thou, two-faced personality," as Murdoch complained of him to me at the time.

Murdoch wanted to use Koch to block Cuomo's nomination in the September primary. With Cuomo out of the way and Koch running against Lehrman in the November general election, Murdoch could then use the *Post,* he believed, to engineer a Lehrman victory by producing a big turnout for him, and against Koch, in Democratic-heavy downstate New York. And after getting the still-youthful, tough-talking Lehrman installed as New York's governor, Murdoch could then groom him as the likely successor to Reagan in 1988. In such fashion Murdoch would eventually have his very own man in the White House and a direct input into the conduct of the American government.

But after Koch agreed unwittingly to function as the vital component of the scenario, he proceeded—just as unwittingly—to shatter it. Not long after the start of his campaign against Cuomo in the early spring of 1982, *Playboy* magazine printed a long interview he had given prior to his Murdoch-assisted entry into the race. In it, he sang the praises of living in New York City and ridiculed the quality of life in the rest of New York State, describing upstaters as "rubes," rural life as a "joke," the suburbs as "sterile," and the prospect of living in Albany, the state capital, as "a fate worse than death."

The early polls had shown Koch to be fairly popular upstate, with an excellent chance to defeat Cuomo in September. But once the upstate press began to publicize his *Playboy* "insults," his prospects nose-dived. His remarks continued to haunt him as he campaigned throughout the summer. By August, it became clear that he could well lose the primary solely because of the upstate vote.

Midway through the same month, the Cowles newspaper chain announced that its *Buffalo Courier-Express,* which was running at a loss of about $8.5 million a year, was for sale. If they could not sell the paper within the month, the Cowles announcement said, they would simply close it down and liquidate its assets. Upon learning of this, Murdoch immediately dispatched a team of his News America financial and editorial executives to Buffalo to investigate its purchase. Buffalo and its industrial surroundings, at the other end of New York State from New York City, had an aggregate population of nearly a million, much of it Democratic. A quick buy of the *Courier-Express,* and then a concerted *Post*-type journalistic campaign over the next few weeks on behalf of Koch, might just save the day for him, Murdoch thought. And even if it didn't, he could still use the *Courier-Express,* as he intended to use the *Post,* to tout the election of the Republican Lehrman in November. Indeed, if Cuomo did beat Koch in the forthcoming September primary, it would almost be imperative for Murdoch to have a major upstate paper to provide additional aid to Lehrman.

But Murdoch was not willing to make a reckless business decision simply to implement an ingenious political scheme. His executives reported back a few days later that the *Courier-Express* was in hopeless financial shape and would require a major overhaul in staff and plant merely to keep it alive. "And once the election was over, what would we do with it then?" said one. "I mean, Buffalo ain't exactly where it's happening."

Two days later, Murdoch flew to Buffalo to see for himself. I saw him hours after his return. "I made an offer," he told me. He described its stiff conditions, most of which demanded sharp and immediate staff cuts—almost 50 percent. "The fools'll probably reject it."

Reject it they did, and a few weeks later, almost on the day of the September primaries, the *Courier-Express* died. As did Koch's gubernatorial hopes and with them Murdoch's scenario. Koch lost the primary to Cuomo by a 52-to-48 percent margin. In the November general election, despite the *New York Post*'s efforts on behalf of Lehrman, Cuomo went on to win the governorship by a narrow plurality. Murdoch seethed, but there was little he could do about it. So he resumed his search for other major-city newspapers.

The year before, the Hearst Corporation had transformed its money-losing Boston daily, the *Herald-American,* into a tabloid in a last-ditch effort to save it. The experiment had failed, and in November 1982, shortly after the New York gubernatorial election, Hearst began to look around for a buyer. Learning that Murdoch was in the market, it turned first to him.

Hearst had to look no further. Within days Murdoch agreed to buy the *Herald-American* for $1 million in cash and $7 million to be paid out of any future profits. The rock-bottom price indicated one of two things. Either Hearst was so eager to get rid of a hopeless financial headache that it was prepared to give the paper away, or Murdoch had stolen it. Whatever the case, by early December, the *Boston Herald-American* was Murdoch's. Aware of his reputation, many Bostonians waited with bemused curiosity to see what he'd do with it. It did not take them long to find out. Given the Australian's history, they were not surprised.

One of the chief attractions for Murdoch of the *Herald-American* was that it had already been "tabloidized," albeit without the journalistic pizzazz he was accustomed to applying to his own tabloids. Boston's other major newspaper was the *Globe,* whose average daily circulation was more than double that of the *Herald-American*'s 236,000 late in 1982. Murdoch's first task was to obtain cost-saving reductions in the *Herald-American* work force. To some degree he succeeded in accomplishing this immediately, using as his primary bargaining lever his threat to shut down the paper at the outset and take a million-dollar loss rather than suffer greater losses later on because of the unions' refusal to agree to job cuts.

Borrowing a leaf from Murdoch's usual approach, the *Globe* warned the unions that it would expect the same concessions they handed to Murdoch. This gave Murdoch the opportunity to accuse the *Globe* of trying to sabotage his attempt to save the *Herald-American,* and it neatly set the stage for his second task, which was to launch a circulation war against the *Globe.*

Murdoch wasted no time. On December 22, 1982, he officially shortened the paper's name to the *Herald* and appointed Robert Page, one of his trusted San Antonio aides, as publisher. To help Page turn the *Herald* into an authentic Murdoch paper, he named Leslie Hinton, an Englishman who had been working on the *Star,* and Joe Robinowitz from the *Post,* to head the editorial staff. He changed the paper's format from four to seven columns per page, expanded its sports section and stock market charts, and got set to introduce a Boston version of Wingo. With the rapid emergence of a combined weekly *Star* and *New York Post* style of news presentation, which concentrated in its usually strident and sensationalist fashion on local crime, sex, and gossip, and with the introduction of a new right-wing editorial slant, the transformation of the *Herald* was completed by the New Year.

Predictably, the daily *Herald*'s circulation climbed during the next two years, going from 236,000 to 381,000 for a gain of 145,000 by the end of 1984. The paper's Sunday edition enjoyed a similar rise, from 227,000 to 319,000. The credit was due largely to Wingo. But despite the increased circulation, Murdoch found himself burdened with the same problem that had bedeviled the *Post* for eight years—no significant increase in advertising revenue. The war with the *Globe* turned out to be no war at all, since the *Herald*'s circulation increases brought about no corresponding decreases in the daily and Sunday *Globe*'s readership. Moreover, the *Globe*'s share of Boston's total newspaper advertising revenues actually grew.

Murdoch, though disappointed that his cheap-jack formula had once again failed to work in America, remained unfazed. The formula continued to flourish in England, where the *Sun* and *News of the World* together poured nearly $30 million into Newscorp's treasury in fiscal 1982–83 and promised to double those figures in 1983–84. In Australia, Murdoch's enlarged television network was beginning to produce major earnings, and Ansett, the airline he half-owned, was due to pay a $65 million dividend to Newscorp early in 1984. The financial squeeze of late 1981 was over, and by early 1983 Murdoch had plenty of surplus cash with which to shore up his failing press ventures further and expand his drive for nationwide political influence in the United States. Consequently, he began to look for a fourth major-city paper. Before he could find one, though, an entirely different media prospect presented itself.

Five years earlier, Murdoch had gone into partnership with Robert Stigwood, the rich Australian pop-music impresario, to produce a motion picture about the World War I Gallipoli disaster. His investment in the big-budget spectacle was partly in response to legislation enacted by the Australian government that was designed to stimulate the growth of the Australian movie industry by providing major tax breaks to wealthy investors who financed the production of domestic feature films.

But Murdoch had other motives, too. One was the sentimental idea of coproducing a movie about an event in Australian history in which his father had played so significant a role and which, if only indirectly, had been the seed of the Murdoch family's rise to prominence. Another was simply to get his feet wet in the financial mechanics of the motion-picture and television-production industries upon which his Australian television network was dependent for so much of its programming. Murdoch had gone as far as he could in television in Australia and England, and he was precluded by law, because he was not an American citizen, from television broadcast ownership in the United States. The production of American movies and television shows was not out of his legal reach, however. It could be another effective way to put his ideological stamp on the United States and at the same time make huge amounts of money. As he said to me in some awe after a special screening of the modestly successful *Gallipoli* in 1982, "Do you realize a single picture like this can clear more in a year than a year's worth of *Sun*s?" By then he was very definitely sold on the idea of getting a piece of the American movie and television-production business. His enthusiasm was in no way discouraged by Stanley Shuman, now his principal financial adviser. Allen and Company, after all, specialized in entertainment-industry financing.

It was the Allen firm, too, that pointed out to Murdoch the vital legal loophole that would allow him to get into actual television broadcasting in America despite the federal laws against foreign ownership of more than 20 percent of any conventional station. The loophole was satellite cable television, where no such restrictions applied. Early in 1983, through Allen and Company, Murdoch bought a struggling satellite-television development company that was grandly called the Inter-American Satellite Television Network. Renaming it Skyband, he proposed to use it, he said in Newscorp's 1983 annual report, to operate "the first nationwide satellite-to-home broadcast network in the United States." He added:

> At first we will function essentially as a distribution system with programming purchased from outside sources. Eventually we will bring our own creative resources into play so that we can produce and broadcast our own entertainment and information services.

Murdoch's plan for Skyband was to lease five transponders on a broadcast satellite and make five channels of programming available to an exclusive untapped market of five million homes in the United States that were unable to receive ordinary cable television because of their rural or semirural locations. The entire scheme depended on the development of a small state-of-the-art rooftop dish antenna that the Murdoch organization intended to lease or sell to subscribers, and additionally on his ability to acquire the necessary programming—mostly movies and syndicated commercial television shows, to start. He hoped to begin broadcasting in the late fall of 1983 and predicted that within three years the network would reap more than $300 million in revenues. So great was his optimism that he hurriedly signed a nearly $20 million contract for the long-term lease of the five satellite transponders, putting down a million-dollar deposit.

Troubles arose almost immediately, however, most of them due to the failure of the antenna manufacturers to solve certain technological problems and then to produce the dishes in any reasonably priced marketable quantity. Adequate programming also proved difficult to assemble. By the time of Skyband's planned launch date in the fall, Murdoch was forced to announce the cancellation of the entire project, at least for the foreseeable future. His decision resulted in an immediate loss to Newscorp of about $20 million.

It was a loss the parent company could easily absorb. But many Murdoch-watchers—especially those in Wall Street—were puzzled by his sudden willingness to write off Skyband and by the seemingly hasty and bad business judgment that was the dominant feature of the venture. Had he bitten off more than he could chew in attempting to expand the American branch of his media

empire beyond newspapers? Had he allowed his political obses-
sions to cloud his business wisdom?

The answer was yes and no. From what he confided to me in
the spring of 1983, Murdoch was thoroughly enchanted by Skyband, not only for its potential to bring in hundreds of millions of
dollars in a few short years, but for the instant nationwide political forum he expected it to provide him. "There are really no lim-
itations on what one can broadcast over this kind of TV," he told
me, intimating that he intended to make the network, like his
newspapers, a vehicle for his pet political, economic, and social
theories.

So, yes, Murdoch leaped before he looked, allowing his
craving for much greater national influence to blur his business
judgment. But no, he hadn't taken leave of his business senses or
bitten off more than he could chew. Once he realized he'd acted
hastily, he accepted his mistake and quickly put it behind him.
What encouraged him to do so was the sudden prospect, in the
summer of 1983, of soon getting into American television in a
much more significant way.

Not long after his arrival in New York in 1974, Murdoch had
gotten to know John Kluge, the German-born creator and chairman of Metromedia, Inc. Metromedia, a New York–New Jersey-
based public company, owned and operated profitable independent commercial television stations in seven major cities of the
United States—New York, Boston, Washington, Chicago, Houston, Dallas, and Los Angeles—as well as a large stable of radio
outlets and other entertainment subsidiaries. Kluge, a tough,
fiercely independent multimillionaire businessman and a strong
believer in the entertainment approach to broadcast journalism,
was one of the few captains of the American media industry who
did not look askance at Murdoch's newspaper techniques once
the Australian started publishing in America. Later in the 1970s,
the two became close social friends and mutual business sympa-
thizers who often talked of one day collaborating in one or more
joint ventures. By 1981, their friendship had grown so intimate
that when Kluge married a onetime British pornographic-
magazine model named Patricia Gay in a lavish ceremony at
New York's St. Patrick's Cathedral, Rupert and Anna Murdoch
served in the wedding party, Anna as a matron of honor.

As early as 1979, mindful of American laws against foreign
ownership of domestic broadcast licenses, Kluge had begun to
urge Murdoch to become a U.S. citizen, a move Kluge had made

two decades earlier. Murdoch, citing the fact that he would be required to renounce his Australian citizenship if he did so, and would thereby be forced to relinquish control over his television holdings in Australia, resisted the advice. However, he said somewhat jokingly, if Kluge ever wanted to sell him Metromedia, he might change his mind. If he ever decided to sell, Kluge joked back, Murdoch would be the one he'd sell to. Kluge would make a citizen of Murdoch yet.

What began as banter soon took on a more serious tone. The early 1980s saw the emergence on Wall Street of the phenomenon known as "junk-bond financing," a sudden rise in huge, unfriendly corporate takeovers by predatory lone-wolf investors with access to seemingly unlimited high-premium stock-purchase funds amassed through the sale of junk bonds. A corollary of the trend, pursued solely to prevent such outsider raids, became the practice of taking large, vulnerable public companies "private." This consisted of top managements buying up most or all of the public stock in their companies in order to concentrate ownership and control in their own hands. Called the "leveraged buyout," this strategy also demanded vast amounts of quickly organized financing, usually of the new "junk" variety.

Junk-bond financing got its name from the high risk–high yield nature of the securities it entailed and from the fact that such securities were among the lowest-rated by Wall Street's financial credit-rating organizations. Although junk-bond financing made hostile takeovers and internal buyouts of large companies much easier than before, it also burdened the acquired or "privatized" companies with so much high-interest short-term debt that the slightest downturn in business could force them to begin selling their most productive and valuable assets simply to meet their massive annual debt obligations.

Early in 1983, John Kluge had closely advised Murdoch on his satellite television venture. When the venture stalled and Murdoch was stuck for $20 million, Kluge consoled him by offering the prospect of a more pervasive and influential television presence in the United States in the not too distant future. With the advent of junk-bond financing, Metromedia had suddenly become vulnerable to a hostile takeover attempt. As a result, Kluge was about to take the company private through a leveraged buyout of its public stock.

Video Visions

Through a syndicate called Boston Ventures Limited Partnership, Murdoch became a major investor in the junk-bond financing Kluge employed to take Metromedia private. The investment was his private signal to Kluge that he had grown more serious about the prospect of one day acquiring Metromedia's television chain. The Kluge buyout had added an enormous amount of debt to the company's books. Based on Metromedia's projected 1984 operating profit of $99.3 million, Kluge would be hard put to keep to a schedule that called for annual repayments of $90 million over the next five years, especially if he hoped to develop the new communications business he'd become interested in—mobile cellular telephones.

It was almost inevitable that Kluge would have to sell Metromedia's broadcast division, perhaps within a year or two. Murdoch knew it, and the two agreed to keep their lines of communication open and current. In the meantime, Kluge advised Murdoch "to go out and buy a Hollywood movie studio, like Marvin Davis did." Davis was the rotund New York–born, Denver-based oil and gas megamillionaire who had acquired control of 20th Century-Fox a short while before. Kluge's advice was based on his theory that if Murdoch could combine his international news organization with an established motion picture and television-production company, he would then be able to join them together with Metromedia to create a fourth major commercial television network in the United States, one that could realistically compete with the other three networks both in entertainment and news programming, and thus for major advertising revenues. Moreover, with such a package, the financing to buy Metromedia, which could cost upward of $2 billion based on its current debt, would be much easier to arrange.

Actually, Murdoch was way ahead of Kluge. He'd been pondering a movie studio acquisition for some time, if only to obtain access to a steady no-cost source of entertainment programming for his Skyband and Sky Channel projects.* He'd even talked to Marvin Davis, also an investor in Boston Ventures, about 20th Century-Fox. Davis hadn't been interested in selling, although 20th's movie and television divisions were struggling financially. Nonetheless the logic behind Kluge's formula intrigued Murdoch. Now he felt he had a double reason to go after a major studio.

What's more, the timing was right. For the fiscal year ending in June 1983, Newscorp's gross revenues for the first time topped the billion-dollar mark in American currency value, and the company's aggregate operating profit came in at $70 million. Further, Murdoch's various newspaper holdings in England provided him with an 11 percent share of Reuters, the international news and wire service that was owned by a consortium of ten British media organizations. Because many of the consortium's members needed cash, plans were afoot to turn Reuters into a public company in 1984 through a massive stock flotation. Estimates were that such a sale might bring in as much as $1.5 billion. On a pro rata basis, Newscorp stood to earn an additional $115 million in 1984 to go with its projected operating profit of about $95 million for that year. Murdoch would have plenty of cash to work with in the coming year, as well as a great deal of increased borrowing power.

Murdoch conferred with Stanley Shuman. What major movie company was available? he asked. Warner Brothers, came Shuman's answer. The only problem was that it wasn't really available in the sense Murdoch meant. He would have to mount a hostile takeover raid to get it. "When do we start?" Murdoch said.

Warner Brothers by then was a subsidiary of New York–

---

* Along with Skyband in the United States, Murdoch had started a similar service in England called Sky Channel. It used a combination of satellite and cable to send English-language news and canned entertainment programs into the television sets of subscribers in several countries of Western Europe. Because Sky Channel did not require individual dish antennas at each home, it was launched with a minimum of delay.

based Warner Communications, Inc., the vast $7 ⌐'llion con-
glomerate that had evolved out of a small chain of loca˙ funeral
homes and parking lots twenty years before and was still ˙ ?d by
its principal founder and chief executive officer, Steven Ros⌐. In
addition to the Warner Brothers movie studios, Warner Communications owned scores of other entertainment and leisure companies, including the Atari computer-game organization, and was
heavily involved with American Express in a major satellite-and-
cable television venture. But Warner, once a high-powered, high-
profit company, was in sharp decline in 1983.

In mid-1983, the company reported a staggering $302 mil-
lion loss for the first six months of the year, most of it due to the
collapse of Atari's computer-game market. The price of Warner's
common stock plunged in a year from $63 to $18. Of all the public companies then being targeted for takeover raids under the
new junk-financing device, Warner was among the most vulnerable. The company had once been viewed as the arrogant Ross's
personal and untouchable fiefdom. Now it was being circled by a
growing pack of hungry financial predators.

Murdoch, who bore a grudge against Ross over a prior dis-
agreeable business encounter, started buying Warner stock secretly during the summer of 1983 through Allen and Company.
By the end of September, he had spent nearly $20 million and
accumulated a little more than a million shares, which represented 1.6 percent of the outstanding stock. When the financial
press got wind of the move, it immediately began to speculate
about his intentions. Ross discounted any threat, caustically describing Murdoch as being without the resources to mount a raid
on a company as big as Warner. Speaking laconically through
Shuman, Murdoch called his stock acquisition a passive investment. But he kept buying.

By early December, he had spent an additional $78 million
and held 6.7 percent of Warner's shares, making him the company's largest single stockholder. As such he was required to file
the obligatory Securities and Exchange Commission registration
statements. In his filings, he assured the government that he had
no intention of seeking control of Warner, or even a seat on the
board. Such assurances were a dead giveaway of his real purpose,
many Wall Street analysts thought. If Murdoch's majority-
ownership investment was friendly, why wouldn't he expect to
move onto the board?

Ross didn't need the analysts' conclusions to arrive at his own accurate assessment of Murdoch's intentions. He had learned of them the week before, when the gauntlet had been laid down in a heated meeting he had with Murdoch, Shuman, and Howard Squadron, who was, as usual, orchestrating Murdoch's legal strategy. By mid-December, when Murdoch's holding had reached 7 percent, Ross was already busy formulating a plan to repel him. By the end of December, his scheme was in place, and he was able to announce that he had made a secret deal with Herbert Siegel, the chairman of Chris-Craft Industries, another large conglomerate, to swap 19 percent of Warner Communications stock for a 42.5 percent stake in a Chris-Craft subsidiary that owned and operated a number of commercial television stations around the country. With Warner Communications now a major television owner, Murdoch, still a foreigner, would be barred by federal law from owning more than 20 percent of its stock. Furthermore, one of the television stations the Chris-Craft subsidiary operated was in San Antonio, where Murdoch continued to publish two newspapers. Other federal laws prohibited a newspaper owner from operating a television station in the same locale.

Murdoch and his strategists were stunned and angered by Ross's announcement. Murdoch, whose reputation for crafty practices was becoming legend, did not take kindly to having a fast one pulled on him. All thoughts of the original purpose of his move on Warner—to acquire Warner Brothers and a few other divisions while selling off the rest of the conglomerate—became moot. To accept defeat would mean an immediate plunge in Warner's common-stock price, which had surged during the course of the previous three months of takeover activity. That in turn would mean a major loss to Murdoch on his 7 percent holding and a deep embarrassment to Shuman and Squadron.

There was only one thing to do: fight back. If nothing else, they might be able to make matters so unpleasant and expensive for Ross that he'd agree to a settlement under a new weapon that had emerged in the corporate-raid wars. The weapon was "greenmail," the device by which a raider consents to end his takeover attempt in exchange for the target company's buy-back of the stock he has accumulated at a price well in excess of what he paid for it.

And so, in early January 1984, Murdoch began a concerted

legal attack on Ross's deal with Chris-Craft. He filed a lawsuit in Delaware, where Warner Communications was incorporated, seeking to block the deal. He brought a similar action before the Federal Communications Commission in Washington. The prose Squadron used to frame Murdoch's complaints about Ross was almost as purple as that which regularly appeared in Murdoch's newspapers. It was laced with accusations of fraud and trickery on Ross's part, and later, allegations of racketeering.

Ross, countersuing, answered in kind. His court papers characterized Murdoch as "deceptive and manipulative" and in reviewing his history, said:

> Murdoch is now well known in the United States and England for purchasing reputable newspapers and converting them into a sensationalist format, emphasizing violence, scandal and sex. Murdoch has already destroyed the journalistic reputations of the *Post* and the *Herald*. . . . Except in publications controlled by him, Murdoch has frequently been described as deceitful and untrustworthy by persons who have worked for him. . . . Recently, he has been using his newspapers to publicize his position concerning his position [*sic*] with Warner.

It was true that along with his other journalistic sins, Murdoch had long used his newspapers to feature and promote his outside commercial interests as well as his personal and political ones. The ordinary reader of the *New York Post* or London *Sunday Times,* for instance, unfamiliar with what those interests were, might read an extensive, flattering business story about some obscure company or business venture and wonder why it deserved such lavish coverage. There would be no hint that the company or venture was one that Murdoch was involved in. Another reader might puzzle over why a particular Murdoch paper gave a full page of startlingly favorable coverage to some local charity event of the night before when such events were otherwise ignored. The reader would not be told, of course, that the event in question was one that Anna Murdoch had organized. This sort of owner self-promotion was not unknown in the American newspaper world; in fact it was done occasionally by just about every paper. Murdoch merely made it more regular and blatant.

What was not so conventional was a newspaper owner's

practice of assigning members of the paper's journalistic staff to conduct an undercover investigation of an adversary with whom he was locked in personal and business litigation that had nothing to do with the newspaper. When it was learned that Murdoch had ordered the *Post*'s metropolitan editor, Steve Dunleavy, and a pair of *Post* reporters to dig up damaging information about Warner's Ross, even the most jaded New York eyebrows were raised.

The various courtroom bouts lasted into March 1984, with the inexhaustible Murdoch losing most of the key rounds but threatening to keep the fight going indefinitely. Finally, in mid-March, he brought the greenmail weapon to bear, offering through Squadron to withdraw in exchange for a Warner buyout of his stock at a stiff premium. The weary Ross agreed, and Murdoch came away with a profit of more than $40 million on the repurchase of his stock, plus an agreement from Warner to pay his $8 million in legal costs. He gained an additional measure of spiritual satisfaction when, soon after, Ross was hit with a series of class-action suits by small stockholders of Warner accusing him of gross mismanagement in his bow to Murdoch's greenmail and demanding his ouster as the company's chairman.

By the time of the Ross-Murdoch settlement, dozens of other takeover entrepreneurs were raiding huge public companies, all of them armed with junk-financing commitments and holding the greenmail weapon in reserve in case their assaults stalled. Murdoch wasted little time in exploiting the environment of corporate confusion and panic he'd helped create with his Warner raid. Targeting the St. Regis paper and timber company, he began buying stock at an average of $36 a share. By mid-July, having spent $65 million, he owned 5.2 percent of St. Regis. He then announced his intention to offer $52 a share, or another $800 million, to acquire enough additional stock to give him 51 percent control. To put a smooth public relations gloss on his bid, Murdoch reminded the press that St. Regis was a major supplier of newsprint and that its takeover by a newspaper publishing company was "a good fit." What he didn't mention was that earlier in 1984, St. Regis had twice paid a modest form of greenmail to fend off previous raiders.

William Haselton, the chairman of St. Regis, reacted much as Steve Ross had done when Murdoch began his attempt to take over Warner Communications. While searching for a friendly corporate "white knight" to help him turn back Murdoch's raid, he filed a series of injunctive lawsuits against the Australian, thereby playing straight into Murdoch's hands. Haselton won in the end, but it was a Pyrrhic victory. He persuaded Champion International, another big paper and timber company, to act as his white knight by allowing Champion to acquire 60 percent of St. Regis in a friendly merger. Part of the deal was that Champion would buy back Murdoch's stock at $55.50 a share, which was nearly $20 more than he'd paid to acquire his 5.2 percent stake. In August, Murdoch walked away with a profit of almost $37 million.

Of course, Stanley Shuman and his banking firm took a generous slice of that profit in fees. Herbert Allen, the head of Allen and Company, when questioned about Murdoch's role as a client, said, "Rupert Murdoch can write his own ticket here anytime." Murdoch and Shuman, along with Squadron, seemed to have hit on a formula for quick and easy big-bucks moneymaking that had infinite possibilities. All of Wall Street waited to see where they would strike next.

There was to be no further strike, however. Murdoch had invited me to be his guest, along with scores of people from his various media companies around the world, at the August 1984 Summer Olympics in Los Angeles, which his Australian television network was covering. Although I declined the invitation, I visited his headquarters at Beverly Hills's Beverly Wilshire Hotel on a few occasions during the Games. There I found a Rupert Murdoch who, rather than exulting over his recent Wall Street triumphs, was seething with anger. Another glitch had reared its ugly head.

Because Newscorp operated in three countries, its money dealings had always been in three different currencies—the Australian dollar, the British pound, and the American dollar. With the constant shifting back and forth among the three of large chunks of Newscorp funds and borrowings, the slightest variation in exchange rates could mean a significant increase or decrease in the value of those funds. Consequently, as with any tycoon who operates internationally, Murdoch made exchange-rate planning an integral part of Newscorp's financial strategy, seeking always to time the organization's fund transfers and loan conversions to coincide with the most beneficial shifts in exchange rates. The practice had produced increasingly aggressive speculation in international currencies within the company. During the early 1980s, as recession took hold in the United States, Murdoch lost faith in the sinking American dollar and parked a large percentage of Newscorp's American and Australian operating funds in European currencies. However, Murdoch was slow to acknowledge the gradual comeback of the dollar beginning in 1983 and the corresponding drop in the comparative value of most key Eurocurrencies he'd sought shelter in. By the time he did, in the summer of 1984, Newscorp had lost nearly $75 million in what in the preceding years had been noted on its books as exchange-rate gains.

So Murdoch did not feel at all like crowing over his Warner–St. Regis financial coups when I saw him at the Los Angeles Olympics, for the profits he'd made in those had been almost completely wiped out by his exchange-rate losses. Nor—despite the steady stream of Wall Street guessing about his next greenmail target—was he inclined to pursue the hostile takeover game any further. During the earlier, quieter stages of his Warner takeover attempt, Murdoch had added the *Chicago Sun-Times* to his expanding American newspaper stable. The purchase had cost him $90 million, the most he'd ever spent for a newspaper. But it had also cost him greatly in psychic drain. That, coupled with the mudslinging controversy over his Warner and St. Regis adventures, had left him wondering about the wisdom of the more than usual public role he'd assumed. An intensive national public relations campaign during the first half of 1984, orchestrated by his New York PR man, Howard Rubenstein, and designed to soften his image, had failed to do so, if only because Murdoch was a lousy actor—or, said some who knew him, a lousy liar. It was time, he said, to "crawl back into the woodwork" and let the country's attention focus on his product, rather than on him. It was a naive hope.

Although Murdoch had grown accustomed to being publicly excoriated for his journalism and business practices, he was not quite prepared for the storm of anguish and invective that poured out of Chicago when it became known in the fall of 1983 that he would be taking over the *Sun-Times.* The tabloid had been started in 1941 by Chicago department store tycoon Marshall Field III. Its primary purpose was to provide a liberal challenge to the virulent right-wing pamphleteering of the *Chicago Tribune,* which was owned and published by Colonel Robert McCormick.

By 1983, the *Sun-Times* and *Tribune,* still competing, were the only surviving major daily newspapers in Chicago. Each had moderated its political partisanship, and each took great pride in itself as a model of dynamic, responsible journalism. The *Tribune* comfortably outsold the *Sun-Times.* But the *Sun-Times* had a large, loyal circulation of its own and usually managed to make a modest profit despite the sharply rising costs of newspapering in the early 1980s.

Murdoch's nasty combat in New York with the *Daily News* and its Chicago parent had given him a taste for further battle with the *Tribune*—on its own turf. When he decided to start expanding his American newspaper barony in 1982, Chicago was one of the cities at the top of his list. At that time, he let the Field family know that he'd be interested in buying the *Sun-Times* should they ever wish to sell.

The paper by then was owned jointly by forty-two-year-old Marshall Field V and his younger half-brother Frederick, both grandsons of the founder. The thirty-one-year-old Frederick, known as Teddy and barely on speaking terms with Marshall, had never been closely involved with the paper, preferring to live in California, where he pursued other interests. Marshall had had a much closer relationship, even serving as the *Sun-Times*'s publisher in the 1970s, but by 1983, his business preoccupations lay elsewhere, particularly in Chicago real estate. The paper was being run by James Hoge, a relatively young but veteran Chicago journalist who, after a term as its editor-in-chief, had succeeded Marshall as publisher in 1980 and deserved much of the credit for the favorable reputation it enjoyed.

Inspired in large part by Murdoch's expression of interest, the Field brothers decided to sell in the spring of 1983. When Hoge learned who the likely buyer would be, he mounted a campaign to dissuade Marshall Field from considering Murdoch, citing his history and reputation. According to Hoge, he succeeded in changing Marshall's mind. He announced to the *Sun-Times* staff that Murdoch would not be permitted to acquire the paper and, with Marshall's blessings, began organizing a group of his own to buy it. Hoge failed to anticipate Teddy Field's vital say in the matter, however. When in the early fall Hoge and his group produced an offer of $63 million, Teddy vetoed it. "I've been talking to Murdoch," Teddy told his brother. "We can get much more from him."

The younger Field was right, and Marshall felt he had no choice but to agree to a sale to Murdoch when the Australian offered $90 million, and Hoge, as well as other potential buyers, could come nowhere close to matching it. The Field brothers' acceptance of Murdoch's offer was formalized on November 1, 1983. It triggered a paroxysm of protest, both from the *Sun-Times* staff, which had continued to rely on Hoge's assurances, and from other Chicagoans. Although some of the vituperation was reserved for the Fields, most was directed at Murdoch and was thunderous with scorn. The *Sun-Times*'s most popular columnist, the irreverent Mike Royko, quit in a hail of public insults about Murdoch and soon started writing for the *Tribune*. Other top journalists and editorial executives began looking for jobs as well, including James Hoge.*

Murdoch had given his usual assurances that he had no desire to change the *Sun-Times* in any significant way. But between November and the following January 9, the date of his official takeover, it became readily apparent to the staff that he intended to "Murdochize" it thoroughly. He brought in Robert Page from the *Boston Herald* to be the paper's new publisher and assigned Roger Wood from the *New York Post* and Charles Wilson, one of his editors in London, to run the editorial side until he could find a permanent editor. Soon the *Sun-Times* began to look and sound like just another trashy Murdoch tabloid. By the end of January, sixty-seven members of the pre-Murdoch staff had left in disgust, and circulation began to drop. It would not be until April, when Murdoch introduced Wingo, that the slide would halt.

In the spring of 1984, although he continued to snap back at his critics with intensifying vitriol of his own, Murdoch admitted to me that, underneath, he was beginning to feel psychically battered and physically worn out. Not that he'd lost any of his ambition to press on with his political crusade, he assured me. It was just that—"Well, perhaps it would be better if I could go about it without all this goddamn fanfare every time I make a move."

The intensely negative publicity he was receiving was hurt-

---

* Hoge, originally a New Yorker, was quickly recruited by the Chicago Tribune Company to become publisher of New York's *Daily News*. His mission obviously was to step up the *News*'s war with the Murdoch *Post*. His success has been only marginal, primarily because of financial restraints and because he has lost some of the *News*'s top local columnists to the better-paying *Post*.

ing his family more than him, he said—his teenaged daughter Elisabeth had just been expelled from her posh Connecticut boarding school for disciplinary reasons, and his two sons, still private-school students in New York, were starting to display behavioral problems of their own. Anna Murdoch, in the meantime, continued to voice her dissatisfaction with many of his activities—though not with the lifestyle they provided—and, he told me, "had buried herself in this novel she's just finished to prove that at least one Murdoch can publish something worthwhile."

Early in the legal fight with Warner Communications, which had just ended, Murdoch, intent on outfoxing Warner's Chris-Craft television ploy, had privately declared: "If they think they can beat me by exploiting the fact I'm not a citizen, I'll become a fucking citizen and shove the deal straight up their noses." He might have, too, had not the greenmail alternative eventually proved more attractive.

Later that spring I asked him about his January threat. "It's no longer a threat," he said. "The way things look now, sooner or later I'll *have* to take out American citizenship." It was then that I learned of his Metromedia plans.

"*Stormy Weather*"

In January 1984, Murdoch was recruited by the controversial Harry Gray, head of Connecticut-based United Technologies, Inc., to become a member of the board of the giant $16 billion manufacturing conglomerate. United Technologies made elevators, air conditioners, and dozens of other "civilian" products, but it was best-known as a jet engine and helicopter manufacturer and as a leading American defense contractor. The controversy surrounding Gray related both to his shadowy personal background and to his allegedly despotic managerial methods, which were widely rumored to include the wire-tapping and physical surveillance of top company executives. When Murdoch accepted his appointment to the United Technologies board, Gray praised him to the press as "my kind of business man," by which he meant, presumably, tough, ruthless, and intimidating.

Why Gray would desire a foreigner on the board of a corporation whose revenues came in considerable measure from its highly classified defense contracts was a question that was never publicly explored. The answer was twofold. First, the Australian government was about to make a major investment in military helicopters, and Gray wanted United's Sikorsky Helicopter Division to get the contract. Second, Gray would soon reach sixty-five, which meant that under the corporation's by-laws he would be required to step down as its chief executive. Although he had already selected and groomed his successor, United Technologies' president Robert Carlson, by 1984 Gray had privately formulated a covert plan to delay his retirement. To make the plan work, he would have to get rid of Carlson, who was waiting impatiently in the wings, and then win the support of his board of directors for an indefinite extension of his position. Murdoch could be very useful in that respect.

An even more puzzling question was why a major newspaper editor and publisher would agree to join the board of a company run by Harry Gray. Gray had gone to great lengths during the latter stages of his career to conceal his past, apparently to hide the fact that he had been born and raised a Jew, the son of Jacob and Bertha Grusin, that until 1950 he had been married to a Jewish woman, and that he had changed his name. Not because he possessed such a past, but because the chairman of one of America's largest corporations so assiduously concealed it, seemed to be grist for any aggressive newspaperman's mill, especially one whose main journalistic currency was churning up scandal and peeking into the private lives of the powerful.

Moreover, Harry Gray, known as the "Gray Shark" to industry insiders, had built a managerial history so fraught with suspicions and allegations of wrongdoing that it seemed inappropriate for a newspaper publisher to join him in a formal business association. Gray's methods as a chief executive constantly made news, much of it negative. What if one day he palpably stepped over the line of legality? Where would the board member-newspaperman's duty lie—to Gray, or to the public?

I queried Murdoch on these points not long after he joined the United Technologies board. He saw no conflict of interest, which didn't surprise me. But later in 1984, a scenario such as the one I had intimated began to play itself out. In August, Robert Carlson, Gray's heir apparent, discovered that his Avon, Connecticut, home had been broken into. Since Carlson knew by then that Harry Gray was out to prevent his succession, he suspected that the break-in had been carried out on Gray's orders by United Technologies' security force. Next, he found his office at the company's headquarters ransacked and looted. Carlson went to the board of directors and accused Gray of launching a campaign to harass him out of United so that he—Gray—could stay on.

On November 2, 1984, Carlson's charges were published in *The Wall Street Journal.* Thereafter, the matter became a running headline story throughout the country. Were the accusations true? Had Harry Gray engaged in a criminal conspiracy? What was really going on in the inner sanctum of one of the nation's largest corporations and most important defense contractors?

United Technologies' public relations staff issued the usual corporate mumbo-jumbo in response to the news media's pressing queries, promising nevertheless that the corporation's board was investigating Carlson's allegations and would eventually make its findings public. All well and good, but what no one mentioned was that a top newspaperman was a member of the board and presumably privy to the real story.

Murdoch remained silent throughout the entire imbroglio. Except for a brief item acknowledging its existence, not a word about it appeared in the *New York Post* or any other Murdoch paper in America. Eventually, Gray was cleared of wrongdoing by the United board and Carlson resigned as the company's number-two man, muttering bitterly of a whitewash. Still nothing, however, of any journalistic substance from Murdoch or his "news" organization. As far as he was concerned, it was a nonevent. Today, he remains a key United Technologies director. And as of this writing, Gray remains largely in charge. Parenthetically, during the summer of 1985, the company's Sikorsky division was awarded the Australian military helicopter contract.

The more Murdoch managed to "get away with" as a newspaper publisher, the more he tried to get away with. He usually succeeded, if only because the rest of the media were reluctant to take him to task. The 1984 presidential election campaign was a case in point. Needless to say, Murdoch was committed to doing everything he could to ensure the reelection of Ronald Reagan— not just by a comfortable margin, but by a landslide. If any single event in recent American history had convinced Murdoch that it might be worthwhile for him to change his citizenship, it was Reagan's 1983 invasion of Grenada. To him, that minor military action represented the revival at last of the United States' resolve to repel Soviet communism at all costs. It absolutely magnetized him, so much so that in his British papers he turned on Prime Minister Margaret Thatcher when she dared to question the need for the Grenada invasion.

"I supported her completely when she went 10,000 miles to invade the Falklands [in 1982]," Murdoch said to me. "How dare she criticize Reagan for going a few hundred miles to enforce an American policy that's infinitely more valid! She waged a war over property rights, and she bloody well botched it up, if you ask me. Reagan's Grenada action has to do with the freedom of the Western World, including England's. Thatcher had no business opening her mouth. I'll see she pays for it."

Reaganism—a hard-line anti-Communist foreign policy combined with an equally resolute domestic program of free-market economics, much-reduced government, and heavy military buildup—had the approval of much of America by 1984. It was still viewed by many of its proponents, however, as a fragile experiment that could all too easily be sandbagged by the traditionally liberal American press. Murdoch was one of those proponents. To him, Reaganism represented a positive change in American thinking, but one that, like a sapling, needed careful nurturing if it was to reach its full potential. "It has the support of the people," he said to me in 1981, "but not the national press. The press here is sitting around doing its usual thing, sneering at Reagan and waiting to pounce on him the moment he stumbles. . . . The whole Reagan package needs much more support by the press. If no one else will provide it, we'll bloody well have to do the job!"

He had done the job to a certain extent in 1980, when he turned the *New York Post* and his San Antonio papers into pro-Reagan pamphlets. Now, in 1984, he had two additional big-city papers under his control, and he was determined to boost Reagan's reelection with even more avidity than he had the President's 1980 election. The *New York Post* was the fourth-largest-selling newspaper in the country, the *Chicago Sun-Times,* with its circulation of 655,000 when Murdoch took it over, the sixth. Factoring in the *Boston Herald* and his San Antonio papers, Murdoch reached nearly two million readers a day in four distinct regions of the country, all of them heavily Democratic in their traditional political orientation.

That, as Murdoch saw it, was his real journalistic challenge for the 1984 campaign—to turn four separate Democratic regions into vast pools of Reagan votes. How? Not so much by selling Reagan, for Reagan was a consummate self-promoter, but by selling the people against Walter Mondale, whom Murdoch viewed as a dangerous throwback to all the New Deal–postwar appeasement liberalism and welfarism that Reaganism stood a good chance of vanquishing permanently.

Murdoch might have had difficulty on that score, however, since Mondale had little in his personal or political past that could be "exposed" except the issues he was already well known for; readers of Murdoch's papers were generally not interested in issue-analysis. He had hoped that Gary Hart, rather than Mondale, would win the Democratic nomination. At least Hart would have been vulnerable to all sorts of journalistic humiliation, given his personal history of marital strife, name changes, and anti–Vietnam War activity. But then Mondale, having won the nomination at that summer's Democratic Convention in San Francisco, turned around and unwittingly handed Murdoch the match he needed to ignite his pro-Reagan newspaper crusade. Her name was Geraldine Ferraro.

The idea of a woman as Vice President of the United States—no less as a candidate for the office—was anathema to Murdoch. Although he had supported Thatcher's election as Prime Minister of England in 1979, it was only the economic and social changes her candidacy promised that persuaded him to do so. Otherwise, he had been highly skeptical of her ability to function effectively as a prime minister, solely because she was a woman. Thatcher's timorous prosecution of the Falklands War, and then her resistance to Reagan's invasion of Grenada in 1983, reinforced his conviction that women were emotionally ill-equipped to hold high office. To him, in the America of 1984, the Democrats' choice of a woman to run for the vice presidency was nothing more than a desperate effort to steal Reagan's thunder. That they settled on Geraldine Ferraro simply doubled the offense.

Ferraro's nomination came just before the start of the Olympic Games in Los Angeles in late July 1984. When I was there with the Murdoch group in early August, I detected a sharp undercurrent of excitement among some of his closest aides. The buzz had nothing to do with the games, I learned, but stemmed from what had apparently been Murdoch's recent orders to his chief editors around the country to launch an immediate no-holds-barred "get-Ferraro" crusade in the Murdoch press. I was not able to get Murdoch to confirm that he'd actually issued such orders. But my knowledge of his negative attitude toward Ferraro—he had recently grown furious when she indicated that she wouldn't take a stand against abortion—made it plausible.

Independent confirmation came at least partially a short while later when a cryptic confidential memo written by Steve Dunleavy, Murdoch's metropolitan editor at the *New York Post,* surfaced. The memo, composed shortly after Ferraro's nomination, was a detailed tactical battle plan for the *Post*'s treatment of Ferraro. "Time we took the gloves off" and "We can balance an anti-Ferraro Page One" and "She has to be nailed on abortion" were just a few of Dunleavy's prescriptions.* By the time the *Post* got cranked up, however, routine investigations by other papers in and around the New York area had uncovered two significant facts. One was that Ferraro's husband had been involved in several financial irregularities in his roles as a realtor and a conservator of two estates; the other, that Ferraro herself, along with her husband, had indulged in questionable income-tax and campaign-finance practices during her term as a congresswoman. Even before the Democrats' post–Labor Day election campaign started in earnest, then, Ferraro's candidacy was in deep trouble.

The Murdoch press made the most of the disclosures, particularly the *Post,* although it had made no contribution to unearthing them. As the election campaign progressed, and Ferraro backed herself more deeply into a corner in her attempts to explain the family's murky money habits, it soon became evident that her candidacy had mortally poisoned the Democratic ticket, and that she and Mondale had no chance of winning in November.

Murdoch, however, angry that the *Post* was getting none of the credit for the Ferraro slaughter, was not content to let events take their natural toll. Like a hungry feral scavenger determined to seize the best part of the kill, he leaped into print with an item that had nothing to do with Ferraro's vice-presidential qualifications but, if true, was merely an interesting footnote to her family history. The *Post*'s "exclusive" was that Ferraro's long-dead immigrant father had been arrested forty years before on a charge of engaging in illegal gambling activities in upstate Newburgh, and that her elderly mother, still living, had also been implicated.

The *Post* bannered the story in the frenzied fashion most tabloids might have used to announce the outbreak of thermonuclear war. The paper had published so many sensationalized but exaggerated or untrue stories since Murdoch had taken it over that few knew at first whether to believe it. Even if true, it hardly seemed worth the multipage, days-on-end hysteria Murdoch obviously tried to generate about it. By her own admission, it devastated Ferraro, if only because she barely remembered her father and was unaware of the incident. But the question was not Ferraro's reaction. It was the relevance of the long-ago incident.

* Dunleavy's memo was first revealed publicly by journalist Geoffrey Stokes in Murdoch's *Village Voice.*

The *Post* had taken a piece of minor information and blown it up out of all proportion to its significance, craftily suggesting in the process that Ferraro was unfit to hold office. The sins of the father, they implied, whether real or imagined, were the responsibility of the daughter.

Murdoch had several motives. First, he was able to wreak personal revenge against Ferraro—generally for having had the audacity to go after the vice-presidential nomination and thus seek to steal much of the nation's female vote from Reagan, and particularly for having refused to condemn abortion. Second, the story enabled him to avenge the humiliating ouster of Richard Nixon from the presidency ten years before. Nixon's enforced departure had been engineered by the 1974 Democrats, and allegations about his own links to the criminal underworld had been a prominent feature of his humiliation. Third, Murdoch was now able to boast of having contributed to the crippling of the Mondale-Ferraro ticket. Although a false boast—the ticket had been crippled well before the *Post* raised the matter of her father—it was one that would be eminently useful once the Reagan Administration moved into its second term.

If anyone in America, or at least New York, doubted up to then that the routine basis of Murdochian journalism was the printed lie masquerading as fact, such doubt was erased for good by the *Post*'s performance following the Mondale-Ferraro defeat in November. Ferraro and her husband owned a condominium on the Caribbean island of St. Croix. Doug Feiden, a Murdoch reporter who had covered the Ferraro campaign for the *Post,* trailed them to St. Croix when Ferraro flew there with her family for a vacation shortly after the election. A few days later, his story, written in the style of a private eye's confidential report to his client, appeared on the *Post*'s front page under the headline: "Stormy Weather in Gerry's Paradise."

The tale centered on Ferraro's visit to Sunday Mass the morning before at the Roman Catholic church in Christiansted, the island's main town, and it quoted two different priests, one a bishop, as sermonizing harshly to Ferraro for her refusal to denounce abortion during the campaign. The only trouble was that the bishop whom Feiden quoted wasn't even on the island that morning, no less at the church, and he later heatedly denied the words attributed to him after Feiden's story ran in the *Post.* So did the other cleric Feiden cited as tearing into Ferraro from the pulpit. The story was obviously designed to get the *Post* off the

hook for its wildly slanted campaign treatment of Ferraro by invoking the disapproving authority of the Church itself. But except
for the fact that Feiden had followed Ferraro and her husband to
the town's church, there was little truth to the story.

Just as revealing was the *Post*'s reaction once its story was
exposed. Not long before, newspapers like *The Washington Post*
and *The Wall Street Journal* had been hoodwinked by journalists
in their employ, as had the New York *Daily News.* In each instance, once falsity had been revealed, the paper fired the reporter, candidly admitted its responsibility, and took measures to
protect against future occurrences. In the Feiden case, however,
the *Post* simply stonewalled the matter in a fashion reminiscent of
the Watergate period.

Examples of such journalistic practices continue to abound
throughout Murdoch's international press empire. They are particularly rampant in those papers over which, through his eager-
to-please surrogates, he exercises a direct and strong editorial
command. For instance, not long before, the *Sun* in London carried a lengthy "World Exclusive" interview with the widow of
one of the first British servicemen killed in the Falklands War, a
sergeant who was posthumously decorated with Britain's highest
award for heroism. It didn't take long for the British public to
learn that the interview never took place, and that what they had
so eagerly read had been concocted. Equally egregious, often, are
Murdoch's efforts to pump journalistic respectability into his
shoddier publications. A representative example was the *New
York Post*'s 1985 Gross-Squadron crusade against *The New York
Times.*

Elliott Gross, the New York City medical examiner, was the
object of increasingly vocal criticism from city minority groups in
1984 over a series of autopsy reports he'd issued in cases in which
blacks and Hispanics had died while in the custody of police officers. At the core of the criticism was the allegation that Gross's
postmortem reports tended to absolve the police of liability for
several of the deaths when it appeared from the known physical
evidence, and from independent eye-witness testimony, that they
might have been criminally responsible. The furor prompted *The
New York Times* to look into Gross's performance. In January
1985, it published a series of four long articles, citing many
sources, that were highly critical of Gross and suggested that
there was some substance to the allegations.

The *Times* series triggered several official investigations of

Gross. He, in the meantime, protesting the *Times*'s conclusions and claiming that he'd been defamed by the series, made tracks to the office of Howard Squadron. Agreeing to represent Gross in his defense against the *Times* findings, and in the official investigations and lawsuits to come, Squadron called in his friend and fellow New York power broker Howard Rubenstein, who also happened to be Rupert Murdoch's and the *Post*'s chief public relations operative. Squadron and Rubenstein, as familiar to Murdoch's top staff at the *Post* as Murdoch himself was, plotted their strategy.

Murdoch wasted no time in putting the *Post* at their disposal. For weeks, the paper appeared with prominently bannered stories defending Gross and attacking the *Times,* mainly for using tainted sources as the basis for its series on Gross. For a day or two at the start, it seemed that the *Post* might have been on to something—that it might be able to satisfy Murdoch's craving to catch the *Times* itself in the practice of shoddy journalism. But when the appearance became reality, it was clear that the *Post*'s "investigation" of the *Times* was more distorted than the latter's probe of Gross had been. In attempting to debunk several of the *Time*'s sources, the *Post* ignored or twisted dozens of facts to give its theory a congenial fit. In the end, the *Times* investigation of Gross stood up for the most part. The *Post*'s rabidly self-congratulatory charges of fraud against the *Times* soon ran out of steam, as well as credibility. Three separate official investigations into Gross's performance as medical examiner concluded that although he had not been guilty of any criminal wrongdoing, his handling of several controversial cases had been riddled with errors and that his conduct of the medical examiner's office in general had been unsatisfactory. Gross has denied the charges and has since instituted a libel action against *The New York Times.*

Nevertheless, Squadron had succeeded for a while in craftily exploiting the *Post* to carry out the standard defense lawyer's tactic of deflecting attention away from his client and pouring it on the accuser. The *Post* was forced to admit early on that Squadron, whom it pictured and quoted extensively, was its chief lawyer as well as Gross's, but the admission was nothing more than a brief parenthetical acknowledgment buried deep in one of its first stories. Thereafter, it made hardly any reference to Squadron's dual role. And when it published a lengthy article by Squadron on May 1, 1985, in which he re-aired his dissatisfaction with *The*

New York Times, the *Post* announced that it was printing it "for the record and as a matter of public interest." Squadron, it added, "served as Dr. Elliott Gross's attorney during the investigation of his office." It neglected to mention that he had long functioned as Murdoch's and the *Post*'s principal attorney.

It was hard to imagine what public interest was served by the Squadron article, unless the *Post* had established a revolutionary new journalistic policy. Not a few other lawyers in New York wondered if the paper would be as accommodating to them if they sought to use its pages to defend their clients before the court of public opinion. No, was the pessimistic conclusion. The *Post* had opened its pages to its own attorney solely to help him get another client off. It was unlikely that it would show the same courtesy to attorneys who were unconnected to Rupert Murdoch.

But Murdoch's blatant misuse of his printing presses to promote and benefit the private interests of friends and family was not confined to *New York Post.* Soon after he took over the *Chicago Sun-Times* and named Robert Page its publisher, Page and Nancy Merrill, a Bostonian, decided to get married. Despite the fact that Page and his new wife had only recently arrived in Chicago and were scarcely known, their wedding received almost a full page of coverage in the *Sun-Times* of June 8, 1984.

Equally lavish attention was paid in London's *Times* and *Sunday Times* to another wedding in the early summer of 1985—the marriage of Murdoch's twenty-six-year-old daughter Prudence. Neither paper, each famous for its Letters to the Editor page, took note of the numerous protests mailed by irate readers in the wake of its prominent coverage of that event.

And Murdoch continued to protect his friends' and family's interests as determinedly as he promoted them. As a result of her 1981 marriage to the aging John Kluge, Patricia Gay, the former London men's-magazine model and belly dancer, acquired instant social cachet in New York, Palm Beach, and the lush horse country of Virginia, each the site of one of Kluge's opulent homes. In accordance with her new status as a rich and respectable young society doyenne, she began to involve herself in various charities designed to bring their wealthy sponsors the most favorable and sympathetic publicity. One of her pet causes became an organization called United World Colleges, which had been founded by oil tycoon Armand Hammer to afford the youth of impoverished Third World countries access to higher education. Patricia Gay Kluge soon was New York's and Palm Beach's most prominent supporter of United World Colleges.

As it happened, Armand Hammer had also interested England's Prince Charles in United World Colleges. As a result, when it was announced that Charles and his fabled young wife Diana would visit Palm Beach in November 1985 to attend a high-ticket banquet for the benefit of United World Colleges—the social event of the decade in that bastion of high society—Patricia Kluge persuaded Hammer to appoint her as the royal couple's official hostess. Thus was set in motion a train of events that would bring profound embarrassment, or outrage, to all concerned.

In early October, a month before the departure of the Prince and Princess for the United States, several London newspapers hit the streets with such headlines as: "Charles to Be Greeted by Ex-porn Queen" and "Former Porno Model to Host Charles and Diana." Laid out for all to see, although judiciously cropped, were nude photos Patricia Kluge had posed for in the 1970s that had been published in magazines with names like *Knave,* along with pulsatingly salacious quotes about her "wanton sexuality" and "hot, hot, hot body" from photographers who claimed they had taken the pictures. The *Sun*'s two main competitors—one of which, the *Mirror,* had recently been acquired by Murdoch's erstwhile foe, Robert Maxwell, and which was engaged in yet another fierce circulation war with the *Sun*—applied the full repertoire of their tabloid skills to milk the "scandal" for all it was worth in the weeks that followed.

The entire episode was a case study in Murdochian journalism. Yet Murdoch's principal London papers remained curiously hushed throughout the affair, as did the *Post* and his other tabloids in the United States, once the story reached the American press. The reasons were obvious to anyone who knew of Rupert and Anna Murdoch's close connection to the Kluges.

Few, though, did know about it, proving perhaps that often what Murdoch didn't print in his sex-and-scandal rags could be as much an exercise in journalistic manipulation as what he did. Patricia Kluge, in the meantime, sheepishly admitted to her pornographic modeling past and, along with her husband, quietly vanished from Palm Beach before the Prince and Princess arrived.

Citizen Murdoch

One of Murdoch's more grandiose public deceptions exploded not just on New York but on the entire world in the spring of 1985—his triumphant announcement of yet another "exclusive": the signing up of Pope John Paul II as a weekly "columnist" for his various newspapers around the globe.

In 1979, John Paul II had come to New York to, among other things, address the United Nations. I was at the United Nations the day of his speech, as were Murdoch and his family. At a large private reception after the speech, the Murdochs were among the first in the long looping line of local dignitaries waiting to be received by the Pope. As Murdoch shepherded his wife and children into the Pope's presence, his manner was cloyingly obsequious; it was the first time I had ever seen him act in such fashion. It was obvious the Pope didn't know who the Murdochs were, since a clerical aide had to whisper their identity to him. It was also obvious that he must have heard of Murdoch, for as soon as the aide completed his whisper, the Pope's sunny if somewhat bemused expression suddenly grew sour with distaste. Murdoch, in the meantime, preoccupied with introducing his family, missed the fleeting change of papal expression. There followed a brief ritualistic conversation, with Anna Murdoch doing most of the talking and the Pope eyeing Murdoch suspiciously.

Later, I jokingly asked Murdoch if the Pope had warned him to mend his wicked ways. Not joking, Murdoch answered that some day he'd have the Pope writing for him. Unlikely, I said, recalling John Paul's stony look upon greeting him. "Wait and see," Murdoch shot back. He had been impressed by the sharp rise in New York newspaper circulation during the Pope's visit.

"The Pope sells papers wherever he goes. I intend to have him selling papers for us."

Murdoch's announcement in 1985 that the Pope would become one of his regular columnists must have been the fruit of the seed that had been planted six years earlier, I thought. The only trouble was that it wasn't true, or at best was grossly misleading. In Rome, when John Paul II was told of it, he was reported to have said, in Polish, "Huh?" Quickly, heated denials began to fly out of the Vatican. The image of Pope John Paul II slaving away at a typewriter for Rupert Murdoch—an image generated by the original Murdoch announcement—quickly blurred as Murdoch left the situation to his underlings to explain.

What had actually happened was that the Murdoch organization had made a deal with E.A.V. Associates, a New York agency that held the English-language rights to certain writings and speeches of John Paul II through a license from the Vatican. Rather than a weekly column written contemporaneously by the Pope, the *Post* and other Murdoch papers had merely purchased a compendium of material culled and lifted from the Pope's old writings and speeches and then organized by E.A.V. into weekly "topics."

None of this became clear, however, until September 1985, when the *Post* and other Murdoch papers around the world published their first papal "column," complete with the byline: "By Pope John Paul II." Immediately, the Vatican denounced it as a fraud, first because it gave the impression that the Pope himself had just written it in the form in which it was printed, and second because he was made to appear to be working for the Murdoch organization. The dispute was eventually resolved when Murdoch, without conceding that he'd tried to pull another fast one on the public, agreed to make radical changes in the way he presented the material. The Pope's byline was omitted and replaced by the title, "Selected Observations of Pope John Paul II." Murdoch was also required to print certain caveats designed to alert readers that each weekly piece was a "synthesis" of old writings and speeches, many of them from the time before John Paul II became Pope, and was edited "in consultation with the Vatican Communications Office" and *L'Osservatore Romano,* the Vatican newspaper.

In England, the Murdoch press's exaggerated stories about the Royal Family were legend. It was obvious that the institution

of the monarchy meant little more to him, or to most other Fleet
Street tabloid publishers, than a daily opportunity to sell papers.
But the papacy was another institution altogether. It was respected and revered by hundreds of millions the world over. That
Murdoch would attempt to use the Pope to continue working his
journalistic con games struck many as a sacrilege beyond justification or redemption.

The issue of Murdoch's newspaper ethics was of little moment to America's Federal Communications Commission, however. The FCC is the government agency charged with passing on
the question of who is and isn't qualified to receive commercial
broadcast licenses in the United States. What concerns it most are
an applicant's compliance with its citizenship requirements and
his financial wherewithal. Murdoch came to the FCC's attention
in the spring of 1985.

A year earlier, he had added *New Woman* magazine to his
stable of American publications. A few months before, at the end
of 1984, he had bought a group of profitable specialty trade journals from the Ziff-Davis Publishing Company for the exceedingly
high price of $350 million, most of it financed. By the start of
1985, Newscorp and its main operating subsidiaries were so heavily leveraged, and their annual interest payments so steep, that
they seemed to many financial analysts to be stretched beyond
the bounds of safety. Thus the astonishment on Wall Street when
Murdoch announced in March that he had spent an additional
$250 million in borrowed funds to buy 50 percent of the ailing
20th Century-Fox from Marvin Davis. And the near disbelief
when, a month later, he let it be known that, in partnership with
Davis, he was about to acquire John Kluge's Metromedia television stations for more than $2 billion.

Although they did not doubt that he could raise the money
for the Metromedia buy, the experts were sure that Murdoch had
finally gone off the deep end. Under Kluge, Metromedia was an
extremely well-run company, with traditionally tight cost controls
and an operating profit the year before of $99.3 million. But by
virtue of Kluge's leveraged buyout, the interest costs alone on its
1984 debt had been $90 million and were scheduled to rise even
higher. Between its debt repayments and the $17.8 million it was
required to remit in taxes, Metromedia had actually suffered a net
loss of $8.5 million in 1984. No one could see Murdoch as being
able to increase its annual operating profit to overcome its yearly

debt-and-tax burden. He would be forced to start selling some of his other properties, went the thinking, merely to sustain Metromedia at or near the break-even point each year.

Murdoch had another answer. He intended to merge 20th Century-Fox and Metromedia into a new combined television-production-broadcast network to compete with CBS, NBC, and ABC. With 20th providing the bulk of the programming through its Hollywood studios and heavily stocked movie library, the television network could operate at much lower annual costs and thus increase its yearly operating profit. Furthermore, he intended to reduce the Metromedia debt he was about to inherit by immediately selling one of the chain's television stations—WCVB in Boston—to the Hearst Corporation for $450 million. The sale had already been arranged by Kluge, and it would lower the actual cost of the Murdoch-Davis takeover of Metromedia television to about $1.6 billion, of which he—Murdoch—would be responsible for only half, $800 million. Or so it seemed.

Marvin Davis, usually a much more flamboyant self-promoter in public than Murdoch, was conspicuously silent through all this. That was because he had no intention of going through with the deal. He had grown disillusioned with his expensive venture into the movie business. Moreover, he was no more willing to have Murdoch as a partner than Murdoch was to have him. He had allowed Murdoch into 20th because by early 1985 he was looking to get out and also because Murdoch needed a financing rationale to make his bid for Metromedia. Without at least half a movie company in his pocket, Murdoch might not have been able to obtain sufficient financing to close his deal with Kluge.

Once Murdoch acquired Metromedia for 20th, Davis intended to sell his remaining 50 percent to the Australian and drop out of the picture altogether. Murdoch not only would be responsible for the total cost of Metromedia, but would pay Davis an additional $350 million for full ownership of 20th. In all, then, even after he sold the Boston station to Hearst, Murdoch would still be paying well over $2 billion to complete the combined 20th-Metromedia acquisition and pursue his ambition to create a fourth national television network.

The transaction went according to plan. Once Murdoch received preliminary approval from the FCC and other government agencies, and once he obtained firm financing commitments from a consortium of banks organized by Allen and Company, he quickly bought out Davis's remaining 50 percent of 20th Century-Fox and announced that he would proceed with the Metromedia takeover on his own. In acquiring Kluge's company, he would be required to pay $650 million in cash and assume Metromedia's $1.3 billion debt. Added to those figures were the $600 million he'd borrowed to acquire all of 20th Century-Fox and the $350 million to buy the Ziff-Davis magazine group, for a total debt of nearly $2.9 billion beyond his organization's ordinary—to many observers extraordinary—ongoing debt liability. The immediate sale of Boston's WCVB-TV would provide him with enough cash to reduce that figure straightaway to about $2.4 billion. Thereafter, he expected Fox Television—the name of the new company he intended to form out of 20th Century-Fox and Metromedia—to earn enough in yearly operating profits to help begin to retire the $2.4 billion debt, much of which was in short-term, high-interest junk bonds.

But "help" was the operative word, and the financial analysts remained deeply skeptical. After looking over the Murdoch organization's balance sheets and reviewing his profit projections for Fox Television from 1986 onward, they saw little chance of his successfully paying off the crushing debt burden he'd assumed without, a few years hence, having to sell several of Newscorp's major assets. It would be either that, they concluded, or else he'd be forced to raise the money by turning Newscorp into an American corporation and taking it public, which, of course, would strip him and his family of much of their nearly 50 percent ownership. What few outside Murdoch's innermost councils knew was that he had another scenario in mind and was just then secretly preparing to implement it.

With his Metromedia master plan launched, Murdoch proceeded to attend to its details. The first centered on the question of his citizenship. Initially, he thought he might be able to obtain an unprecedented waiver of the FCC rule prohibiting a non-American from directly owning more than 20 percent of a commercial television company. He had, after all, grown accustomed to receiving special favors from the governments of Australia and Britain when faced with sticky regulatory hurdles. Why not the government of the United States, particularly in view of his six years of devoted service to the Reagan inner circle, which, for all practical purposes, controlled the FCC?

The FCC had indicated from the very start that it would

look favorably on Murdoch's Metromedia takeover. One of its commissioners, James Quello, had rhapsodized to the press: "With this one move, Rupert Murdoch will become one of the major players in broadcasting, not just in the United States but worldwide." But a waiver of the citizenship rule? It would be too obvious, Reagan Administration insiders informed Murdoch, particularly in view of the accusations of favoritism that had been leveled against him five years before in connection with the Eximbank-Ansett loan. The Democrats in Congress would jump all over the Administration with investigations of any such waiver.

Although he thought the Reaganites were being excessively cautious, Murdoch had been realistic enough not to put too much hope in getting a citizenship waiver. Thus, he solved the problem by applying for immediate American citizenship. At the same time he transferred his waiver hopes back to Australia, whose citizenship he would lose by becoming an American. He was sure he would figure out some way to get around the similar Australian law that barred noncitizens from owning television stations there. Perhaps the government would name him an "honorary citizen."

Murdoch was sworn in as an American citizen at the Federal Courthouse in New York in September 1985. Jimmy Breslin, the star columnist of the *Daily News,* had been attacking him in print for years as a rich foreigner who had come to New York to reap further wealth through the journalistic exploitation of the city's poor minorities and the deliberate heightening of racial tensions. After taking the citizenship oath and being asked what it meant to him, Murdoch said drily, "It means Breslin will have to stop calling me an alien."

With the citizenship problem solved, Murdoch turned to the drama's second act, which related to an exemption of another sort—a waiver of the federal rule that barred the same person, citizen or not, from owning a newspaper and television station in the same city. Here the possibilities were more flexible. In the first place, such waivers had been granted before, usually on grounds of economic hardship. If Murdoch was forced to get rid of the *New York Post* and *Chicago Sun-Times* because of his acquisition of Metromedia's New York and Chicago television stations, he would be required either to sell or to close each paper. If he couldn't find a buyer for each, he would have no choice but to close them. One way to avoid selling the papers would be to put a price on them so high that no one would want them. Unable to sell them, he would therefore be faced with the only other alternative under the FCC rule—their permanent closure. That would mean the loss of thousands of jobs, as well as punishing shutdown costs to him in the form of pension guarantees, union settlements, and the like. He intended to request a permanent waiver on those grounds.

When Murdoch raised the issue with the FCC, he was told that the commission would give it due consideration, but that it might be more realistic for him to apply for a temporary waiver of a year or two so that he could at least have some breathing room and the commission could see how matters developed. At the end of two years, if he hadn't been able to sell one or both of the two papers, he could apply for a further extension. For now, though, Murdoch was almost guaranteed a two-year waiver if he applied for it. He did, and he got it.

The third and final phase of Murdoch's master plan had to do with the immediate financing of his Metromedia takeover. It proved the most nettlesome. The FCC was required to assure itself that Murdoch's financing was both sufficient and legitimate. The original commitments he'd received had been made on the expectation of a joint Murdoch-Davis purchase. With Davis no longer part of the venture, a significant portion of the promised financing had departed with him. Allen and Company was forced to reassemble the entire financial package.

But Allen was using as one of its lead financing sources the First National Bank of Boston, which had been convicted earlier in 1985 for failing to report to the U.S. Treasury more than a billion dollars in cash transactions. Although government prosecutors had not pressed the issue, the government's concern was that those transactions were part of an international money-laundering scheme, possibly Mafia-related.

That raised a question in many Wall Streeters' minds: was Murdoch, whether knowingly or not, being financed in some way or another by money whose sources were suspect? And that question triggered another. The original 50 percent share of 20th Century-Fox that Murdoch purchased in the early spring of 1985 had been owned by Marc Rich, the notorious Wall Street oil speculator who had recently fled to Switzerland as a fugitive from American justice after being indicted as a Mafia-connected embezzler.

In any case, as Murdoch got ready to present his entire takeover package to the FCC for approval in the fall of 1985, his financing had run into trouble. Whether that was due to the background of the financing, or to the fact that the international banking community viewed the debt burden Murdoch was about to assume as too risky, was another question that could not be definitively answered. The answers I received from several bankers, however, indicated the latter.

In any event, to ensure the FCC's financial approval of his purchase of Metromedia, Murdoch announced in early November 1985—three months after he'd expected his acquisition to be completed—that he would likely have to take his new Fox Television public. His plan was to offer six million common shares to the general public and 1.15 million preferred shares to the holders of Metromedia junk bonds in lieu of debt repayments. Assuming that a market could be made in the common stock issue at a minimum of $20 a share, and that the preferred-stock issue would be fully subscribed, Murdoch stood a good chance of making up his financing shortfall and of winning the government's final approval of the Metromedia takeover.

Murdoch got the approval later in November, at the same time receiving his two-year waiver of his obligation to dispose of the *New York Post* and the *Chicago Sun-Times.* Now, in addition to nearly two million daily newspaper readers in the United States, he had a potential nationwide market of about 40 million televiewers. What he would do with his American newspapers remained to be seen. Although he professed undying loyalty to them, it quickly became clear that his new television presence and power had radically changed his perspective. Having already sold New York's *Village Voice* during the summer of 1985 for a very profitable $55 million, he had few qualms about divesting himself of the *Chicago Sun-Times* at a similar profit rate—$150 million if he could find a buyer.

Find a buyer he did. Backed by several investors, including the Equitable insurance company, Robert Page, its Murdoch-appointed publisher, purchased the *Sun-Times* for $145 million in the summer of 1986.

As for the *New York Post*—well, that was another matter. Putting a mid-nine-figure price on the paper he had bought in 1976 for a mere $30 million, he hoped to recover the more than $100 million he'd lost during his ten-year ownership of it, and then some. But who would buy the *Post* at such a steep price? Its record had proved that Murdochian journalism was not a money-winner in New York, and by the spring of 1986 its circulation had tailed off sharply. Yet it had been so thoroughly "Murdochized" that any purchaser would have to make wholesale changes in it to overcome its terrible reputation. What's more, upon Murdoch's divestiture, most if not all of the paper's Australian and British journalistic staff would depart with him. That would leave any purchaser with the expensive task of restaffing as well as radically revamping the *Post.*

There certainly still is room for a lively and entertaining, but journalistically responsible, afternoon-evening tabloid in New York. Perhaps an enterprising and imaginative new ownership could make such a paper work, using the skeleton of the old *Post* as its base. But the economics of embarking on such a project are so daunting as to make it seem impossible. Moreover, in 1985, Long Island's *Newsday* began to make impressive inroads into the New York City afternoon market with a special city-oriented tabloid edition. *New York Newsday,* in fact, was largely responsible for the *Post*'s sharp circulation drop in 1985 and 1986.

Provided he gets no further FCC waivers, the likelihood is that by 1988 Murdoch will simply close the *Post* and either sell its downtown plant or convert it into a production adjunct of Metromedia's—now Fox Television's—cramped uptown East Side television studios. Given the plans he has for Fox in New York and the five other major cities in which it broadcasts, especially in the news domain, his retention of the *Post* building would make sense.

And what are Murdoch's plans for Fox as he tries to shape it into the nation's fourth network? Plenty of retread entertainment, to be sure. He has not decided yet whether he will take the upmarket or downmarket route in his attempt to draw viewers away from the other networks—that decision will turn, he says, on the results of viewer surveys in 1986. However, Murdoch has gambled practically his entire media empire on his 20th Century-Fox–Metromedia acquisition. He cannot afford to fail. And since the most lucrative print-media successes of his career have been in the downmarket arena, the likelihood is that the network's entertainment programming will be aimed at the lowest-common-denominator sector of its six regional markets, and that its programming will bristle with considerable right-wing political cant. These tendencies have already evinced themselves.

The same can be predicted for the network's national and

local news programming, which is where Murdoch—on the theory that he is basically a purveyor of news—will have his sharpest immediate impact. During John Kluge's reign, Metromedia's seven stations developed a formula for local news reporting that strove for a blue-collar tabloid newspaper urgency but managed to produce only a bland, watery soup. Murdoch will keep the self-important urgency, but will dress it up even more with a video version of the grating frenzy, alarmism, hysteria, and trivia that have been the trademarks of his newspapers. His principal targets nationally, of course, will be the nightly network news shows, which he'll seek to undercut with heavy doses of such "reporting" coupled with, again, a strong right-wing political bias and much factual distortion.

It has been said that it is much harder to lie on television than it is in print, especially when presenting the news. That may be so. But Rupert Murdoch has built his career, his empire, and his $300 million personal fortune on the basis of printed deceptions and distortions. There is no reason to believe that he will suddenly break the habits and patterns of a lifetime or that he even wants to. Nor is there reason to expect that he won't intentionally carry those habits and patterns into his new career as a television mogul.

The only question is whether the American television public, or that considerable portion of it that Murdoch's new network reaches, will let him get away with it. The fate of his entire media empire rests on the answer.

"Mr. Prime Minister"

Murdoch's takeover of the Metromedia television chain was formalized in March 1986. For months prior to that, many Murdoch-watchers were convinced that by reason of the massive new financial liabilities he'd be taking on, he had reached the end of his globe-girdling expansion. Such was not the case. In the interim, he added a small Anglo-American book-publishing firm, Salem House. Then he started an American version of the glossy French fashion magazine *Elle*. He followed that with plans to launch a slick new magazine for car enthusiasts called *Automobile*. And no sooner had he begun to position his pending Metromedia–20th Century-Fox combination as America's fourth network, he then took steps to weave a similar and even more powerful video web throughout Western Europe.

With more television sets than the United States, continental Europe has long been potentially the largest and most lucrative television advertising market in the world. Until now, that potential has been virtually untapped because most television broadcasting in Europe has been the exclusive preserve of state-owned and operated networks. As a result, commercial broadcasting and private ownership have been severely limited. But no more. Soon the major countries of Western Europe will be opening their airwaves to privately owned commercial networks. In the forefront of the trend is France, which in 1985 authorized the granting of two private nationwide broadcast licenses. And in the forefront of those competing to acquire a share in one of them was Rupert Murdoch.

Murdoch's approach was to establish a partnership with Groupe Bruxelles Lambert, Belgium's largest financial and industrial holding company and a major owner of Compagnie Luxembourgeoise de Tèlèdiffusion (CLT), the biggest independent radio and television operator in Europe. CLT already broadcast to parts of France, Germany, and Belgium from Luxembourg, as well as throughout tiny Luxembourg itself. With extensive experience in the commercial aspects of the industry, it had been all but promised one of France's two new private licenses by key members of the French government. Murdoch's partnership with Lambert, through the joint company they hastily formed and called Media International, gave him a head start in the race to enter the pan-European market. Or so he thought.

The prospective rewards were compelling. In the first year alone, 1986–87, the two new French networks were expected to produce advertising revenues in excess of $450 million. Assuming that half of that, or $225 million, accrued to the Murdoch-Lambert partnership, half of *that* amount, $112.5 million, would constitute Murdoch's share.

And that was just for starters. Combined gross revenues for the next four years were conservatively projected at a billion dollars or more annually. At least a quarter of that, $250 million, presumably would go to Murdoch each year. Since much of the programming for the Murdoch-Lambert network would be supplied through 20th Century-Fox's 2,500 movie and television show library, its production expenses and other overhead costs would be relatively modest, thereby generating a munificent operating profit for Murdoch from his $250 million annual gross—perhaps as much as $175 million a year. (It was Murdoch's 1985 acquisition of 20th Century-Fox and its invaluable library that had made him such an attractive partner to the Lambert organization.) Poured into the Newscorp kitty, that profit would go a long way toward helping him pay off his punishing annual Metromedia debt obligations. It would also calm the nerves of his bankers.

Beyond those rosy profit considerations, Murdoch could also expect to have a significant political impact on the French nation through his television programming. In his eyes, with its hardline Socialist—nearly Communist—Mitterrand government, the France of the first half of the 1980s represented a dangerous trend in Western Europe and a terrible example for the rest of the industrialized free world. France needed a voice like his, he assured himself, to rectify its political errancy.

Alas for him, his sugarplum visions were not to ι ˀ realized, at least for the moment. It was precisely Murdoch's repuι ˼ion for uncompromising right-wing politics that scared off the ŀ ˀnch authorities once they learned that he was an integral part oι ˍhe Lambert bid. Early in 1986, the two licenses went to other more politically amenable applicants.

Murdoch was neither surprised nor daunted by the setback; he knew there would soon be further chances elsewhere in Europe. Besides, the French rebuff appeared only temporary. François Mitterrand's exercise in state socialism had already produced considerable disaffection and unrest in France, and his government's power was almost certain to be severely curtailed in the general election of early spring 1986. If so, there was a likelihood that its license awards would be canceled by a more conservative successor regime and that a second Lambert bid would succeed. With the election now history, that outcome seems certain.

Murdoch's involvement with Lambert had been a spontaneous last-minute venture entered into in response to a sudden, unforeseen opportunity. Despite the potential rewards, he'd only partly expected it to succeed. Infinitely more vital to him at the time was the plan he had simultaneously set in motion in England, which was the secret scenario to which I alluded in the last chapter. Until then, Murdoch had been tentatively relying on the scheme to silence the many experts on Wall Street and elsewhere who doubted his ability to survive his forthcoming Metromedia megadebt unscathed. Now, its success became an urgent imperative. It was the only way he could engineer the quick and large-scale increase in profits he would need to begin meeting his monumental new American debt without endangering the assets of Newscorp or his nearly 50 percent ownership of it.

Starting with the 1986–87 fiscal year, Murdoch was going to have to pay about $400 million annually over the next ten years to service the debt and fulfill other Newscorp financial obligations. The figure was well beyond Newscorp's projected yearly operating profits over the same period, even adding the net earnings expected from the Metromedia stations and 20th Century-Fox. Indeed, it was beyond the corporation's most optimistic yearly cash-flow projections. Only by rapidly creating a large new source of profit within the Newscorp umbrella could Murdoch come close to meeting his $400 million annual debt load. Otherwise, financial experts predicted, he would soon be forced to sell two of the company's most valuable assets—probably its 50 percent ownership of Ansett in Australia and its 10 percent share of Reuters in England. Although the two holdings represented convenient financial cushions for Murdoch, he was loath to consider such a possibility. Hence the vital importance of his secret British strategy.

But the strategy was highly risky. It had originally been inspired by Murdoch's threat, four years earlier, to see the British newspaper unions "pay dearly for their idiocy" in refusing to accede to reasonable job cuts and other labor economies. Now, at the end of 1985, it had a much more pressing business function. If it failed, at best it would leave Murdoch with no increase in profits and a host of further labor troubles in London; at worst it could result in the disastrous collapse of his British organization, still by far his most profitable.

As previously noted, Murdoch's four London newspapers together remained the financial linchpin of his global empire, with the *Sun* and *News of the World* its principal collective profit center. In 1980–81, prior to his purchase of the *Times* and *Sunday Times,* Murdoch's British operations had earned a pretax profit of $62.4 million, most of it coming from the *Sun* and *News of the World.* In 1981–82, following his acquisition of the *Times* papers, profits dropped to about $40 million. In 1982–83, they sank to $12 million. Much of the shrinkage was due to the exorbitant and often extortionate labor costs imposed on the four papers by their unionized work forces. They were extortionate, Murdoch insisted, because his refusal to bow to the unions' increasingly extravagant demands would inevitably have resulted in company-wide strikes, for all practical purposes shutting down his London operations and cutting off the lifeblood cash flow and profits he needed each year to shore up his money-losing ventures elsewhere. As it was, as the 1980s progressed he was forced to contend with a regular pattern of mini-strikes, work slowdowns, and sabotage that continually interfered with the papers' production and further ate into yearly profits.

Most of the verbal combat between Murdoch and the Fleet Street unions revolved around the question of introducing up-to-date newspaper-production technology into the papers' two old-fashioned and dilapidated plants, thereby reducing their work forces in wholesale numbers. The unions would have none of it, and the archaic status quo remained. Actually, the huge, ancient, three-reel printing presses still in use could be operated by fewer than six men. Thanks to union intransigence, eighteen people had to be paid to run each press, most at salaries and fringe benefits five times those of the average British worker. As English journalist Bernard Levin sardonically observed about Fleet Street union practices in 1984, "It was quite impossible for 18 men to get anywhere near the machines. But there was no congestion, as most of them were never there, or even expected to be."

By 1982, the arithmetic was simple. The year before, Murdoch's London operations had made a profit of $62 million, notwithstanding their already bloated labor and other production costs. Had he been able to publish his papers without union labor, he determined, his profits would have been at least double that figure.

In fiscal 1984–85, the arithmetic was similar. Profits had bounced back from their 1982–83 nadir to about $35 million. Without the unions, Murdoch would have saved about $85 million in costs that year, which would have translated into a profit of $120 million. Until then, he had not dared attempt to dispose of the unions; indeed, he'd had no way of doing so short of sacrificing his entire London business complex. But now, as 1986 approached, and with it his pending takeover of Metromedia, he desperately needed that potential $120 million or more a year for the annual payments on his vastly expanded debt. To get it, he would have to get rid of the Fleet Street unions.

That goal became the focus of Murdoch's secret plan, if only because he realized in 1985 that he had a way—at last—of achieving it.

Four years before, not long after he took over the *Times* newspapers and first made his threat to "get" the unions, Murdoch proceeded to modernize his London printing resources despite the further union fights he'd be letting himself in for. He was encouraged in large part by recent and anticipated changes in British labor law inspired and sponsored by the Thatcher government—in fact, by Prime Minister Margaret Thatcher herself, with Murdoch's persistent personal prodding and journalistic support.

By then, Murdoch was perceived by some in England as one of "the main powers behind the Thatcher throne," to cite the words of Charles Douglas-Home, the man who succeeded Harold Evans as editor of the *Times*. There was little reason to doubt the reality of the perception. "Rupert and Mrs. Thatcher consult regularly on every important matter of policy," Douglas-Home told me with some acerbity in 1984, "especially as they relate to his economic and political interests. Around here, he's often jokingly referred to as 'Mr. Prime Minister.' Except that it's no longer all that much a joke. In many respects, he *is* the phantom prime minister of this country."

Indeed, Murdoch himself continued to boast privately to friends, as he had to me earlier, of the power he purportedly exercised over Thatcher, particularly after he claimed to have dressed her down for her criticism of the Reagan Administration's invasion of Grenada. Following her landslide reelection in 1983, aided in no small measure by Murdoch's London papers, it could be reasonably deduced that Thatcher was more heavily in his debt than ever. Unknown to most, the apparent calling of that debt two years later would have near-disastrous personal and political consequences for Thatcher and her government.

One of the principal labor-law changes enacted in the early 1980s was a new statute that made it illegal for British unions to engage in sympathy strikes. Sympathy strikes had been the bane of private and public industry in England for decades, more than once bringing the production of most vital goods and services to a nationwide halt through the device of the "general strike." They had been the bane of Fleet Street as well, with a strike by a single union at one paper usually mandating a walkout by all its other unions and often spreading to other papers in the same organization and beyond.

The new law was justified by Thatcher as an absolute necessity for the revival of the long-depressed fortunes of British industry and for the rescue of the country's dismally performing economy, both of which ailments she was credibly able to blame on previous Labour Party governments. Predictably, it was condemned by her Labour and other adversaries as "the start of a massive, aggressive anti-labour drive on the part of the reactionary capitalist establishment and its political lackeys," as one left-wing magazine exclaimed.

Nevertheless, the new law stuck, as did further changes that severely curtailed the rights of striking unions to picket and gave employers the right to sack striking union workers en masse on breach-of-contract grounds. Just as the Reagan Administration could summarily fire the entire complement of unionized air traffic controllers in the United States when they struck in 1981, so, too, could British industrialists now dismiss an entire striking work force. This became the keystone of Murdoch's secret plan to rid himself of the Fleet Street unions.

The question might be asked: in light of the new labor laws, if Murdoch was so financially beleaguered by the unions at his four London newspapers, why didn't he refuse their demands outright earlier on and incite them to strike, thereby providing himself with an immediate legal opportunity to dispense with them for good?

The answer was simple. If he had, he would have been forced to organize and hire a totally new work force to operate his existing plants' dated and cumbersome production machinery. Most skilled printing workers elsewhere in England were also union members, however, and the unions would certainly not allow them to replace the fired workers. To recruit a reduced but unskilled corps of new workers to run the complicated old machinery would have been of no use, since it would have taken too long to train it, during which time his papers would have been forced to remain closed and tens of millions of pounds would have been lost. So long as Murdoch and the other Fleet Street proprietors were tied to the archaic mechanical methods of getting out their papers, they were at the mercy of the unions. That fact was not lost on the unions, and it accounted for their ability to hold the publishing establishment in their thrall despite the new "Thatcher laws."

But the new laws *did* inject the cells of a potential tumor into the powerful, militant muscle of Fleet Street unionism. The incipient lesion was one that, when sufficiently nourished and formed, could atrophy the muscle into enervated flab, perhaps even kill it. Murdoch was among the first to detect that possibility, and he quickly took steps to cultivate it.

The potential was primarily an opportunity for publishers to mount an end run around the impenetrable wall of union resistance to the introduction of the new labor-saving technology. It gave every major publisher the option of building a state-of-the-art printing plant outside the union-dominated production confines of Fleet Street and its immediate environs and then transferring all of his operations to such a facility. Once a new high-tech printing plant was established, and with it the need for fewer workers to run it, the unions would have little choice but to accept sharply reduced manning quotas—as dictated by the publisher—if they wished to remain on the scene. If they didn't, their only alternative would be to strike. Thereupon the publisher would be in a good legal position to close his old plant, fire the striking work force, and hire a smaller and lower-salaried complement of nonunion workers to man his greatly simplified and more efficient new plant.*

In 1982, after acquiring a large parcel of land in the dreary industrial district of East London known as Wapping, nearly two miles from Fleet Street, Murdoch began construction of an ultra-modern $140 million printing plant and newspaper headquarters. When completed and outfitted with the latest in automated machine and electronic printing technology, the plant would theoretically be able to produce all four of his papers, and several more besides, at about half the cost of his existing facilities in Gray's Inn Road and Bouverie Street. Rather than announce his intention eventually to move all his operations to the new plant, however, he remained vague about his plans for it. At first he told the suspicious unions its purpose was solely to handle the overflow from the old plants. Later he hinted that he might use it to start his fifth London paper, a tabloid afternoon daily designed to meet the challenge posed by Eddie Shah.

Murdoch's coyness was eminently practical. If he revealed his intentions too soon, the unions operating at his existing plants would surely rebel and thus intensify their already regular pattern of harassment and work disruption. But union leaders were not fooled; at least they claimed they weren't. In mid-1984, as the new plant neared completion, they pressured Murdoch into negotiations over manning requirements and other job conditions at Wapping. By doing so, they played straight into his hands.

Murdoch and his News International management deputies held periodic discussions with the Fleet Street unions well into

---

* In 1984, a relative newcomer to British publishing, Eddie Shah, announced his intention to start a new national newspaper in the style of America's *USA Today*. Seizing on the benefits provided by the government's labor-law changes, Shah, a cousin of the Aga Khan, was able to build a high-tech printing plant from scratch outside London and exclude union labor altogether. Much of Murdoch's subsequent antiunion strategy was guided both by Shah's success and by the competitive threat his new paper posed. The paper, however, proved to be a dud once it was launched.

1985, when the Wapping plant—constructed in the architectural style of a modern maximum-security prison—was ready. It soon became clear that the unions were prepared to negotiate little in the way of job-reduction concessions and other labor economies, notwithstanding the fact that the new plant was designed to be almost fully automated and that such automation would produce higher quality newspapers, physically, than Britain was accustomed to. The union leaders continued to insist that the traditional Fleet Street work practices, job duplications, and wage-and-benefit extravagances be shifted, more or less in toto, to Wapping.

Murdoch stretched out the talks, seemingly in good faith, until the prospect of his debt-laden acquisition of Metromedia in the United States seemed a certainty later in 1985. Then he raised the curtain on the penultimate act of his scenario, which by that time was no longer much of a secret within the inner circles of Fleet Street.

The overture was sounded in a confidential "legal opinion" letter delivered to the Murdoch organization by one of its London lawyers on December 20, 1985. The letter endorsed Murdoch's conviction that the time had come for him to provoke a strike by all the unions at his two Fleet Street plants, and it provided the ammunition he needed to get rid of them once and for all.

Again, although the tactic was risky in other respects, by successfully pulling it off he would instantly cut his annual labor and production costs by $85 million or more. Most if not all of that saving would convert into the same amount of additional profit for News International at the end of the first year of operations at Wapping. What's more, with his costs so radically reduced, Murdoch could afford to lower the cover price of each of his papers by several pence, thereby undercutting his competitors and generating major increases in circulation and advertising sales, which would result in further substantial profits.

Murdoch wasted no time pondering the risks. Only two questions concerned him. First, how to persuade the unionized journalistic and clerical staffs of his four papers to refuse to join the other union workers in a strike, for he could not make the switch to Wapping without editors, reporters, photographers, and their supporting office personnel. Second, how to rapidly create the relatively small but entirely new printing-plant work force he would need to run "the Fortress," as the heavily protected Wapping site began to be called. Ringed by high, razor-wire steel fences and concrete sentry bunkers, bathed at night by prowling floodlights, and patrolled by trained attack dogs, the bleakly modernistic facility by then resembled an ICBM launch base.

Murdoch attacked the first problem by setting out to break the journalists' union at each of his papers. Although the weakest of the Fleet Street unions, the National Union of Journalists was bound by its solidarity pacts with the production unions to make no separate deals with him regarding Wapping. Murdoch guessed that with a little encouragement, most of his journalistic employees would put their jobs ahead of any collective bargaining principles they might subscribe to; it remained his theory that reporters, editors, and other such "professionals" were by nature incapable of being slavish unionists. He provided the encouragement by an offer of a $2,800 cash bonus, along with a few lesser rewards, to every journalistic staffer who consented to move to Wapping. Most, however grudgingly, accepted the terms, and in the process abandoned the NUJ.

In the meantime, the Wapping plant was secretly equipped from the United States with a full range of computerized typesetting and printing machinery. That action led to the solution of Murdoch's second problem. The new equipment had been installed by a small labor force represented by Britain's electronic and electrical workers' union—the EETPU—which for some time had been regarded as a maverick by the British labor establishment because of its frequent willingness to make significant concessions to management. Said Murdoch to his aides, "If the electricians can install and test the new gear, why can't we hire them to operate it? Who knows more about it? Who's better qualified for the job? Let's talk to them."

Talk he did, and soon he had a simple, binding, no-strike commitment from the EETPU whereby its members would run the Wapping plant at wages and manpower levels far below those demanded by SOGAT, SGA, and the other major Fleet Street production unions. The 500 necessary EETPU workers were quickly recruited from England's hinterlands, most of them from the union's unemployment rolls.

With those problems put to rest, on January 22, 1986, Murdoch announced the impending consolidation and removal of all his London newspaper operations—news-gathering, printing, and distribution—to Wapping. The Fleet Street unions reacted in

a chorus of wounded outrage, claiming that Murdoch had fraud-
ulently misled them into believing that their previous year of negotiations over Wapping had related only to his desire to start a
new afternoon paper there. He stoutly denied the fraud charges
and, with sly innocence, publicly invited the unions to join in the
move to Wapping—pursuant to his manning, wage, and benefit
terms, of course. As expected, the unions refused and immediately struck the *Times* and *Sun/News of the World* plants.

Murdoch could not have asked for a more favorable outcome. The next day, citing the illegality of the unions' strike
under the Thatcher labor laws, he promptly closed the struck
plants, declared their more than 5,000 workers summarily and
permanently fired, and commenced operations at Wapping.

The rapid-fire succession of events, which received lavish
coverage in the rest of the British news media, briefly transfixed
the nation at the end of January. To many, particularly those of a
conservative bent, Murdoch's moves were nothing less than a val-
iant, much-needed, one-man revolution against a fifty-year reign
of despotic, corrupt trade-union power in England. To others,
they constituted a sinister attack on the country's working classes,
a cynical, greedy attempt to destroy a century of progress in industrial relations and workers' rights. Britons waited with bated
breath to see if Murdoch's revolution would succeed.

It did, beyond even the hopes of Murdoch himself. The terminated print-union forces marched en masse on the Wapping
site, only to be swallowed up in a maelstrom of government-
backed criminal and civil law-enforcement measures that turned
their protest into violent but ineffectual rantings. After a few
weeks spent getting the bugs out of the plant's operations and
making new arrangements with his distribution networks, Murdoch restored the production and distribution of his four papers
to normal. Shortly thereafter, undeterred by further union violence directed at Wapping and by the burning-down of one of his
newsprint warehouses, he proceeded with his plan to inaugurate a
new afternoon-evening daily.

Once the move to Wapping was completed in early February
1986, Murdoch's major remaining concern was the possibility of a
popular backlash against his overthrow of the print unions. He
had, after all, put more than 5,000 people out of work in a country already afflicted by cripplingly high unemployment. Union
leaders throughout Britain, along with many left-wing politicians

and journalists, feverishly urged a boycott of all Murdoch's papers, and it seemed in the beginning that such a mass embargo might indeed organize itself. But as time went on and emotions cooled, Murdoch's anxiety became academic. Like other people, Britons are creatures of custom and habit, and it takes a lot more than an event like Murdoch's Wapping venture to shake them out of their lethargy. In fact, the daring and decisive "bad boy" image they attached to Murdoch worked to his advantage. There even grew a powerful sentiment within certain conservative circles that he would make a better—a much better—prime minister than Margaret Thatcher, who at that very moment was losing control of her government.

The sentiment had a double if unintended irony. The first was that having recently taken out American citizenship, Murdoch would not have been eligible for the prime ministership. The second had to do with the fact that, unrealized by practically everyone in England, at the time of the Wapping controversy it was likely that he was connected to the separate events that had thrust Margaret Thatcher into the deep and dire political trouble she was in.

Since the time of her landslide reelection in 1983, which had also given the Conservative Party a huge majority in Parliament, the British public's approval of Thatcher had taken a nosedive. This was attributable in large measure to the widely perceived failure of her still-militantly conservative policies to halt the nation's achingly long economic slide. But it was due also to the increasingly petulant and imperious style of her public leadership. By mid-1985, the prospect of the conservatives' continuing in power after the general election scheduled in 1987 seemed dim. Indeed, only the lack of suitable prime ministerial candidates in the opposition Labour and Liberal/Social Democratic parties protected the Thatcher government from having to call for a special midterm "vote of confidence" election that otherwise would likely have resulted in its removal. But then came the Westland Affair.

Westland Ltd. was Britain's only major helicopter-manufacturing company, and in 1985, it found itself on the verge of bankruptcy. Because the company had contracts with the British defense establishment, the Thatcher government decided it must engineer its rescue. The method it hit upon was to invite a larger aeronautics company to make a substantial investment in Westland through a stock buyout. Assigned to coordinate the rescue was Thatcher's Defense Minister, Michael Heseltine, with the support of her Minister of Trade and Industry, Leon Brittan.

Although the ideal political outcome of the government effort would have been Westland's rescue by another British company, none could be found—the British aircraft industry in general was in a sorry financial state. Therefore, Heseltine and the Defense Ministry were forced to solicit interest from foreign companies. Soon a trio of manufacturers from France, Germany, and Italy, each eager to get a piece of Britain's defense work and gain entry into its civil helicopter market, formed a consortium with two British organizations to acquire a major share of Westland. Stoutly recommended by Heseltine, the "European consortium" received the preliminary approval of Thatcher and was asked to make a tender offer that would satisfy Westland's board and public stockholders. The self-admiring Heseltine smugly accepted the plaudits of his Whitehall colleagues for "a job well done" in masterminding the prospective survival of Westland. He didn't reckon on what was about to occur, however.

Just as eager to enter the British—and by extension the European—helicopter market was the Sikorsky Helicopter division of America's United Technologies, Inc. And still a key member of the board of United Technologies was Rupert Murdoch, Margaret Thatcher's alleged prime ministerial alter ego and the man with whom, as I have previously mentioned, according to Charles Douglas-Home, she consulted "regularly on every important matter of policy, especially as they relate to his political and economic interests." Suddenly, United Technologies/Sikorsky announced its desire to acquire the share in Westland that was being offered. Forming a partnership with Italy's giant Fiat industrial organization, Sikorsky promised to better any specific bid made by Heseltine's European consortium.

Defense Minister Heseltine had been a longtime political ally of Thatcher. A man with a fierce sense of his own worth, Heseltine saw himself as a natural successor to Thatcher as leader of the Conservative Party and, one day, prime minister. Assured by her that his sponsorship of the European consortium had her full blessing, he had gone public with the plan for the purpose, among others, of enriching his personal political capital. By doing so, he put his governmental authority and political credibility on the line.

Much of that credibility centered on a separate issue, namely the recent alarm in England over the rapidly expanding investment and management participation in British industry by large American financial and industrial corporations. It was feared by many in and out of government that if such investment were allowed to continue at the rate it had, Great Britain would eventually be transformed into little more than an economic and industrial satellite of the United States. In theory, the Thatcher government had strongly committed itself to maintaining and protecting Britain's economic sovereignty, and Heseltine had been among the most outspoken opponents of the growing American encroachment. In that context, the European consortium was in his view the only politically viable means by which to save Westland, and he spent much of his time late in 1985 drumming that point into the public mind through the media. That he would be credited with the orderly rescue of Westland, that the event would be perceived as a demonstration of his personal leadership qualities, and that the two together would become a distinctive feather in his political cap—all were to be beneficial by-products of his advocacy of the European consortium.

Thus Heseltine's profound shock when he learned in December that Thatcher had suddenly, and unaccountably, reversed herself; she was no longer in favor of the European consortium but now supported, and was vigorously promoting to the rest of her cabinet, the Sikorsky-Fiat bid, in effect, to take over Westland. Outraged, he tried to learn directly from her the reason for her turnabout. He was, he said later, treated like an errant child commanded by a dictatorial parent to mind his own business, to "keep my nose out, shut up, and go along with the P.M."

Heseltine did not shut up. Instead he started complaining, and within days his complaints were on the front page of every newspaper in England. The subsequent public furor, with Thatcher by then faithfully supported by Trade Minister Brittan and Murdoch's papers, climaxed a few days later in Heseltine's dramatic and loudly public resignation. With it came sinister hints that there was "something extremely fishy about all this." He claimed that Thatcher was acting irrationally and was seeking to conceal some "deep, dark secret," that she had "sold out" her principles for the sake of political expediency. Quickly, the phrase "another Watergate" began to be bandied about.

That left the always contentious British House of Commons,

where by then even Thatcher had bitter Conservative Party enemies, with a mandate to discover, or try to discover, what was really going on at 10 Downing Street. The more Commons probed, the more Thatcher and her closest aides—including Brittan—stonewalled, to use the verb that entered the language with Watergate. Finally, in late January 1986, Leon Brittan was forced to resign from the government after being exposed in a series of lies and misrepresentations to Commons while attempting to explain and defend Thatcher's last-minute shift to Sikorsky-Fiat. Thatcher herself came perilously close to being forced to step down as prime minister.

That she survived was due only to the fact that her government was in total disarray, and that there was still no one with enough command of the public's respect in any political party to succeed her. In the end, Sikorsky got its piece of Westland and the furor seemed to subside. But in reality it didn't. For all practical purposes, both Heseltine and Brittan, among the brightest stars of the Conservative Party, were finished in British politics, at least for the foreseeable future. And Thatcher's reputation was damaged almost beyond salvation, as to a lesser degree was the status of the Conservative Party. Thatcher was further injured by her support of Murdoch's Wapping revolution and by the impression most Britons retained that she really hadn't come clean on what had motivated her to back Sikorsky's financial and managerial takeover of Westland. The two major opposition parties immediately laid plans to capitalize on the scandal—and on the host of still-unanswered questions—in their drive to oust Thatcher and the conservatives from power in 1987. Their plans got a further boost later in 1986, when Thatcher, despite the British public's strong sentiment against it, allowed the Reagan Administration to use England as the launching pad for its air raids on Libya.

Murdoch's footprints were all over the Westland affair, and if anyone personally benefited from it, he did. The gain was two-fold. First, of course, a major American corporation in which he had a significant interest had achieved an advantageous position in a multibillion-dollar market that until then had eluded it. Second, and arguably more important to him in the short term, the scandal diverted much of the nation's attention from his Wapping adventure, thereby diminishing left-wing outrage and minimizing his public relations losses among the working classes that constituted the great bulk of his newspapers' readership. Ancillary to that, it probably helped to neutralize any sentiment about a national boycott of his papers, for most Britons had become too focused on the fate of Thatcher to care.

Oddly, though, Murdoch's likely behind-the-scenes role in the Westland affair was never explored by the British press. In fact, his intimate personal involvement in Sikorsky never even saw the light of print. Only later was it learned that a major shareholder in Westland was TNT Ltd., Murdoch's partner in Ansett, the Australian airline.

What was odder still was the news media's failure to detect the irony of Sikorsky's partnership with Fiat of Italy in the Westland rescue. Several years before, the government of Libya had acquired a substantial ownership position in Fiat, as well as two seats on its board of directors. Libya, of course, was ruled by the iron hand of Muammar Qaddafi, the despotic, self-proclaimed spiritual champion of international terrorism and often its direct sponsor. Margaret Thatcher had spent much of her recent time in office decrying terrorism, and had been a near-fatal victim of it herself two years before when a bomb blew apart an English seaside hotel where she was staying and killed or maimed a number of people in her official party. Moreover, months before that, a young policewoman had been murdered in cold blood by a Libyan terrorist sniper shooting from his government's embassy in London.

Also, Murdoch had constantly used his newspapers around the world to condemn terrorism—particularly the Arab brand of it, and more particularly, Qaddafi's—even while his papers sensationalized, exploited, and profited from it. But now here was Murdoch, hand in hand with Margaret Thatcher, advocating in his newspapers the virtual takeover of a bankrupt British helicopter company by a major American corporation that was in partnership with an Italian organization owned in significant part by none other than the Libya of Muammar Qaddafi.

The saga of Rupert Murdoch remains both a remarkable and troubling one. Out of a modest family inheritance, he has, with great business skill and guile, and in a mere thirty years, constructed what will soon be the most far-reaching and pervasive media empire in history. And he will not stop there, if all the clues from his past are prophetic. As advancing computer-and-satellite communications technology turns us all into citizens of a single global village, Murdoch is determined to be one of those who controls the main channels of information and its transmission.

That is the troubling part. More than anything else, Murdoch's journalistic past forms a record replete with deceptions and falsehoods in the transmission of vital information, done either for profit or for imposing his political, economic, and social beliefs on large masses of people. Nor is that record merely a manifestation of Murdoch's early days of journalistic and business struggle; it is a habit he has not outgrown even now that he has reached maturity and financial success, as a review of any of his most important contemporary media properties starkly reveals.

We can expect to have Rupert Murdoch expanding his influence in our everyday lives for years to come, including his by now predictable brand of news-and-information peddling. The questions are: will the world continue to accept it, and thereby continue to reward him as lavishly as it has? And how will he affect our cultural and political values as he continues to hawk distortion and exaggeration in the guise of fact and truth? The answers, of course, remain to be seen, since Rupert Murdoch has only just begun to build his empire of power and influence in America.

Properties in Rupert Murdoch's Empire

Through the vehicle of Newscorp Ltd., Rupert Murdoch's international empire currently takes the following form. All properties are wholly owned unless otherwise indicated.

1. AMERICAN NEWSPAPERS   APPROXIMATE CIRCULATION

New York Post	675,000 (Daily ex. Sunday)
Boston Herald	350,000 (Daily)
	280,000 (Sunday)
San Antonio Express	92,000 (Daily ex. Sunday)
San Antonio News	75,000 (Daily ex. Sunday)
San Antonio Express-News	205,000 (Sunday)
Houston Community Newspapers	270,000 (Daily/Weekly)
Star	3,750,000 (Weekly)

   (It should be noted that in recent years the *Star* has been promoted as a magazine rather than a weekly newspaper.)

2. AMERICAN MAGAZINES

New York	435,000 (Weekly)
New Woman	1,250,000 (Monthly)
Elle	(Monthly)
Automobile	(Monthly)
European Travel and Life	(Monthly)

   (The last three of the above-named magazines were launched only recently; their respective circulations have not yet been determined.)

3. AMERICAN MOTION PICTURE & TELEVISION

20th Century-Fox, Inc. (Motion Picture and Television Production and Distribution)

Fox Television Stations, Inc. (Television Broadcasting)

WNYW, New York (Formerly WNEW-TV.)

KTTV, Los Angeles
WFLD, Chicago
KDAF, Dallas & Fort Worth
WTTG, Washington, D.C.
KRIV, Houston
WXNL (Cable), Boston
Skyband (Inactive—Satellite TV)

Combined market
of approximately
40 million
households.

4. OTHER AMERICAN PROPERTIES

Salem House (Book Publishing)
World Printing, Inc. (Printing and Paper)
News Air, Inc. (Airplane leasing)
Computer Power (Computer Software—33% owned)

5. BRITISH NEWSPAPERS

	APPROXIMATE CIRCULATION
The Times	400,000 (Daily ex. Sunday)
The Sunday Times	1,200,000 (Sunday)
The Sun	4,380,000 (Daily ex. Sunday)
News of the World	4,250,000 (Sunday)
Times Literary Supplement	32,000 (Weekly)
Times Educational Supplement	91,000 (Weekly)
Times Higher Education Supplement	15,400 (Weekly)

6. BRITISH TELEVISION

Sky Channel (Satellite TV broadcasting to approximately 2 million households in 9 European countries— 73% owned)

7. OTHER MAJOR BRITISH PROPERTIES

Wm. Collins & Sons (Book Publishing—42% owned)
Times Books (Book Publishing and Distribution)
Eric Bemrose (Printing & Paper)
Townsend Hook & Co. (Printing & Paper)
Convoys Group (Printing & Paper)
Newscorp Plc. (Investments)

8. AUSTRALIAN NEWSPAPERS

	APPROXIMATE CIRCULATION
The Australian	120,000 (Daily)
Sydney Daily Mirror	330,000 (Daily)
Sydney Telegraph	303,000 (Daily)
	640,000 (Sunday)
Adelaide News	176,000 (Daily)
Adelaide Sunday Mail	250,000 (Sunday)

Brisbane *Sun*	115,000 (Daily)
	377,000 (Sunday)
Perth *Sunday Times*	254,000 (Sunday)
Cumberland Newspapers	940,000 (Daily/Weekly)
Northern Territory *News*	17,000 (Daily)
Other Provincial Newspapers	190,000 (Daily/Weekly)

9. AUSTRALIAN MAGAZINES   APPROXIMATE CIRCULATION

New Idea	812,000 (Weekly)
TV Week (50% owned)	836,000 (Weekly)

10. AUSTRALIAN TELEVISION

Channel Ten-10, Sydney ⎰	Combined market of approximately
Channel ATV-10, Melbourne ⎱	3 million households.

(Control of the above television stations is presently in a state of flux due to Murdoch's abandonment of his Australian citizenship.)

11. OTHER MAJOR AUSTRALIAN PROPERTIES
    Angus & Robertson (Book Publishing)
    Bay Books (Book Publishing)
    Independent Newspapers, New Zealand (22% owned)
    Progress Press (Printing & Paper)
    Associated R & R Films (Motion Picture Production—50% owned)
    Festival Records
    Ansett Transport Industries (Airline—50% owned)
    Shell Consortium (Oil and Gas Exploration and Production—20% owned)
    News-Eagle Partnership (Oil and Gas Exploration and Production—95% owned)
    F.S. Falkiner & Sons (Sheep and Cattle Raising/Breeding)

Index

DATE			
FEB 2 0 1989			